Visitor's G
GREEC

KEY TO FORMER YUGOSLAVIA

S	SLOVENIA
C	CROATIA
BH	BOSNIA-HERZEGOVINA
YU	YUGOSLAVIA

About the Authors

Brian & Eileen Anderson relished the idea of early retirement to pursue their lifelong interests in travel, flowers, photography and history. Brian read botany 2 years full time at Manchester University before they launched into a new career as travel writers. They have spent a number of years living and travelling around the Mediterranean including around 2 years living in various parts of Greece. When at home, they lecture up and down the country on travel and wild flowers.

Acknowledgement

The authors would like to thank the Greek National Tourist Offices in both London and Athens for their tremendous support and help.

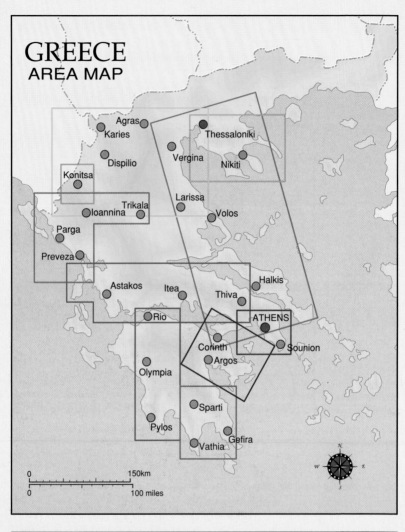

GREECE
AREA MAP

Agras
Karies
Dispilio
Konitsa
Trikala
Ioannina
Parga
Preveza
Astakos
Rio
Olympia
Pylos
Sparti
Vathia
Gefira
Thessaloniki
Vergina
Nikiti
Larissa
Volos
Halkis
Itea
Thiva
ATHENS
Corinth
Argos
Sounion

| 0 | | 150km |
| 0 | | 100 miles |

KEY TO AREA MAP

———	Chapter 1	———	Chapter 6
———	Chapter 2	———	Chapter 7
———	Chapter 3	———	Chapter 8
———	Chapter 4	———	Chapter 9
———	Chapter 5	———	Chapter 10

● Denotes where a street plan is available.

VISITOR'S GUIDE
GREECE

Brian & Eileen Anderson

MPC
HUNTER

Published by:
Moorland Publishing Co Ltd,
Moor Farm Road West, Ashbourne,
Derbyshire DE6 1HD
England

Published in the USA by:
Hunter Publishing Inc,
300 Raritan Center Parkway,
CN 94, Edison, NJ 08818

ISBN 086190 603 9

British Library Cataloguing in Publication Data:
A catalogue record for this book is available from the British Library.

Colour origination by: Sele & Color, Bergamo, Italy &
GA GRAPHICS, Stamford, Lincolnshire ☎ 01780 56166

Printed in Hong Kong by: Wing King Tong Co Ltd

Cover photograph: Corfu's magical coastline (*B. & E. Anderson*)
Rear Cover: (left) Monemvassia, (middle) Convolvulus, (right) Acropolis,
Athens (*B. & E. Anderson*), (below) Parga (*Lindsey Porter*)
Page 3: An old way of life can still be seen in rural areas
(*B. & E. Anderson*)

The Illustrations have been supplied by Brian & Eileen Anderson

MPC Production Team:
Editor: Tonya Monk
Designer: Ashley Emery
Cartographer: Alastair Morrison

CONTENTS

Key to Symbols Used in Text Margin and on Maps

Recommended walks

Garden

Castle/Fortification

Other place of interest

Winter sports

Birdlife

Cave

Water Sports

Church/Monastery

Building of interest

Archaeological site

Museum/Art Gallery

Beautiful view/Scenery,
Natural phenomenon

Beaches

Airport

Key to Maps

Multilane Road

Main Road

Minor Road

Unsurfaced Road

Nome Boundary

Country Boundary

City

Town /Village

How To Use This Guide

This MPC Visitor's Guide has been designed to be as easy to use as possible.
Each chapter covers a region or itinerary in a natural progression which
gives all the background information to help you enjoy your visit. MPC's
distinctive margin symbols, the important places printed in bold, and a
comprehensive index enable the reader to find the most interesting places
to visit with ease.

At the end of each chapter an Additional Information section gives
specific details such as addresses and opening times, making this guide a
complete sightseeing companion.

At the back of the guide the Fact File, arranged in alphabetical order,
gives practical information and useful tips to help you plan your holiday
before you go and while you are there.

The maps of each region show the main towns, villages, roads and places
of interest, but are not designed as route maps and motorists should always
use a good recommended road atlas.

INTRODUCTION

Greece is a land of natural forces boldly traced in fierce mountain ranges. A land blessed with a richness of flora and a wealth of people; a land where a glorious past fashioned in rock invades the present. It is more than a visual experience, it invades the senses, it stimulates and questions the mind. Lawrence Durell expressed it so elegantly in three short lines: 'Other countries may offer you discoveries in manners or lores or landscape; Greece offers you something harder — the discovery of yourself.'

It is the independent traveller who has most to gain in mainland Greece. This does not seek to deny that there are some fine resorts, like Nafplio and Pylos in the Peloponnese or Parga in the western mainland or Halkidiki in the north, where tourists may delight in spending the whole of their holidays in the traditional way, enjoying the sun, sea and sand. But the mainland offers so much more which is impossible to ignore. It offers glimpses of the past in the remains from civilisations which thrived two or three millenniums ago. Evocative Delphi, a 'mecca' for tourists, Mycenae and Nestor's Palace, so bound up in Homeric tales and Pella, home of Alexander the Great, are not just a rich tapestry of the past but are strongly woven into the fabric of the present. It offers also unrivalled scenery from wandering coastlines to majestic mountains, none more so perhaps than Mount Olympos itself, the home of the gods. Adding colour to all this are the people. Life in the many towns, villages and hamlets scattered throughout the mainland is totally unaffected or influenced by tourism and the culture and customs are there to share.

Practicalities are part of touring but few find time for the hours of planning required to find the best routes and to work out which places are of most interest. Then there are the imponderables, how long it will take? Where are the hotels located? What will the food be like? The list is endless but this guide offers practical help on all these points. Tours are described in enough detail to guide the visitor through all the important regions of mainland Greece. Where the principal interest of a region is its historical sites they are presented with a brief summary of the relevant background. Where the region is best known for the beauty of its countryside, as Zagorohoria, tours on foot are also described with some indication of the flowers which might be found and where a region is one for general sightseeing then it is included as a car tour. Athens is the natural starting and finishing point but the tours can be joined at any convenient point. If Epirus is the prime region of interest (Chapters 6 and 7), to visit Ioannina or Meteora or the Zagorian villages, then a fly-drive to Preveza would eliminate a lot of driving and save time. This same starting point could also be considered for central Greece and Delphi (Chapter 5) and for access into the Peloponnese (Chapters 2, 3 and 4). Similarly, Thessaloniki provides a good starting point to all the northern regions, for Kastoria and Edessa (Chapter 8) for Halkidiki (Chapter 9) and Mount Olympos (chapter 10). In fact it is only necessary to use Athens as a starting point if Athens and Attica (Chapter 1) is firmly on the itinerary.

People And Culture

It is the conviviality of the people and their hospitality to strangers which makes Greece so special. Unfortunately, these characteristics are seen less in the tourist areas where the Greeks are too hard pressed looking after visitors in great numbers. In all other parts, it takes only a cheerful greeting, sometimes only a smile, to be on the receiving end of their hospitality. It may take the form of an orange pulled from a bag or a handful of freshly grown broad beans but whatever it is, it is considered bad manners to refuse. Language barriers do not exist for the Greeks and mostly they will chatter away in their native tongue in the full expectancy that you will understand some or part of whatever they are saying. Body language and gesticulations play a full part too. The head is frequently used this way. Assent is signified by a slight nod to the side and no is indicated by a slight toss of the head upward often accompanied by a slight 'tchh' sound. If words fail, an invitation to come or to follow is mostly by a downward pawing movement of the hand. If this is an invitation into the home, the first offering will be some sweet preserves served with a glass of water. To refuse this is to refuse their hospitality but it is not essential to eat all of it. No matter how poor the hosts, any suggestion of payment will cause deep offence but a small present for a child would be acceptable. The surprise arrival of a bottle of wine or ouzo on your table in the taverna may well be the gift of a new acquaintance. The custom here is to pour a glass to toast the sender and drink at least a little of the bottle but there will be no expectation that it is all consumed. The penetration of polite conversation often takes visitors by surprise. After the usual health enquiries, which are taken seriously by the Greeks, the conversation quickly moves into questions about the family, how many sons, daughters and their ages. Unreserved admiration is expressed for parents of large families especially with many sons. From this point enquiries continue about work and will invariably contain a question which throws unprepared visitors almost into a state of shock; 'How much do you earn?' In Greek society it would be considered impolite not to ask this question.

The family unit is strong and still the basis of Greek society, although there are signs that the bonds are starting to weaken under western influences. It is sons who receive the adulation and are totally spoilt by their parents. This does not mean that daughters are not welcomed, as in some societies, and the ideal family is regarded as one son and one daughter. It is remarkable just how many Greek families comprise just two children. In reality they have been using abortion as a means of birth control for a long time. Parental influence is still strong when the time is right for their children to marry. Arranged marriages have not entirely disappeared but they are no longer the norm although parents still have a dominant role in satisfying the demands of society and tradition. It is the duty of the son to stand by his parents to ensure that suitable matches are made for all his sisters before he can contemplate marriage. Although a dowry is no longer a legal requirement, and this repeal was only in recent times, it is still perpetuated. A girl goes into marriage with the gift of a furnished house or apartment from her parents. It remains the girls property and her security. In the same way gifts of gold to the bride are not unusual. The parents have a working lifetime to prepare for providing a home for their daughter or daughters but, such is the pressure from society, failure to succeed may mean that they have to relinquish their own home when the time arrives. At least the newly wedded couple start life without the burden of debt and are able to build and plan a future for their own children. The family unit extends into business too. The Greek preference is for self employment, failing that a secure job with the state, and most of the small businesses employ only family which are eventually passed down via sons and daughters.

It is a male dominated society in which it is demeaning for a man to indulge in women's tasks. This distinct role division is ingrained into society and a woman would lose face if her man was seen sweeping floors or washing dishes. Attitudes are slowly changing amongst the younger generation. The segregation of the sexes too is inbuilt into society. When family or friends enjoy a meal in a taverna, which can be quite a boisterous affair, there is usually a polarisation where the men cluster to one end of the table and the women to the other. Only young men have the freedom to go out alone and it is not uncommon to see them dining out in groups but mostly they head for the bars and congregate there in large numbers. Again signs of change are evident even in this area. The role of the women in the broader society has been recognised in legislation. They acquired the vote only in 1952 and the first woman Deputy was elected to Parliament the following year. Sexual discrimination in career opportunities and in the place of work has been outlawed. Many practical steps have

Happily watching the world go by is a favourite Greek pastime

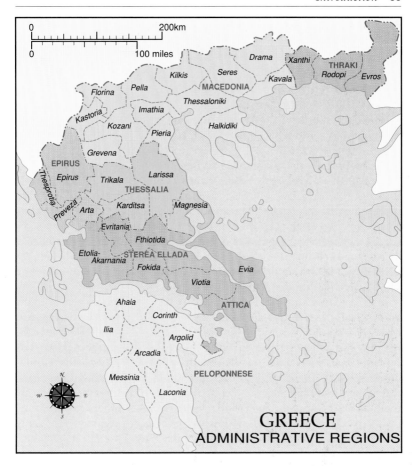

been taken to assist the integration of women as equals in society. Low cost nurseries providing child places have been provided to free women to work and they have acquired rights of ownership after marriage and an equal share of communal property on divorce. Women now hold important posts in all branches of the Civil Service and in commerce but, in spite of all their progress, equality is only accepted in the big cities. Throughout rural Greece it remains contrary to the culture and fundamental change will only be fully accepted very slowly. For women travelling alone in Greece there are no exceptional problems. The incidence of violent crime, including rape, is much lower than in other western societies. But it is not unknown and the same wariness of the possible situations should be observed. Greek men firmly believe that they are irresistible to all women so their attentions can be expected. Women alone in bars or tavernas may cause some raised eyebrows but they will be served without question.

Geography And Topography

Occupying the southern tip of the Balkan peninsula, Greece is firmly located in Europe. With a land area estimated at 131,944sq km (51,540sq miles) and only around 10 million people it approximates to a population density of 76 people/sq km (200 people/sq mile). That assumes an even spread but it is not evenly spread. Since some 4 million people alone live in Athens or its immediate surrounds this leaves many of the other areas very thinly populated.

Geographically the mainland is divided into seven regions and each of these is further divided into administrative units known as *nomes* (*nomoi*), making a total of thirty-nine. Excluded from these is the monastic republic of Mount Athos which has its own administration. Each *nome* has a chief town regarded as the capital which often also serves as the hub of the regional bus service. The visitor is perhaps most aware of the existence of *nomes* in the Peloponnese where Arcadia and Argolid are already familiar names. Pick up any accommodation list in Greece and it is almost certain to be subdivided under *nomes*.

In spite of this huge land mass, not all of it is cultivable or even freely accessible for four-fifths of the country is mountainous. The backbone is a range of mountains running north to south for virtually the length of the country and persisting even in the Peloponnese. The northern part of this range is known as the Pindos mountains. Starting in the north central is another, interrupted, range which runs parallel to the Pindos down to the Pilion region and includes Mount Olympos. In the Peloponnese, there are a number of ranges of which the Taygetos, in the southern part running down into Mani, is the best known. Just to the north-west lies the Parnes which runs almost parallel and in the north is a cluster of ranges which includes the Aroania and Mount Helmos. There are many peaks over 2,000m (6,560ft) with the highest mountain, Olympos, peaking at 2,917m (9,568ft). Winter snow which covers the tops of all these mountain ranges persists throughout the spring months into early summer. There may be permanent snow patches in the hollows around the mountain tops but there are no glaciers. With such high mountains and so much snow around, it might be expected that there would be many fast flowing rivers. In fact there are relatively few rivers and none of them navigable. There are plenty of dry river beds around which take away the flash floods from the winter storms and are almost instantly dry again.

Politics

Politics is an overriding obsession with the Greeks. Free political expression arrived only in 1974 with the fall of the dictatorship. All the three hundred seats in the single chamber parliament are filled by parties formed after 1974. Essentially a two party system is evolving with the

contestants being the socialist PASOK, the Panhellenic Socialist Movement and the New Democracy party (ND) with conservative leanings.
Not without some support is the Communist Party of Greece, the KKE. All
these symbols are liberally painted on bridges and buildings throughout
the country. After years of socialist rule, the New Democracy under
Mitsotakis currently holds the balance of power by the slenderest of
margins, one seat but for how long is anybody's guess. The political
system is slowly maturing but it still faces some serious problems in
bureaucracy, nepotism, petty corruption, low productivity and poor social services. Greece's membership of the EEC has itself been a stabilising
influence and the country has benefited greatly from grants, enormous
loans and subsidies over recent years. A stabilisation programme imposed from Brussels is currently in place trying to reduce government
spending and bring inflation under control. Regardless of which party
holds the balance of power, strikes are a way of life in Greece and barely
a week passes without some sector providing the action. It does occasionally become a serious problem for the traveller when the action moves into
a concerted phase and banks, transport and tavernas, for example, all co-
ordinate their strikes.

For the Greeks, politics is a passion akin to football and demands the
same loyalty. The uncommitted or floating voter is a rare species. Prime
time Saturday evening television is often filled with 2 hours of political
debate which is avidly followed even in the tavernas. Visitors will not
escape being drawn into political discussion and are likely to be tested on
three main topics; relations between Greece and Turkey, the Cyprus
question and Macedonia. The latter problem is of passionate interest in
northern Greece and the locals are very interested to learn the views of
foreigners and to press their own views. It has arisen with the disintegra-
tion of the former Yugoslavia and the request for Macedonia there to be
recognised as independent. The Greeks are deeply troubled by this and
fear that it may lead to future territorial claims on their northern province
of Macedonia. Passions run high. Rooted deep in history, from the time
when King Philip was King of Macedon, the belief is that the Greeks hold
the true title and that the former Yugoslavia Macedonia should be recognised as Skopje and they refer to it that way.

Economy

Traditionally, Greece's economy was based on farming and small scale
manufacturing but there has been considerable change over recent years.
After the war years, up to around 1970, about half the labour force worked
on the land and agricultural products contributed significantly to the
countries exports, as they still do. Unimpressed with the hard life and
poor returns, the younger generation started to move to the cities and to
the developing tourist centres for better paid work. The exodus seriously

depopulated some areas, like the hill villages, where farming was nothing more than an existence. Since joining the EEC in 1981, the farming sector has benefited considerably from subsidies and has enjoyed a considerable improvement in its standard of living. Shipping and tourism are two of the major stabilising factors in the Greek economy, both big earners of foreign currency. With so much coastline and the sea offering easier travel than the mountainous interior, Greece has had a strong shipping sector from ancient times. With troubled times for too many years this century and with unfavourable government policies, many of the shipping magnets had registered ships under a flag of convenience and moved their centre of operations away from Greece. All that has changed in the last few years under the influence of revised government policies. Many have returned to the Greek flag and maritime earnings have steadily increased. Currently, Greece has the largest merchant fleet in the EEC and the fifth largest in the world. There is a view that if all Greek ships were Greek registered then it would have the largest fleet in the world. Piraeus, close to Athens is the countries biggest port and this is in the throes of a modernisation plan to improve facilities and handling for shippers. Other major ports include Volos, Igoumenitsa, more important following closure of the land route to Europe through former Yugoslavia, Thessaloniki and Patra.

Tourism is a more recent success story. Boasting 3,000 hours of sunshine a year, a host of beautiful islands and a wealth of historical interest, it has succeeded almost in spite of itself. It is generally acknowledged that there are more things wrong in Greek tourism than right. Unlike other nations which have perhaps tried harder, the Greeks have not gone overboard building water-chutes, theme parks and all the other features regarded as desirable. Unwittingly, they may have found the key to the successful development of tourism. Tourist resorts in Greece are as near natural as any in the Mediterranean and their lack of sophistication and the natural charm of the people are important elements which attract visitors back and back again. Infrastructure improvements in terms of new roads, water supplies and better support services are in hand which the government hope will promote new developments in the quality sector. At the moment the season is limited to the main summer months and the longer term strategy is to develop all year round tourism.

The third major source of foreign income is from the remittances sent home by the emigrants. For a period after World War II and civil war which followed, when the country was truly devastated and the prospects for employment very poor, there was a period of mass emigration in which many thousands of Greek men and their families departed overseas, mainly to Australia but also to America and Africa. It is often jokingly said that if all the expatriates returned home the population would double. The Greeks seem to work harder abroad and many proved successful in business enterprises. They did and still do send money home to support their parents and brothers and sisters although there has been something of a drift back in recent years, especially in retirement.

To complete the economic picture, the country still has little manufacturing capacity and its main exports are in fruit and vegetables, wine, tobacco, textiles and jewellery.

Law And Order

The incidence of violent crime, theft and robbery is still far lower than in most other western cultures, although there are signs that it is on the increase in Athens. It is not something that need concern the tourist and to be able to move around in the evening without feeling threatened in any way is one of the pleasures of this country. It still pays to be sensible with personal property and protect it as at home. Generally, the Greeks have their own moral code for living in which there are some distinctly eastern traits and ambiguities. They have a basic honesty which means that if you leave your change in their shop then they will chase down the street after you to return it. On the other hand, the same owner may well have twisted you out of a few *drachmas* by quoting a wrong price. This is regarded as smart and foreigners are fair game. Their attitude to the laws in general are not always easy to comprehend. There are many laws which the public just totally and completely ignore. Parking is one of them. It is hard to find a parking space even where a street is littered with no parking signs. Periodically the police come along with parking tickets but so few ever get paid for various reasons so the parking continues. It is the same with safety belts in cars. The law is very explicit on this, safety belts are compulsory but drivers rarely wear them. Every few months there is an announcement that the fine is to be increased for this offence and that there will be a check in a few days time. On the day of the check seat belts are worn and on the following day everything reverts to as it was. There is also a law that motorcyclists should wear crash helmets but motorcyclists do not wear them and bikes for hire are offered without crash helmets. Disobedience of these driving laws is visible, it can be observed every day of the week but the same philosophy applies to many laws in every day life.

Religion

The Greek Orthodox Church is firmly established and dominates the religious scene. Other denominations are tolerated but proselytisation is not. The Archbishop of Athens and All Greece heads the church which is governed by a synod of the bishops and other leading members. Some of the church's income arises from the state but more from its massive real estate interests acquired in earlier years. Priests move about the community in their black ankle-length cassocks, black hat and full beard. They may be seen drinking coffee in the kafeneon and travelling by bus when, more than likely, someone will spring up to offer a seat but they are rigidly church based without the role of social worker in the wider community. As in many other western cultures, the church is slowly losing its power amongst the people, especially the younger generation. The acceptance of civil marriage was forced on the church by the government following reforms in 1981. Up until that time, Greeks married abroad by civil ceremony were not accepted as married under the Government's own civil law. Abortion too was legalised, also against church opposition, but this did nothing more than legalise the existing high rate of abortion. It has long been used as a means of family planning and remains, even now, the most widely practised form. Other forms are still very much under the counter. The Church still controls a lot of agricultural land and unused land which the government is trying to wrestle away to put into the hands of farmers and cooperatives.

On high days and holy days, and there are many in the Greek calendar, the church comes into its own and, for a brief time becomes the focus of community life. Easter is the most important event of the year and this and other religious events are discussed in the Fact File. The church played an important role throughout the Byzantine years as guardian of the Greek culture. It organised secret schools to educate the children and preserve the language.

Folk Art

Folk art in Greece is very distinctive and shows regional influence. Pottery, textiles, woodwork and other expressions of folk art tend to be very traditional and conservative. Designs and techniques are handed down from generation to generation with little change or evolution. As in any poor society, the object must also fulfil a function even though it may be decoratively coloured or crafted. In country areas, carved walking sticks or the distaff used in spinning are prominent, representing the items which command a local sale. Decorative pottery is made throughout the country and is characterised by its vivid coloration with reds, greens and blues. Work aimed specifically for the tourist market relies heavily on designs from early history or from Greek mythology. Woven and embroidered textiles are also commonly found throughout the country. Embroidery, which is seen more in the southern part of the region, has proved popular with visitors and it is not uncommon for village ladies to arrange displays along the roadside of tourist trails. Museums of folk art are also becoming increasingly popular. There is at least one to be found in all the larger towns and they are particularly interesting for their displays of national costumes.

Food And Drink

Eating out in Greece, traditionally inexpensive, is a national pastime but even that is under threat with rising prices and high rates of inflation. It was unthinkable for a Greek family to entertain friends or family to a meal at home. As a party they would head for the taverna and the host would collect the bill. Not only was the taverna a place to eat but it was also a place of entertainment. After the meal, tables would be pushed back, the owner would produce a bouzouki or similar instrument and the menfolk would rise to dance. Perhaps later the women might join the dancing too. Sadly this now happens only on festive occasions. Gone is the bouzouki to be replaced by the television and the atmosphere of the taverna is generally more subdued. Watching the Greeks eat is a pleasure in itself. Seldom do they order individually, instead they order a vast number of communal dishes which fill the table to overflowing. There is no rush to eat the food either, conversation continues at a high pitch whilst the diners pick and nibble their way steadily through the dishes. They are far less concerned about cold food and many dishes which arrive hot are cold before they are eaten. Some tourists find it a bit disconcerting when their meals are actually served on the cool side but, in most tourist areas, the message that tourists generally like their food hot has registered.

Although the Greek cuisine is quite extensive, tavernas tend only to have a limited menu. Lunch time, between 2 and 3pm after work finishes, is the only meal of the day for which the chef will prepare a range of cooked dishes. For the evening trade, and the Greeks are notoriously late eaters, the menu offers whatever is left over from lunch, which has often been kept warm for hours, and a range of grills which are cooked to order. Charcoal is generally used for grilling and it is not unusual to see large charcoal grills by the doorway or outside in summer. Although the tavernas are the traditional eating places, cities and larger towns may also have restaurants which provide a better standard of decor in particular and tend to have a more international cuisine.

Tavernas are obliged to have a menu but many still do not. Instead diners will be shown a glass show case exhibiting the range of dishes available or, and this is still very common in the villages, they will be led into the kitchen to see exactly what is cooking. If difficulties are experienced in the final choice then spoons may appear for a tasting session. In an effort to improve standards, there has been a recent government decree instructing that all tables should have a cloth table cloth. Previously it was usual just to have a plain piece of polythene which was changed for each new client. It served a double purpose because at the end of the meal all scraps from the plates would be tipped into it and the whole lot bundled up and removed. Now the situation has changed. Tables are fitted with a decorative table cloth but this is securely protected by a polythene sheet covered by a paper square and only the latter is laid fresh each time. Should there be a menu on the table then it will probably be in Greek and

Fast Food Greek Style

The Greeks are great nibblers so there is no shortage of fastfood. 'Pies' with various fillings, usually made with filo pastry and looking like a Cornish pasty or sometimes pieces cut from one large pie are:

Savouries
Tiropitta: cheese.
Spanakopitta: spinach only or with cheese and eggs.
Kreatopitta: minced meat.

Souvlaki: small pieces of meat on a wooden skewer served with a lump of bread or with pitta.

Doner me pitta: slices of meat from the *gyros* (meat cooked on a vertical spit) placed in a pitta parcel with a little yoghurt, tomato and onion.

Tost: usually a slice of ham and cheese toasted between bread.
Koulouria: sesame seed encrusted rings and *Loukouma* , sugar coated rings like doughnuts are sold by street vendors.

Freshly pressed orange, carrot and apple juice is widely available in the cities.

Sweets
Milopitta: apple.
Bougatza: vanilla custard.

A variety of nuts for sale on Athens market

English but it will only show a partial correspondence with the dishes on offer so it still pays to ask. It is unusual to find the table laid, apart from the oil and vinegar flasks, paper napkins and the inevitable toothpicks, but the cutlery arrives with bread after an order is placed.

There is no special form in a taverna and no conventions to follow. The Greeks often go in for a plate of chips and a beer and make it last half the night. For diners though, it is usual to begin with one or a selection of the starters or *mezedes* on offer. These include *tzatsiki* (a yoghurt, cucumber and garlic dip), *taramasalata* (fish roe mixed with potato, oil and vinegar, the pinker the better), *melitzano salata* (an aubergine dip with tomato and garlic) and *humus*, another dip this time from chick-peas. Fresh vegetables are rarely available but two vegetables which turn up as *mezedes* are *gigantes* (butter beans cooked in tomato and oil) and peas (*arakas*). *Saganaki*, fried cheese is another interesting starter. The waiter will raise an eyebrow if *mezedes* are ordered separately by each individual, even tourists are expected to order a selection and share in Greek style. Salads may be preferred as starters or as part of the starters and the most popular is the village salad or *horiatiki salata*. The content of this mixed salad is laid down by regulations and it should include lettuce, or cabbage, tomato, onion, cucumber, a certain weight of feta cheese and olives. A few years ago, a salad like this constituted a meal in itself and many tourists were perfectly happy to make a lunch from it. Unfortunately, this made the taverna owner less than happy, consequently the price has risen considerably and they are not always the generous portions they were. Tomatoes, cucumbers, feta cheese and lettuce (*maruli*) are all offered as separate dishes. Ready cooked dishes may include the familiar *moussaka*, a mince dish with aubergines, potato and bechamel sauce, veal in tomato, *stifado* (veal stew with onions) or *giovetsi* (oven cooked lamb served with pasta). Chicken cooked on the spit is popular and an inexpensive dish but favoured amongst the grills is *souvlaki*, veal or pork on a skewer. Chops, pork, lamb or veal, are ever present on the evening menus as are *keftedes* (spicy meat balls) and *biftekia* (mince burgers). Fish is sometimes on offer but for a selection it is better to find a fish (*psaria*) taverna. Lobster (*astakos*) and red mullet (*barbounia*) are usually top of the menu and are expensive as are shrimps (*garides*). Octopus, grilled or cooked in wine is less expensive as is squid (*kalamari*). At the cheap end is the small whitebait (*marides*) which is eaten in its entirety, head and all. This dish is often available as a starter in a fish restaurant. Trout is sometimes on the menu in mountain areas. Desserts are very limited, usually fruit, but the popularity of yoghurt and honey amongst the tourists is now recognised. If you have tucked into your meal with obvious enjoyment, the proprietor may produce a plate of fruit, peeled and presented with his compliments.

Some Greeks prefer to drink ouzo with meals and this is served in small bottles and usually taken with water. Others choose *retsina*, a resinated wine, which is an acquired taste. Often the *retsina* is from the barrel and locally made. Some of this can be very good, especially if lightly resinated, and it is worth trying a glass to start with. It is more than likely that the wine list will contain some good wines like *Boutari, Naoussa* and *Lac des Roches* as well as some medium priced popular wines like *Kambas* and *Rotonda*. Labels such as these are generally available throughout the country but there are a large number of branded local wines which are equally good. Many Greeks themselves have vines on their own farms and it is worth asking for *krasi dopio* (wine of the house), which at least is cheap and can vary from excellent to undrinkable but is usually exciting enough to risk the experiment. In most regions there is a locally made unbranded wine and this too is worth a try although some of it might be lightly resinated.

Flora And Fauna

Greece is one of the most floristically rich areas of Europe and boasts over 6,500 species. There are many factors contributing to the success of the plant life in this region but important amongst them is that the country escaped the destructive ravages of an ice flow in the Quarternary Ice Ages. Also to be considered are the climatic influences, the huge variety in habitats in this mountainous country and the fact that it lies on plant migration routes to and from the area. Many of the species are endemic and cannot be found outside the region. W. B. Turrill *(The Plantlife of the Balkan Peninsula. A Phytogeographical Study*, Oxford 1929) estimated the number of endemics at 1,754, almost a quarter of the whole flora. A number of these are paleoendemics, or relic species, which have survived in the area from the Tertiary period some 20 to 50 million years ago. It is guessed that they once had a much wider distribution but climatic changes of this period have decimated the wider populations leaving only small isolated pockets here in Greece and the Balkans. Two examples of this, both from the Gloxinia family, are *Ramonda serbica* which is found in the Vikos Gorge (see Walk 1 Chapter 7) and *Jankaea heldreichii* which survives only on Mount Olympos (see Walk 1 Chapter 10).

The geology is particularly favourable to plant life throughout the region. The western range of mountains stretching down into the Peloponnese formed in the Alpine earth movements some 50 to 100 million years ago and comprise sedimentary rocks of limestone, sands and conglomerates. The mountains to the east which include Mount Olympos are part of an ancient rock system composed of marbles, schists and gneiss.

As far as the plant life is concerned, Greece has two distinct climates. Lowland and coastal areas generally enjoy a Mediterranean climate which is quite simply described as a mild wet winter and a hot dry summer. Winter temperatures are high enough throughout even the coldest months to sustain plant growth, especially when combined with adequate amounts of water and plenty of sunshine. Summer is just the opposite. It is too hot and dry for all but the most deep rooted, like the trees and shrubs, and for other plants it is a question of resting and survival. This results in totally reversed growing seasons compared with the rest of Europe. The olive tree is regarded as as a good indicator which grows only in the regions where a Mediterranean climate exists. One consequence of this climate is that Greece is rich in geophytes, plants with bulbs, corms tubers and rhizomes which have their resting buds below the soil, and annuals which survive the summer as seed. Plant growth in these regions commences with the first rains of autumn. This leads to an initial flush of flowers which includes *Cyclamen hederifolium*, *Scilla autumnalis*, the yellow crocus-like *Sternbergia lutea* and others. Progress throughout late autumn sees the development of leaf growth, including grass, and everything takes on a green hue before the start of the main flowering period in early January. First are the anemones and perhaps some muscari species but others quickly join throughout February until late March and early April sees the peak of the spring flowering period. Beyond this time, the number of species in flower starts to decline and by the end of May most are receding to their resting state. The lambing season in many parts starts at the end of the year to take advantage of winter grazing. Winter vegetable crops too are sown to take advantage of this natural growth period and, unlike summer crops, mature without irrigation.

If winter temperatures can sustain plant growth in the lowlands, this becomes less certain with increasing altitude. Summers in the mountains too are different with a much greater incidence of summer rain. In these areas of sub-Mediterranean climate, growth largely follows the normal pattern of winter resting and summer blooming. Whereas spring may be in full bloom around the foot of Mount Olympos in March, it is June for spring flowers around 2,000m (6,560ft) and July and August at higher levels.

There are a number of very distinctive plant communities which can be easily observed while touring around Greece. The scrubland which covers much of the arid lowland hills is either *phrygana* or *macchie* (or *maquis*). *Phrygana* is the knee-high dwarf scrub vegetation widespread throughout the region. It contains a number of characteristic species both woody and herbaceous. Holly oak (*Quercus coccifera*), is commonly present as are two prickly domed species, *Sarcopoterium spinosum* and *Euphorbia acanthothamnos*. Many of the plants are spiny including the yellow flowered *Genista acanthoclada* which lights up the hillsides in spring until the spanish broom takes over. Cistus species are common too as are many of the aromatic herbs, like *Origanum onites*, which the Greeks use in the kitchen. Although the *phrygana* looks distinctly drab and boring in summer, the opposite is true in spring when it plays host to many annuals and to a range of orchid species.

The *macchie* is taller and usually denser scrub reaching up to 2 or 3m (7 or 10ft). It occurs more in coastal regions and often prefers acid soils. Like *phrygana* it has a range of typical species which aids its identification. Some of the more interesting ones include *Myrtus communis*, *Arbutus*

Greece, one of the most floristically rich areas of Europe; Iris Attica

The Swallowtail Butterfly (Papilio machaon), *is one of the best known species in Europe and fairly widespread throughout Greece*

unedo, Erica arborea, Rosmarinus officinalis, Phlomis fruticosa, Pistacia lentiscus and *Cercis siliquastrum.*

At sea level and in the more arid regions, the forest trees are mainly of *Pinus halepensis* but in cooler conditions inland and in the hills mixed deciduous forests take over. Oaks feature strongly here and include the white oak (*Quercus pubescens*), and the valona oak (*Q. macrolepis*), whose acorn cups are still used in the dyeing and tanning industry. A number of other trees are present too including *Ostrya carpinifolia, Lauris nobilis, Pyrus amygdaliformis, Rhus coriaria* and *Fraxinus ornus* amongst others. At higher altitudes the firs come back into the picture. In the Peloponnese, black pine (*Pinus nigra*), forms forests above 800m (2,624ft) and the Greek silver fir, *Abies cephalonica,* also becomes dominant. In northern Greece it is a different fir which is found, *Abies boris-regis.*

There is a characteristic association of flowering species for each type of habitat but it requires a good Flora to ascertain full details. Good places to look for flowers are on the sea shore and the nearby cliffs where species like *Malcomia flexuosa, Medicago marina* and the pink *Silene colorata* are commonplace. Old undisturbed olive groves and meadows are ideal for finding anemones, orchids, arum species, muscari, ornithogalums, iris, gladioli and a whole spectrum of typical Mediterranean flowers. As mentioned, the phrygana is good hunting ground too for orchids and a wide range of annuals. In the mountains the flora is more typical of central Europe. Hellebores are common, campanulas, lilies and even species which extend into Britain, like the twayblade (*Listera ovata*). Higher still and the flora takes on an alpine character where saxifrages, violas, gentians and similar species are found. The search for plants in this zone should include rock crevices and ledges which are important habitats and provide some of the most exciting species. Certain areas of the country are richer in flowers than others, like Mount Olympos. Where these areas have been visited, a more detailed account of the flowers is included.

As far as the fauna is concerned, most contact is likely to be with the reptiles. Small lizards are everywhere, basking in the sun to adjust their body temperature and perhaps the commonest of the small ones is the wall lizard (*Podarcis muralis*). Much larger are the green lizards which tend to live in thick vegetation. They can run quite speedily on their hind legs and it is not an uncommon sight to see them charging across the road. Tortoises are often heard before they are seen but all three European species can be found in Greece. Hermann's tortoise (*Testudo hermanni*), is found in the Ionian islands and the west, the spur-thighed tortoise (*T. graeca*) in Macedonia and the marginated tortoise (*T. marginata*), from Mount Olympos southwards. Terrapins too can sometimes be seen in freshwater ponds or slowly moving streams. Snakes often cause some concern. There are plenty around but the majority are harmless and move rapidly away if disturbed. It is the vipers which are dangerous, especially the horned viper (*Vipera ammodytes*), but the danger only arises if you are unfortunate enough to stand on one which is why it is essential to wear stout shoes, protect the ankles and wear long trousers when walking in the countryside where they might be found.

There are plenty of small mammals about but, missing out the rats and mice that nobody wishes to see, the red squirrel is not uncommon amongst the pine trees or rabbits in the countryside. Foxes too are around but they are mostly seen when caught in car headlights at night. The bigger mammals are confined to the isolated mountain regions where wolves, wild goat, chamois, wild boar and the brown bear survive although some are living on the edge of extinction.

Bird life is plentiful, especially species like the swift, swallow, chaffinch and goldfinch. Meteora provides an opportunity to see some of the birds of prey hovering amongst the towering monasteries; Egyptian vultures, peregrines and golden eagles are all possible sightings as well as the white stork. White storks are commonly seen throughout Epirus too. Nearer to Athens, the Marathon marshes are worth a visit for the purple herons, little egrets and other wetland species.

There is a growing awareness of conservation in Greece but as yet the movement is in its infancy. Certain areas have been designated National Parks which include Mount Parnassos, Mount Olympos, the Vikos and Aoos Gorge region of the northern Pindos mountains and Lake Mikri at Prespa in the extreme north-west. Apart from Mount Olympos, and that only by the vigilance of the warden at the refuge, the areas are not policed to prevent the destruction of the flora and fauna. Goat and sheep are still grazed and hunting still continues. The local inhabitants have done this through the centuries and old habits die hard.

History

Historical Greece, long regarded as the cradle of civilisation, attracts archaeologists, historians and researchers as nowhere else on earth. Already the knowledge and understanding of historical events in this part of the world is enough to fill volumes and it continues to grow. This brief account aims at nothing more ambitious than to lend some perspective to your travels. In this respect it will concentrate largely on events on the mainland and dwell more on the age when the great temples and cities were built. Nowhere else in the world does the force of history overwhelm the mind in such a startling fashion as when you are standing amongst rocks fashioned and placed by the hand of man with such architectural brilliance. It is sometimes necessary to pinch yourself to remember that they were built millenniums of years ago.

Early history is conveniently divided into periods. Convenient in that, once recognised, they provide a time scale reference which is easier than remembering individual dates. These key periods are:

3000BC-1100BC	(Bronze Age)
1100BC-800BC	(Dark Age)
776BC-480BC	(Archaic Period)
480BC-338BC	(Classical Period)
338BC-146BC	(Hellenistic Period)

Bronze Age (3000BC-1100BC)

A significant point to start the story is with the development of two great civilisations within the Bronze Age. The first to crystallise was the Minoan civilisation on Crete around 2200BC. It was a remarkable, structured culture which built palaces, developed religion, traded by sea throughout the Mediterranean and developed art and pottery to a degree of sophistication not seen before. Historians have learnt much about the culture from the wall frescos depicting scenes of daily life and from the decorated, elegant pottery. The Minoan civilisation showed many stages of advancement over the long period of its history. Natural disasters were believed to have hastened the decline of this civilisation, especially the massive volcanic eruption on Thira (Santorini) around 1450BC.

Greece at this stage of its history did not exist as a single nation nor did it conform to the political boundaries as they are now understood. There existed a large number of independent tribes occupying, not just the lower part of the Balkan Peninsula, but many parts of the Mediterranean including settlements on the Black Sea. It was easier to trade and communicate using the seas than the mainland. On the mainland, tribes were isolated by the mountainous terrain and the difficulty of travel. They shared common features of which the most important was language; they all spoke the Greek language or a recognisable dialogue. People who did not speak Greek were thought to make noises which sounded like bar-bar and were referred to as *barbaroi* (barbarians).

The second great civilisation formed in the Peloponnese, around Mycenae, and soon dominated southern Greece. The culture grew slowly from an early date with the migration of Indo-Europeans down from the Balkans and rose to dominance from 1600BC to 1100BC. Much of its art was influenced by the Mycenaean culture on Crete and possibly its lifestyle too. It was not until the destruction and decline of the Minoans that the Mycenaeans had their chance to develop trade throughout the Mediterranean which they soon came to dominate. At the height of their power, they had constructed some 320 citadels throughout mainland Greece and the Aegean. Today the most important of the ruins associated with the Mycenaean cultures are found at Mycenae, Argos, Tiryns and Nestor's Palace at Pylos.

It was an ordered society ruled by a King who was also chief priest and supreme judge supported by an aristocracy and a warrior class. Evidence for this comes from the royal graves. These were magnificent circular domed tombs a few of which were discovered unplundered. They yielded bronze weapons and gold, gold in the form of diadems, cups and funeral masks.

The Mycenaean culture had certain strong characteristics most evident in its architecture. They built simple, austere stately palaces which were strongly fortified by enclosing walls built in massive masonry and sited for defence. It was an autocratic rule which relied on wisdom and strong leadership from the King who used his knowledge of astronomy to set the calendar for all the important events of the year from religious festivals to cycles of nature, when to sow and when to harvest. Knowledge of the history of this period was gleaned from the artefacts from excavation, from epic poetry and history written at a later time and from Linear B script which was interpreted finally in 1952. The Mycenaean age was an age rich in folklore, in heroes, personalities and events which are captured and encapsulated for posterity in the works of Homer, especially *The Iliad*. Agamemnon was a giant amongst the personalities of that time. King of Argos, he led his warriors to besiege Troy in revenge for the abduction of Helen, his sister-in-law and the most beautiful woman in the world.

The reasons for the eventual decline of the Mycenaeans are not entirely clear. One by one the citadels were sacked and burnt but whether by internal revolution or invasion remains unresolved. The Dorians moving down from the north with superior weapons of iron are believed to have some influence. Slowly, as the autocratic structure of society crumbled, Greece entered a new period known as the Dark Age.

The Dark Age (1100BC-800BC)

The label Dark Ages is often used to disguise the fact that little is known about a period. This period spanning 300 years falls into that category. It was one of chaos and transition. Greek speaking Dorians from the north moved down to occupy the whole of now mainland Greece including the Peloponnese. It was a merging of tribes rather than an annihilation of some. Artistic and material advancement ground to a halt but slowly a new vision of political and social organisation emerged.

The Archaic Period (776BC-480BC)

The rapid spread of the Phoenician alphabet across the Mediterranean marked the beginning a new phase. A phase which re-appraised the basis of society and laid foundations for the growth and development of city-states.

(preceding pages) Delphi; the Sacred Way was adorned by a succession of monuments and treasuries like the Treasury of the Athenians seen here and the alcove, where a statue once stood

It was an energetic period throughout. Written records started which gave the first reliable insight into early history. The works of Homer, thought not to be the works of one man, were written down by 750BC and around the same period Hesiod formalised Greek mythology. New levels of artistic expression surpassing those of the Mycenaean period are observed in the many artefacts from this period including the monumental work. Architecture did not quite match the pace of advancement but new materials and principles were being explored which were to flourish in the Classical Period.

City-states developed to replace the old autocratic rule. The leaders were usually aristocratic warriors but they ruled by consensus in an early form of democracy. Public debate was encouraged and inscribed codes of law started to appear. Cities (*polis*) differed in construction too. Usually a defendable position like a hill top (*acropolis*) was still favoured but the palace structure of the Mycenaean period was now replaced by a temple to the gods of the city and life revolved around the market place (*agora*) where public debate and business took place. Various city-states started to associate to form regional power bases raising cities like Sparta in the Peloponnese and Athens to greater prominence.

Stone replaced wood as the material for building columns leading to the appearance of Doric columns in the Peloponnese (around 650BC) and Ionic columns in eastern Greece (around 600BC). Philosophy too had its roots in this period. With new found freedom of expression, thinkers started to reflect on the new political order and the effect on the individual. Over in the east the Persians had begun to expand their empire towards the Mediterranean which was soon to threaten Greece.

The Classical Period (480BC-338BC)

Classical as a term is now widely used to describe ancient Greek history in general but historians adhere steadfastly to the narrower definition.

The epic battles of the Persian wars are well chronicled. Leading his army against Athens, Darius failed when his fleet floundered on Mount Athos as he tried to round the peninsula. Two years later (490BC), after rebuilding his fleet, he sailed directly across the Aegean to land at Marathon, 42km (26 miles) north-east of Athens. The Athenians left the safety of their city to carry the attack to the Persians before they had time to deploy their superior military force on land. Athens won a famous victory and Phidippides, running with the news back to Athens only to die on reaching the stadium, became a legend. Darius died in 486BC leaving his son Xerxes to continue the fight against the Greeks. With renewed determination, he raised a massive force and entered Greece to fight the battle of Thermopylae in 480BC. An heroic force lead by Leonidas, the Spartan King, delayed the advance of the Persians at the cost of their lives. The Athenians evacuated their city to regroup at Salamis where the more manoeuvrable ships of the Greeks crushed the superior Persian fleet. The Persian army returned to capture and sack Athens in that same year. One year later, the Persians were finally annihilated by a combined army of Athenians, Spartans and other allied city-states.

The end of the war against the Persians marks the start of the Classical Period, a new golden age which saw the rise of Athens and a considerable advance in political and cultural achievements. More than 200 city-states joined the league of Delos to contribute money to a defence fund which was used to liberate the eastern Greek cities in Asia. Pericles used the remains of the fund for a lavish rebuilding programme of Athens, the Acropolis, the Parthenon and the whole complex. It became a period of temple building throughout the region using new mathematical skills to introduce subtleties into the design to enrich the harmonious appearance. Drama advanced and theatres were built using the natural contours of the land. Art and sculpture too evolved and reached new levels of attainment and it was in this period that Pheidas sculptured the Parthenon marbles. Columns of the Corinthian order which use the acanthus leaf decoration at the capital were first used about 450BC. The temple of Apollo at Bassae is an early example.

The outlines of democracy which had emerged earlier were formalised and further developed. A code of law was established in Athens. Power was exercised initially by representatives from important families but this evolved into a council of 500 drawn by lots from neighbouring tribes. Pericles remained an important figure and retained power for almost 30 years.

Sparta and Athens remained in competition with each trying to expand its power. While Athens formed the Delian League based on the sacred island of Delos, Sparta established the Peloponnesian League which included mainland cities such as Delphi. Skirmishes between Athens and Sparta which started in 457BC developed into a full scale war in 430BC. Sparta emerged the eventual winner at the close of the fifth century. Athens lost imperial power but soon regained much of its influence.

The second part of the Classical Period is characterised by a gradual unification of the city-states under the power and leadership of King Philip II but not without some resistance on the way. Against slow but profound political changes of the fourth century, the influence of philosophers made their own impact. Plato and Aristotle started their own schools and Plato's Academy in Athens could lay claim to being the world's first university.

In 338BC, King Philip of Macedonia won a decisive battle which saw the final unification of the city-states and marked the end of the Classical Period.

Hellenistic Period (338BC-146BC)

The assassination of King Philip in 338BC brought the young, 18-year-old, Alexander to power and started a new phase in Greek history. Already blooded in battle and with great powers of leadership, he took the fight right into the enemies camp, the Persians. The first task was to liberate the

A traditional pension in Megalo Papingo with the towers of Astraka rising high above

Greek colonies in Ionia and from there he continued to sweep through Asia. He had the wisdom not to sack the cities but to preserve and enslave the people. Under his leadership, the Greek Empire spread rapidly and soon extended as far as India in the east and Egypt in the south. Alexander died in 323BC at the age of 32 and is remembered as Alexander the Great. Proclaimed a god by the Egyptians, he founded his own city, Alexandria, which eventually replaced Athens as the centre of Greek culture. Throughout his massive Empire he spread Greek art, literature and philosophy and scholarship which were to have their influence through the following centuries.

After his death, the kingdom was divided into territories ruled by generals but the system was too loose to survive very long and the political structure soon dissolved. Away to the west, the Romans were gradually increasing their power and by 200BC Rome was in control of the city-states of the Italian peninsula. Over the next 50 years Rome steadily increased its influence over Greece.

The Roman Domination (146BC-AD330)

Attacks by the Greeks on the Roman envoys in Corinth in 146BC proved to be a significant event. The Roman army descended on Corinth and completely destroyed it and continued to establish control over the whole Greek Empire. They abolished democracy and substituted their own military control making Greece nothing more than a province of Rome. This marked the end of independent ancient Greek history. As far as the traveller is concerned, the other significant period in Greek history which is still present through its architecture is that of Byzantine and medieval times stretching from AD395 through until the Turkish occupation in 1453.

In the decline of the Roman Empire, Constantine became the emperor in control of both east and west. The site he chose for a new capital was Byzantium on the Bosphorus which was originally founded by Byzas in 630BC. From Byzantium emerged the new spiritual and political capital of the Byzantine Empire, *Constantinople*, which was to hold power for almost a thousand years until its ultimate collapse in 1453.

Constantine died in AD337 and was baptised a Christian on his death-bed but it was not until AD380 that Christianity became the state religion. Shortly afterwards a proclamation was made to close the heathen temples like Delphi and the Parthenon. Even the Olympic Games were discontinued because of the nudity. Temples were now converted into Christian churches and new elements entered the architecture. It was in this period that basilicas with double colonnades appeared and domes, representing heaven.

Constantinople was besieged by the Persians then the Arabs in the seventh century but the Empire survived except for the loss of Egypt. From the ninth to the twelfth centuries, under strong leadership and more settled conditions, a period of cultural advancement was reflected in church architecture. Small stone built churches appeared in the shape of a cross with four arms of equal length and with a central dome. Internally, Christ was positioned centrally in the dome with the Virgin in the Apse and angels, apostles and saints placed hierarchically. The monastery at Osios Loukas was built in this period. Towards the very end of the Byzantine period churches were constructed combining the basilica and the cross structure and incorporating several small domes.

In 1204 *Constantinople* was sacked by the Fourth Crusade when the Germans, Franks and Venetians turned their armies against it. Two centuries of conflict and shifting power followed with the increasingly expansionist Turks taking over much of mainland Greece. On 29 May 1453 *Constantinople* fell to the Muslim Turks and the Turkish occupancy of Greece was all but complete, many of the islands still free fell later.

The Turkish Rule (1453-1830)

Memories of the Ottoman occupation, which lasted almost 400 years, still fester in the mind of the modern Greek. Greece as a nation sank into obscurity and took refuge in rural provincialism. The Greek Orthodox church was tolerated by the Islamic doctrine and designated by the Turks as a secular administrative body. By default, the church became the custodian of Greek identity. The preservation of Byzantine culture rested with the monasteries which sometimes secretly schooled the children.

Gradually the Ottoman administration started to disintegrate becoming more decentralised. In these changing circumstances some regions were achieving more autonomy, Greek merchant fleets started to grow and trade throughout the Mediterranean. Widespread resentment of Turkish rule largely remained isolated but increasing support and co-operation between rival groups finally led to the War of Independence in 1821-1822.

On 25 March 1821 the Greek flag of independence was raised at the monastery of Agia Lavra in the northern Peloponnese which is now remembered as National Independence Day. The struggle continued for some time with European public opinion enraged by the well publicised slaughter by the Turks of 25,000 Greeks on Chios and Psara. In 1827 Ioannis Kapodistrias was appointed by Greek leaders as the first president of independent Greece. His autocratic style of government was widely resented and he was assassinated in 1831. Otto, a young Bavarian prince gained support and approval to become the first King of Greece in 1833. Greek independence was confirmed by the western powers in 1830 and the borders were drawn to include part of central Greece, the Peloponnese, the Cyclades and the Argo-Saronic islands

Monuments of the Turkish rule are scattered throughout Greece but are remarkably few in relation to the length of occupation. Mosques and minarets can still be seen around Ioannina and Turkish-style houses with projecting wooden upper storeys still survive in places like Pilion and Kastoria.

1
ATHENS AND ATTICA

The lure of Athens (Athena) lies in a romantic vision of an age long since past. A pastoral vision of graceful architecture, greenery and tumbling streams. The present day reality is a high density sprawl. A huge concrete monster with an insatiable appetite intent on devouring all in its path. Even the restraining hills seem in danger of being swamped. Add to this noise, dirt and pollution and one may wonder why anyone still bothers to go at all but go they do. In the middle of this concrete jungle still lie the remains of Athens' ancient glory where it is still possible to escape into the past. Byron's view of Athens in 1809 was succinctly expressed in this apt couplet and there has been no improvement since. 'Shrine of the mighty! Can it be That this is all remains of thee?'

The removal of the capital of newly liberated Greece from Nafplio to Athens in 1834 provided an ideal opportunity for improvement. There followed a period of planned building construction in neo-Classical style but dreams of repeating Pericles achievement were abruptly ended in 1922 as a result of the Greek-Turkish war in Asia Minor. The ethnic population exchange which ensued witnessed an influx of political refugees. Unable to keep pace with housing demands, shanty towns mushroomed in outlying areas. The problem was further aggravated by World War II followed by Civil War and a subsequent massive population movement from rural areas into the city.

Athens lies in the Attica basin surrounded by the mountains of Parnes (1,413m/4,635ft), Pendeli (1,107m/3,631ft), Hymettus (1,026m/3365ft) and Egaleo (468m/1,535ft). Its current problems are compounded by its geographical position and a population which has almost quadrupled to around four million people in the past 40 years; over a third of the population of Greece. The attendant pollution from industry and cars is trapped by the surrounding ring of mountains and, in summer, the *nefos* lies like a yellow blanket over the city.

A word of warning; do not be tempted to underestimate the pollution. It is usually at its very worst during the heat of summer when traffic can sometimes be stopped for days at a time to give it chance to clear. Even the

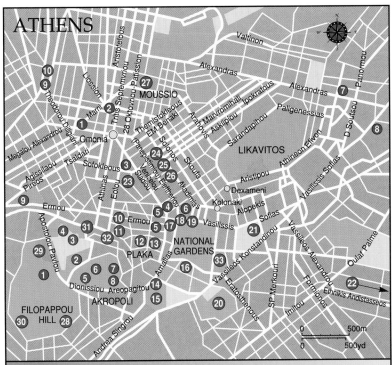

KEY TO STREET PLAN

● Places to Visit

1 The Pynx
2 The Areopagus *(Hill of Ares)*
3 The Agora
4 The Temple of Hephaistos
5 The Herod Atticus Odeon
6 The Acropolis
7 Acropolis Museum
8 The Theatre of Dionysos
9 Kermeikos & Museum
10 Kapnikarea
11 Agios Eleftherios Church & Athens Cathedral *(Metropolis)*
12 Popular Art & Tradition Centre
13 Popular Art Museum
14 Hadrian's Arch
15 The Temple of the Olympian Zeus
16 The Zappeion Exhibition & Congress Hall
17 Syntagma Square
18 Tomb of the Unknown Soldier
19 Greek National Parliament Building
20 The Stadium
21 War Museum
22 Monastery of Kaisariani
23 Agia Theodoria Church
24 Library
25 University
26 Academy
27 National Archaeological Museum
28 Filopappou Monument
29 Observatory
30 Filopappou Theatre
31 Flea Market *(Monastiraki)*
32 Tower of the Winds & Roman Agora
33 Presidential Residence *(Last Royal Palace)*

● Public Services

1 Athens Traffic Police
2 First Aid Station
3 Antiques & Restoration Bureau
4 Greek National Tourist Office *(EOT)*
5 GNTO Information Desk *(EOT)*
6 Press & Information Bureau
7 Aliens Bureau
8 Automobile & Touring Club
9 Railway Station–Peloponnese
10 Railway Station–Northern Greece

healthy can become ill so if you suffer from any respiratory complaint do not contemplate a visit then. November to April are the best months to visit with early spring perhaps the best time of all.

The major sites are confined to a relatively small area within the city centre and, with an early start, easily viewed in one day. A stay of a few days however, allows for wider exploration and a chance to discover some easily accessible oases like the delightful monastery at Kaisariani, the National Gardens and Filopappou Hill.

Driving in Athens is a nightmare of congestion, one-way systems, vague signposting, parking restrictions, wheel clamping and confiscated number plates to name but a few of the problems. For these reasons all tours in the city described, with one exception, are either by foot, on public transport or an organised trip. If you do arrive with your own car some hotels provide parking, check beforehand if possible. There are also a number of storage garages in Athens and Piraeus (details follow).

Most of the accommodation in Athens is centrally situated. Hotels close to Syntagma and Plaka providing the most convenient base for getting around on foot. There is no premium on the price of hotels in Athens compared with other parts of Greece thanks to tourist office control. For those not wishing to stay in the city there are plenty of hotels by the coast out at Glyfada, Voula and Vouliagmeni close to the airport. These coastal resorts are connected to the city by a regular bus service, a journey of about 45 minutes, but when it is very busy this can be a long hot journey.

Tour 1 • Ancient Athens

π A visit to Athens is synonymous with a visit to the **Acropolis**. As long ago as 7,000BC Stone Age man was attracted to the hill and built one of the earliest settlements in Greece on its slopes. During the Mycenaean era it was peopled by successive priest-kings and their retainers who lived in a palace on the site. The remains of cyclopean walls stem from this time. From 1100BC there followed a period of transformation which saw the decline of the palace culture of the Minoan-Mycenaean world. This Dark Age, about which little is known, lasted for several hundred years and ended with the emergence of the *polis* or Greek city-state and the beginnings of democracy. Temples to the gods of the *polis* replaced the palace and other secular buildings on the Acropolis but these were destroyed by the Persians in 480BC. Athens' brief period of glory or 'Golden Age' lasted for 32 years from 461BC during the time Pericles was head of state. Using the Delian League funds, which had been transferred by the Athenians from Delos to the Acropolis, Pericles embarked on an ambitious building plan. His construction programme was executed in an amazingly short span of time, the Parthenon itself taking only 10 years to complete. After Pericles' death Athens never regained the prosperity and growth it had enjoyed under his rule falling prey to various uses and misuses of successive conquerors.

The most pleasant way to approach the Acropolis is through Plaka, from Syntagma via Nikis, Nikodimou, Flessa and up left off Lissiou, thus avoiding the busy road which runs beneath its southern flank. A paved path, just below the Acropolis, passes an entrance to the Agora and the Areopagus, visited later in the tour, before joining the main route up to the Acropolis. Facilities close to the main entrance include a bank, post office, refreshments, cloakroom/left luggage (in season) and toilets. To avoid the sizzling heat in summer make an early start. Beware of the treacherous highly polished marble underfoot!

The Sacred Way: This ancient route (20km/12 miles) ran between the Sanctuary of Eleusis (Elefsina) passing through the ceremonial Sacred Gate, adjacent to the Dipylon Gate, and through the Agora before rising up to the Propylaia.

The Beule Gate: A Roman addition built in the third century AD and the entrance to the Acropolis site.

The Propylaia: Is the name given to the group of buildings which make up the original entrance complex. The Propylon being the actual entrance built, in this case, to resemble a temple.

The Temple of Athena Nike: An exquisite temple situated high up to the right of the Propylaia.

The Erechtheion: The Temple to Athena and Poseidon built on the most sacred part of the Acropolis. On this site the two gods were believed to have held their contest to decide who ruled Athens. Its appeal today is sight of the six graceful Karyatides (copies) and the deceptive ease with which they support the porch. The original Karyatides have been removed, one by Lord Elgin and the remainder into a protective atmosphere within the Acropolis Museum.

The Acropolis Museum: Unobtrusively built on lower ground to the east of the Parthenon. Here, in addition to various pottery finds and statues, are the original Karyatides, fragments of friezes, the Almond-Eyed Kore, the Kritios Boy, the Calf-Bearer and a sculpture of the graceful, winged figure of Athena Nike untying her sandal.

The Parthenon: The Temple of Athena Parthenos (Temple of the Virgin Athena) stands proudly aloof from crass modernity, despite its tumultuous history, and continues to epitomise all that was ancient Greece. Rampant erosion is the present enemy and constantly threatens to overwhelm restoration work.

The Theatre of Dionysos: The most famous theatre of the Greek world nestling into the south-east side of the hill beneath the Acropolis. Most of the present day remains are Roman.

The Asklepion: A healing sanctuary built close to the Theatre of Dionysos. A natural location considering the close relationship between drama and healing.

The Stoa of Eumenes: Constructed in the second century BC as a shelter and promenade along a section of the peripatos close to the Theatre of Dionysos. It was later connected to the Odeon of Herod Atticus by the Romans.

Odeon of Herod Atticus: Built into the south-west slope of the hill in the

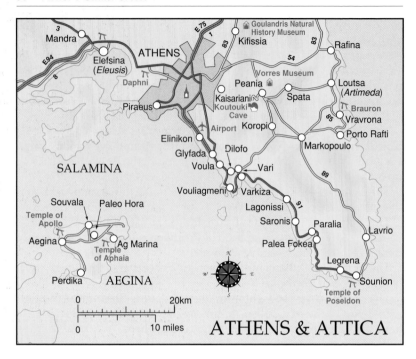

ATHENS & ATTICA

second century AD and restored for present day use. The Odeon is normally closed, except for performances, and the best view of it can be had from the Acropolis.

The Peripatos: The ancient road around the lower Acropolis.

The Areopagus (Hill of Ares): A small hill across a saddle to the north-west of the Acropolis hill. It was on this site the Council of Areopagus met to rule on matters of justice and in AD 51 St Paul preached the new gospel. Provides an excellent vantage point for a bird's eye view of the Agora.

The Agora: Once the hub of ancient Athenian life, now a welcome retreat. Amongst the ancient foundations stand the tenth century AD Church of the Holy Apostles and the Stoa of Attalos now rebuilt and housing a museum. On a rise in the north-west corner of the Agora is the excellently preserved Thesion or Temple of Hephaistos. From the temple there is a good view over the Agora to the Acropolis.

Tour 2 • Hill Of The Muses: Filopappou Hill and The Pnyx

Filopappou Hill, with its huge monument, and Pnyx Hill are usually only accorded a passing glance by most people as they pause in their scramble around the Acropolis. Their wooded slopes though, criss-crossed with footpaths, provide a welcome retreat from the city heat. The reward for a walk up to the monument is a clear view of the Acropolis and over the city.

A view of the Acropolis with Likavitos Hill prominent in the background

The Karyatides support the porch of the Erechtheion with deceptive ease

Follow the same route through Plaka as for Tour 1 but continue on the main path down to Dionissiou Areopagitou road. Cross the road and head right towards the roundabout from where a cobbled road leads up onto Filopappou Hill and over to the Filopappou Theatre.

Filopappou Hill: Known also as the 'Hill of the Muses' provides extensive walkways amongst its tree clad slopes. Follow a path off left of the cobbled road to take you up to the huge monument dedicated to a Roman senator and consul, Filopappos. On the way up there are pleasant areas with old marble seats where you can rest and drink in the views over Athens. Heading back down towards the Pnyx, pass the Prison of Socrates and the Byzantine church of Ag Demetrios with its original frescos.

Pnyx Hill: Questions relating to public policy were debated by the Athenian Assembly on this hill. The area is now used for a Sound and Light show in summer. On the south-west side of the hill is a large picnic area with tables and drinking water fountains. Extensive views stretch beyond Piraeus to the sea.

Hill of the Nymphs: The site of the Observatory and gardens. Only occasionally open to the public.

Tour 3 • City Panorama

The narrow streets off sophisticated Kolonaki Square teem with boutiques for the fashion conscious and, without the constant roar of traffic, drinking coffee and people watching could be a pleasant pastime at one of the pavement cafés in the square itself. On the plus side, a rarely encountered feature are public toilets kept in pristine condition. The 15 minutes walk to Likavitos funicular station starts from this square and takes you up through Dexameni Square with its quieter ambience.

Likavitos Hill (277m/909ft), the ultimate destination, is the highest point in Athens and the place to go for a complete panoramic view over the city and beyond. It is particularly renowned for viewing spectacular sunsets. Start your wander up pedestrianised Skoufa and on the corner of Iraklitou, where you turn right, is 'Everest' one of the best take-away food shops in the area.

Head up into leafy Dexameni Square with its outdoor café tables and the site of a reservoir begun by the Emperor Hadrian. Continue along Dinokratous as far as Ploutarchou. A left turn here will take you directly up to the funicular station for the 2 minutes ascent of Likavitos. One of the many footpaths and the most direct (15 minutes) starts 2 minutes along to the west of the station. The winding path passes a café/bar around halfway up and emerges by the small white chapel dedicated to St George, on the very top above a restaurant. An alternative path down from the lower terrace leads past the Likavitos Theatre used for Greek Dance performances in summer.

Tour 4 • Museums

One thing Athens is not short of is museums. There are more than enough to keep the most ardent buff going throughout a long holiday. This programme highlights just two. The not to be missed National Museum and the fascinating Goulandris Natural History Museum out at Kifissia. Those with an appetite for more might like to consider the closely grouped Benaki Museum for Greek folk art and handicrafts, Museum of Cycladic and Ancient Greek Art, Byzantine Museum and War Museum on Vasilissis Sofias Avenue. The National Gallery is located in front of the Hilton Hotel and there are many small galleries to be found in the city centre.

The National Archaeological Museum: Situated north of Omonia Square in Patission, this vast museum demands at least a good half-day of your time. Time, and lots of it, is required to fully appreciate the sheer quality of artistry in such volume. To reap the benefit of a visit you do need a guide or a detailed guide book as the wonderful exhibits are unimaginatively displayed and labelling is almost non existent. Despite these drawbacks, the displays are housed in defined areas of the museum. By far the biggest draw is the Mycenaean Hall (Room 4) housing Schliemann's gold finds from Mycenae including what he wrongly believed to be the gold death mask of Agamemnon. How long they will remain on display in Athens is a moot point as they are scheduled to be rehoused in an on-site museum at Mycenae. Amongst the Classical Art collection can be found the bronze fifth-century BC Statue of Poseidon (Room 15) and the Little Jockey (Room 21) both reclaimed from the sea off Evia. Lifelike sculptures of the Youth of Antikythera (Room 28) and the heads of a Boxer, Philosopher and Man from Delos with his superbly captured poignant expression (Room 30). A naked Aphrodite (Room 31) excites a great deal of attention but the many sensitively sculpted Stelai provide an insight into the everyday life of the people of the time. Also not to be missed are the fantastic Thira frescos, upstairs in Room 48, restored to their original position on the walls to show how they would have looked about 3,450 years ago. Add to this rooms full of pottery and smaller finds plus an extensive Numismatic Collection, in a separate museum, on the first floor and you will almost certainly be left with the feeling that you have not been able to give full justice to your visit. The Numismatic Museum can be entered from outside, from Tositsa, or from inside the Archaeological Museum on payment of a separate entrance fee.

The Goulandris Natural History Museum: A 35-minute journey north on the metro takes you as far as its last stop, the pleasant, leafy suburb of Kifissia where this delightful and excellent museum is situated. Interesting and informative displays make it a pleasant and worthwhile trip out from the city centre for adults and children alike. To locate the museum, about a 10-minute walk, turn left outside the station along Dragoumi. Reach a T-junction and turn right into Othonos. Keep ahead across the

Flea market souvenirs in Monastiraki

The Tower of the Winds in Plaka

Fresh coconut, one of the more unusual snacks sold by street vendors

The salepi *seller.* Salepi *is a milk made from the tubers of wild orchids and is believed to be an aphrodisiac*

busy mainroad at traffic lights and continue to the next T-junction where you turn right into Levithou. The museum is sited in the large house immediately on the right.

The museum is divided up into easily viewed sections starting with plants. A big three-dimensional model of a plant cell sets the tone for this simplified but highly accurate display, set up in collaboration with the Natural History Department of the British Museum in London. Insects comprises a collection of thousands of insects from all parts of mainland Greece and the islands. Birds are displayed in lifelike settings and there is even a cast of the fossilised remains of Archaeopteryx said to be the first bird that appeared on earth. The three main groups of mammals are explained and there is a fascinating collection of amphibians and reptiles. Here is an opportunity to learn how to identify the different species of tortoise to be found in the Greek countryside. Last but not least are sections covering dinosaurs, molluscs and other invertebrates, fossils and minerals and rocks. There is a café and shop in the museum.

Tour 5 • Old Athens

A stroll round Plaka's narrow streets conjures up a romantic image of an age past and is particularly atmospheric in the evening. Monastiraki on the other hand is a noisier more bustling quarter during the day and the location of the Flea Market but for a little solitude escape to the site of Athens' ancient cemetery, Kerameikos.

Start out from Syntagma Square (Platia Syntagmatos) down Mitropoleos, which leads past the Cathedral to Monastiraki, and turn left up Nikis to locate the souvenir shopping streets of Kidathineon and Adrianou.

❋   **Plaka**, the oldest residential area in Athens on the lower northern slope of the Acropolis Hill, is a pleasure to explore. Its many narrow streets and alleyways hiding a few quiet backwaters especially in Anafiotika where mid-nineteenth-century construction workers from the island of Anafi built their homes. Busy, pedestrianised Kidathineon and Adrianou are lined with numerous souvenir shops their wares spilling out onto the streets in a kaleidoscope of colour. Adrianou stretches from the Thesion by the Ancient Agora almost to Hadrian's Arch passing the metro station at Monastiraki and the Monument of Lysicrates which carried the bronze tripod he won in a drama contest. Squeezed into an area off Adrianou at its junction with Eolou, below the Acropolis, is the Roman Agora and the first century BC Tower of the Winds, a water clock, compass, weather vane and sundial. As a change from shopping there are the Popular Arts Museum, Popular Arts and Traditions Centre and an open-air cinema. Tavernas and cafés abound for mellow evenings spent eating and drinking in one of Plaka's leafy squares to the sound of a bouzouki or, for more robust Greek evenings, in a night club environment.

Merging into Plaka, **Monastiraki** and its bazaar-like atmosphere is where to head for a taste of more authentic Greek life, especially to the west of Monastiraki square. The **Flea Market** starts down Pandrossou which runs from the bottom corner of the cathedral square on Mitropoleos. Along this more touristy section can be found the 'poet-sandalmaker' of Athens, Stavros Melissinos, who made sandals for John Lennon of 'The Beatles' fame. Across Monastiraki Square the Flea Market fills narrow Ifestou with an amazing array of goods for sale and exudes a more homespun air. The square itself has been the core of a market area since Turkish times. A past which is still very much alive today in the cacophony of sound from barrel-organ players to the many street vendors touting lottery tickets, nuts, fruit, drinks and various snack foods. Every Sunday the Flea Market cascades into the surrounding streets attracting throngs of Athenians in search of a bargain. Even the Flower Market, close to the Church of Ag Irini (St Irene) a little way up Eolou, becomes drawn into the carnival-like atmosphere.

Entered from Ermou and tucked into the wedge of land between Ermou and Pireos lies **Kerameikos** a little visited and unexpectedly peaceful haven. This is the site of the main cemetery of ancient Athens where the ruins of the Long Walls, which ran to the port at Piraeus, and the Dipylon and Sacred Gates can be seen. Some plots have been excavated and their original or replica stones replaced in position. Terracotta figurines, vases and intricately sculpted stelai form an extensive collection of finds from the site which are housed in the on-site Oberlaender Museum.

Tour 6 • Shopping And Byzantine Churches

Compared with most other major cities Athens' shopping centre is contained within a relatively small area. Situated on the north side and adjacent to the city's ancient quarter, it is easily accessible to most tourist hotels. Also to be found in the same area are a clutch of Byzantine churches all fighting for survival amidst the concrete and car exhaust fumes. The suggested route provides a good overview but, with more time to spare, further exploration of narrow streets like Leka and Praxitelous are worthwhile.

Syntagma Square makes a good starting point for a shopping expedition and is also where airline and tour company offices can be located. Ferries and organised trips can be booked at travel agents along Filelinon and Nikis on the Plaka side of Mitropoleos en route to Athens Cathedral (Metropolis) which dwarfs its much more interesting predecessor the twelfth-century AD church of Ag Eleftherios.

Leave the Cathedral Square along Evangelistrias to reach the clothing shops and Byzantine **Church of Kapnikarea**, now a traffic island in the middle of the road, on Ermou. Escape the traffic by turning up towards Omonia into a pedestrianised section of Eolou to pass the colourful

Flower Market alongside the **Church of Ag Irini**. Spare time also to pause and look back for the best view of the Tower of the Winds against the backdrop of the Acropolis hill before turning left towards Athinas on reaching Evripidou. (Diverting briefly right at this point leads to the **Church of Ag Theodori** at the end of Evripidou.) A right turn into Athinas and the clamour of human activity competes with the roar of traffic around the Meat and Fish Market on the right and the Fruit and Vegetable Market on the left. Past the markets on the right is fenced off **Kotzia Square**, containing excavated remains, around which a Greek version of a car boot sale is held on Sundays.

Hurtling traffic, squealing tyres and scurrying crowds epitomise **Omonia Square**, the heart of the student quarter. Traffic converges from many directions, circling the controversial glass statue of an olympic runner on the island in the centre, most of it heading down Ag Konstantinou in the direction of Corinth and the Peloponnese or Pireos to

The pristine façade of the Hellenic Academy, Athens

Piraeus. Passageways and arcades lined with shops and quick-food outlets run off the square and provide a welcome diversion from the constant noise and congestion. The larger department stores are also situated in the vicinity.

The route continues out to the east of Omonia Square crossing Ermou then back down Eleftheriou Venizelou, better known as Panepistimiou, in the direction of Syntagma. Three buildings of note stand side by side about half way down on the left the **Library** (Bibliothiki), the **University** (Panepistimiou) and the **Academy** (Akadimia). They are easy to pass by and admire from a distance but frescos depicting the arts and science which adorn the porch of the University are worth a pause. The photogenic and pristine façade of the Academy gives the appearance of having been plucked straight out of an ancient Greek setting.

The fashionable shopping area around **Kolonaki Square** almost completes the circuit. As a change from designer boutiques, a lively fruit, flower and vegetable street market is held close by on Friday mornings along Xenokratous.

Tour 7 • Constitutional Heart

Syntagma or Constitution Square with its garden and cafés is possibly the most familiar square and meeting point in Athens. The sentries guarding the **Tomb of the Unknown Soldier** outside the Parliament building draw the crowds but fewer people venture into the restful ambience of the National Gardens close by. Built between 1834 and1838 as a palace for Greece's King Otho, the **Greek National Parliament Building** or 'Vouli' looks disdainfully down over Syntagma Square. The focus of interest though is not the building but the ceremonial guards or *evzones* who stand guard at the front. With their unusual costumes, based on those of the *klefts* from northern Greece, and their strange clockwork movements they are a constant source of fascination. Every Sunday at 11am there is an official changing of the guard when a troop of soldiers, all dressed in their 'best' uniforms, march on parade accompanied by a band.

The **National Gardens** (Ethnikos Kipos) spread out behind the Parliament building. Access from Syntagma is along Leoforos Amalias or up Vassilissis Sofias past the flower sellers. First designed, landscaped and planted between 1839 and 1860 they became the first Royal Gardens of King Otho and Queen Amalia. Dedicated more to ornamental plants than flowers, there are more than 500 species and varieties most of which are not native. During a period of democracy in 1927 the gardens were renamed the National Gardens and opened to the public. Signposted footpaths weave through tangled foliage which creates a cooling protective canopy from the relentless summer sun. Tucked away amidst this greenery is a Botanical Museum, close to the Parliament building, tranquil pools and what could be loosely termed a menagerie.

The rear of a large crescent shaped building, the Zappeion, and a wide boulevard mark the southern end of the gardens. The **Zappeion** was built especially for the 1896 Olympic Games by the Zappas family. It was used to house the competitors and effectively became the first Olympic village of modern times. At the front side of the building, closest to Irodou Attikou (Herod Atticus Street), is the famous 'Aigli' café/restaurant/ open-air cinema complex but only the café is open year round.

To the east of the Zappeion at the junction of Irodou Attikou and Vassileos Konstandinou is the **Stadium** (Stadiou). It was rebuilt over its ancient predecessor for the 1896 Olympic Games but is too narrow for competitive use today. A short way up Irodou Attikou is the last Royal and now the Presidential Palace where more *evzones* can be seen on guard outside.

South from the Zappeion leads through the Zappeion Gardens and crosses Leoforos Olgas to the **Temple of Olympian Zeus** and Hadrian's Arch. The temple, completed by Hadrian, was the largest Corinthian temple in Greece with 104 columns of which only fourteen remain standing today. **Hadrian's Arch** was erected by him to mark the boundary between 'the city of Theseus' and 'the city of Hadrian'. Something of their former glory is restored at night when they can be viewed floodlit.

Tour 8 • The Monastery Of Kaisariani

Peace and solitude lie no more than 5½km (3 miles) from the heart of Athens at Kaisariani (Kessariani). The grounds of this eleventh-century monastery, on the lower slopes of Mount Hymettus, are a botanists' delight and an ideal setting for a picnic even when the monastery itself is closed. Raised above the infamous 'nefos' by its position at a height of 450m (1,476ft) above sea level it is arguably the loveliest country site closest to the city. If quietness is a priority avoid weekends and holidays.

Take blue bus number 224 to Kaisariani, boarding at the first blue shelter up Vassilissis Sofias, to the left of the Parliament building. The monastery is a 2½km (1½ miles) walk of about 30 to 40 minutes from the terminus so it is advisable to take refreshments as there are no shops or cafés en route or at the monastery. Stay on the bus for the 15 to 20 minutes bus journey as far as the terminus. Walk back to the road the bus has just left, turn right, and continue up the road with the cemetery on your right. There is no pavement but once past the cemetery a path winds through the trees alongside the road to the right. Flower lovers will definitely want to linger in spring to inspect the scattering of flowers along the way including the bee orchids *Ophrys lutea, O. fusca* and the beautiful saw-fly orchid *O. tenthredinifera*. Amongst the Orchis species are the delicate *Orchis quadripunctata* and the fascinating naked-man orchid *O. italica*. Standing above all is the giant orchid, *Barlia robertiana*, which can reach a height of half a metre. Muscari species also abound but difficult to spot amongst the foliage is *Fritillaria graeca* and the iris-like *Hermodactylus tuberosus*.

Keep right to pass under the motorway bridge. The road continues directly to the monastery but by far the more interesting route is to turn immediately right now up the steps alongside the motorway. Take the path up diagonally left, just before the paved area ends by the motorway, which runs into a stronger path. Keep left, rising steadily, with the motorway now behind. More of the same flowers brighten the way but keep up right at a fork in the path and climb a little more steeply before crossing a track. Soon after, before the next bend, take the well defined path up to the left. Rise up into a clearing where there are the ruins of the tenth-century AD Church of the Assomaton Taxiarchon and chapel of St Mark. To the right is a pine fringed picnic area from where there is a wonderful panorama over Athens.

Continue on the path past the ruins and descend on the far side towards the monastery which can now be seen through the trees ahead. Conservationists will be pleased to learn that Athens Friends of the Trees Society are responsible for the upkeep of the cypress, pine, plane, olive, almond, apple and eucalyptus trees which shade the site. Stepping into the leafy enclosure which houses the monastery and its two churches is a refreshing world away from the twentieth century turmoil outside. On the opposite side of the monastery to the entrance is a ram's head fountain. It is fed by waters from a spring, a little higher up, which was once purported to enhance fertility. The same spring also used to supply Athens with drinking water.

Return to the bus terminus via the same route or down the road. On the ride back into Athens the Hilton Hotel provides a timely reminder that the bus is entering Vassilissis Sofia. Alight opposite the War Museum, as the bus then shoots off to the right into a maze of back streets away from Syntagma.

Tour 9 • Daphni And Eleusis (Elefsina)

Follow the route of the Sacred Way to the site of the Sanctuary of Demeter and its famed Eleusinian Mysteries. Stop off at Daphni, the half way point, to admire the mosaics in one of the oldest Byzantine monasteries.

Blue buses (ticket only) for Daphni and Elefsina depart from Platia Eleftherias, off Pireos, at frequent intervals. Numbers 853, 854, 855, 862 and 880 start from close to the corner where Dipilou and Milerou cross.

The bus roughly follows the route of the Sacred Way through uninspiring suburbs and industrialisation. A more country atmosphere and the sight of castellated walls, after a journey of about 20 minutes, heralds your arrival at Daphni.

Approach the monastery down the wide track across the road from the bus stop. **Daphni** was named after the laurels, sacred to Apollo, which grew in the area. His Sanctuary stood on the same site and remnants from

that building were incorporated into the construction of the boundary wall and the monastery. Rebuilt in the eleventh century AD little remains of the earlier fifth-century AD structure dedicated to the Virgin Mary. Fragmentary remains of mosaics and newly restored frescos are worth viewing. A Wine Festival is held in the grounds each year.

Continue by bus a further 20 minutes along the Sacred Way to **Eleusis** at **Elefsina**. Ask for Arkaos (Ancient) Eleusis. To locate the site look for a fluttering Greek flag atop an elevated pale blue clock tower. Walk along the street and through a pedestrianised platia to the site entrance which is on the left. The surroundings might be industrial but the attractive site, on the slopes of a low rocky hill, manages to distance itself from present day intrusion. In the museum is a model of the layout of the Sanctuary of Demeter which helps give substance to the many foundations.

The Sanctuary at Eleusis was a centre for the worship of Demeter — Kore, the Earth Mother and her daughter Persephone. Greeks believed the Eleusinian Mysteries held the universe together and that life would end without them so they were also connected with cycles of lunar and solar movements. Initiates, sworn to a vow of secrecy, underwent rituals which centred around death and rebirth, in their quest for immortality. Return to Athens from the bus stop on the main road.

Tour 10 • Koutouki Cave And Vorres Museum

Mount Hymettus hides a different face on its eastern slope from the one most usually viewed from Athens. Stark it may be, when compared with its softer lower slopes to the west, but visitors to the cave are rewarded with sweeping views across the Mesogeia Plain eastwards over the coast to Evia and beyond.

Catch a blue bus number 125 or 310 for the 50 minute journey to **Peania**, (Paiania) from the terminus at Thissio close by the junction of Eptahalkou and Apostolou Pavlou. Ask to be told when you reach the platia in Peania where you can catch a taxi for the 5km (3miles) up to **Koutouki Cave**.

There are conducted tours of the cave every half-hour which take about 20 minutes. It is advisable to wear suitable footwear as the floor is fairly wet and can be slippery. Inside the cave the concealed lighting highlights the more spectacular stalactite and stalagmite formations enhancing the varied hues and shades of colour in the rock formations. The green coloration is man induced; it is algae growth in response to the artificial illumination. A sound and light finale where the changing colour temperature of light is sequenced to match that of natural daylight, a rosy dawn for example, makes a fitting end to the visit. Refreshments and souvenirs are available and there is a large terrace on which to sit and admire the views.

(opposite) Tranquility at Kaisariani, close to Athens centre

Return to Peania and, if it is weekend, there is the opportunity to visit the **Vorres Museum** and gardens. The museum, situated near the square, houses what began as a private collection of Greek art and covers a variety of styles as far back as Mycenaean times.

Tour 11 • The Apollo Coast

Pink hued dawns and blazing golden-red sunsets create a mystical aura around the majestic white marble Temple of Poseidon at Cape Sounion. A commanding landmark down the centuries for sailors approaching the Saronic Gulf from the Aegean and, more recently, for air travellers on the descent into Athens airport.

It is a 65km (40 mile) winding run down the Apollo Coast to Cape Sounion. Orange buses leave Athens regularly from Mavromateon at its junction with Leoforos Alexandras (south-west corner of Areos Park) for the trip down to Sounion. The quicker bus goes via the coast road and the other via Markopoulo and Lavrio through the middle of Attica. Either can be a long hot journey especially in summer. The advantages of hiring a car are that you can stop where you like when you like. The disadvantages are more noticeable in summer when the coast road is crowded and driving slow. The most comfortable way to go is on an organised trip on an air-conditioned coach run by companies such as CHAT, KEY and GO and with an accompanying guide who dispenses interesting information en route as well as leading a guided tour of the site.

Exit Athens along Leoforos Syngrou for the 1 ½ hour drive to Sounion. Go left at Old Faliron on approaching the coast. The island of Aegina is clearly visible in the gulf to the right as the coast is followed down in the direction of the west airport at Elinikon. Once past the airport the area becomes visibly more upmarket. Glyfada, with its fish restaurants and high class shops and apartments where wealthy Athenians spend their weekends, merges with Voula. After Voula where the road divides keep to the longer and prettier coastal road. The inland road, to the left through Dilofo and Vari, is lined with tavernas frequented by Greeks who flock there for specialities such as suckling pig and goat. Continue following the coast through Vouliagmeni passing the Astir Beach promontory which is the site of the sixth-century BC Temple of Apollo from which the Apollo Coast gets its name.

Exclusive beach homes are more in evidence now as the dense building development closer to Athens is left behind. After Varkiza, where the shorter road through Vari rejoins, the route continues close to the coast through the smaller resorts of Lagonissi, Saronis and Palea Fokea which are popular with the Athenians. Buildings give way to rolling phrygana covered hills and the white columns of the Temple of Poseidon soon come into view ahead.

The **Temple of Poseidon** sits 60m (197ft) above the sea on the highest point of **Cape Sounion**. A fitting setting for the god of the wild sea and earthquakes. An earlier temple from the sixth-century BC stood on the site until it was destroyed by the Persians. The present temple was constructed at the same time as the Parthenon in the same Doric style but smaller. Today only sixteen of its thirty four columns remain standing. It is possible to make out the foundations of a small temple dedicated to Athena Sounias, the protector of Attika, on the isthmus connecting the cape to the mainland.

To really capture the mood of the site you need to visit early in the morning or in the evening. In spring there is the added delight of wild flowers amongst the mass of yellow *Medicago arborea* bushes. There is a feeling of being surrounded by the sea from the terrace of the café adjoining the site but be prepared to pay over the odds for a beer. **Lavrio**, which used to be an important centre for silver mining, is 10km (6 miles) further along the coast from Sounion. Ferries from Lavrio to the Island of Kea, more popularly known as Tzia, leave daily.

Tour 12 · The Island Of Aegina

An opportunity to enjoy refreshing sea breezes and swim in clear turquoise green water; to sample octopus, pistachios and the local retsina and visit the beautiful wooded site of the Temple of Aphaia from where there are fine views out over the Saronic Gulf. Aegina is one of the most ancient kingdoms of Greece and the first, albeit temporary, capital of Greece in 1828 before the seat of government was transferred to Nafplio then later Athens.

Ferry boats and hydrofoils ply daily between the main harbour at Piraeus and Aegina Town. The former takes 1½ hours and the latter 35 minutes. In summer there is a ferry service directly to **Ag Marina** which is convenient for visitors to the Temple of Aphaia. Tickets for ferry and hydrofoil are available from different kiosks close to where they depart. Take the metro to the harbour at Piraeus (Pireas) which takes about 15 to 20 minutes. Leave the station by the bottom exit and turn left for the 5 to 10 minutes walk to the harbour. Cross the road towards the seafront and the left-hand side of the bus station in Platia Karaiskaki. On reaching the harbour, look for the ferry and hydrofoil to the left.

On arrival in **Aegina Town** book your return ticket, especially in high season for the hydrofoil, from the kiosk on the harbour. The narrow streets are lively and colourful with souvenir shops, tavernas and a small fish market. On a headland to the left as you reach the harbour is the site of the Temple of Apollo which is open to the public. Just beyond the temple site is a narrow sand and shingle beach backed by pine and tamarisk trees which shade a pleasant picnic area.

Buses and taxis are located to the left as you disembark on arrival. It is advisable to arrive on the island early in the day as buses are more frequent in the morning. The bus to the main resort town of Ag Marina (25 minutes), with its sandy beach, passes close to the island's ruined old capital Paleohora before reaching the **Temple of Aphaia**. This late sixth century BC Doric construction, which was built on the site of two earlier temples, stands on a hill amidst pine trees about 3km (2 miles) outside Ag Marina. Many parts of the temple have been preserved or restored and with twenty four of the original thirty two columns now standing it is an impressive sight. Aphaia was an ancient goddess and patroness of Aegina but was replaced by the better known Athena at the time of the Trojan War. Thus the temple is known today as the Aphaia-Athena. The fishing village of Perdika to the south is also accessible by bus from Aegina Town (20 minutes).

Eastern Attica

The whole of the east coast of Attica is fast developing as a playground for Athenians who shun the glitz and glamour of Glyfada and Vouliagmeni. There is nothing much to attract the visitor to the central region except for those with an insatiable appetite for Byzantine churches. Hiring a car for two days would allow time for a visit to Sounion and the lesser sites of Amfiaraion, Ramnous, Marathon and Vravrona (Brauron).

The Temple of Poseidon at Sounion

Additional Information

Places to Visit

Athens
Acropolis Archaeological Site
Open: Monday-Friday 8am-5pm
Saturday-Sunday & Holidays 8.30am-3pm.

Acropolis Museum
Open: Monday 11am-5pm. Tuesday-Friday 8am-5pm. Saturday-Sunday & Holidays 8.30am-3pm.

Ancient Agora, Thision and Stoa of Attalus Museum
Open: Tuesday-Sunday & Holidays 8.30am-3pm. Closed Monday.

Benaki Museum
1 Koumbari & Vas Sofias, Open: Monday-Sunday & Holidays 8.30am-2pm. Closed Tuesday.

Byzantine Museum
22 Vas Sofias
Open: Tuesday-Sunday & Holidays 8.30am-3pm. Closed Monday.

Centre of Folk Art and Tradition
6 Hatzimihali (off Kidathineon) Free entry. Open Tuesday, Thu 9am-9pm Wednesday, Friday, Saturday 9am-1pm & 5-9pm Sunday & Holidays 9am-1pm. Closed Monday.

Dionysus Theatre
Open: Monday 11am-5pm, Tuesday-Friday 8am-5pm. Saturday, Sunday & Holidays 8.30am-3pm.

Greek Folk Art Museum
17 Kidathineon
Open: Tuesday-Sunday & Holidays 10am-2pm. Closed Monday.

Kerameikos Archaeological Site and Museum
148 Ermou
Open: Monday 11am-5pm. Tuesday-Friday 8am-5pm. Saturday, Sunday & Holidays 8.30am-3pm.

National Archaeological Museum
44 Patission
Open: Monday 11am-5pm. Tuesday-Friday 8am-5pm. Saturday, Sunday & Holidays 8.30am-3pm.

Numismatic Museum
1 Tossitsa
Open: Tuesday-Sunday & Holidays 8.30am-3pm. Closed Monday.

Roman Agora
Open: Tuesday-Sunday & Holidays 8.30am-3pm. Closed Monday.

Temple of the Olympian Zeus
Vas. Olgas & Amalias
Open: Tuesday-Sunday & Holidays 8.30am-3pm. Closed Monday.

War Museum of Greece
Vas. Sofias & Rizari
Open: Tuesday-Saturday 9am-2pm. Sunday & Holidays 9.30am-2pm. Closed Monday.

Athens Suburbs
Daphni Monastery
Open: Monday-Sunday & Holidays 8.30am-3pm.

Eleusis (Elefsina) Archaeological Site & Museum
Open: Tuesday-Sunday & Holidays 8.30am-3pm. Closed Monday.

Kaisariani Monastery
Open: Tuesday, Sunday & Holidays 8.30am-3pm. Closed Monday.

Kifissia, Goulandris Natural History Museum
13 Levidou
Open: Monday-Sunday & Holidays 9am-2.30pm. Closed Friday.

Aegina (Island)
Temple of Aphaia
Open: Monday-Friday 8am-5pm. Saturday, Sunday & Holidays 8.30am-3pm.

Temple of Apollo & Aegina Museum
Open: Daily 8.30am-3pm. Closed Monday.

Attica
Kalamos, Amfiaraio Archaeological Site
Open: Monday-Sunday & Holidays 8.30am-3pm.

Marathonas Tomb Museum
Open: Tuesday-Sunday & Holidays
8.30am-3pm. Closed Monday.

Peania, Vorres Museum
Open: Saturday, Sunday & Holidays
only 10am-2pm.

Ramnous Archaeological Site
Kato Souli
Open: Tuesday-Sunday & Holidays
8.30am-3pm. Closed Monday.

Sounion (Sounio), Temple of Poseidon
Open: daily & Holidays 10am-Sunset.

Vravrona Archaeological Site
(Brauron) Open: Tuesday-Sunday &
Holidays 9am-2.30pm. Closed Monday.

Vravrona Museum
Open: Tuesday-Sunday & Holidays
8.30am-3pm. Closed Monday.

Useful Information

Athens

POST OFFICE
The Post Offices located at Omonia
Square, Syntagma Square and the
Acropolis are open on Sundays from
9am-1.30pm in addition to their normal
weekday opening hours. There is also a
mobile Post Office at Monastiraki
Square open weekdays 8am-6pm and
Sundays from 8am-5pm.

LOCAL TRANSPORT
Buses run from 5am-12midnight.

Buses
Blue: Athens & Suburbs from various
stops in centre.
Green: Athens to Piraeus. Yellow
'trolleys'. A flat rate fare applies for the
above 'ticket only' services and tickets,
singly or in tens, are available from
kiosks throughout Athens. Validate in
ticket machine as enter vehicle.
Orange: Attica destinations. Most start
from Mavromateon Street.
Blue & Yellow double-decker: 24-hour
frequent express lines A &A and B &B
from the East and West air terminals stopping at Syntagma (Amalias Ave) and
Omonia (Stadiou St) to Bus Terminals A
and B and return. The B &B lines pass the

main railway stations. Port of Piraeus to
airports #19.

Bus Terminals (K.T.E.L.)
Well north of the city centre but
frequent bus links.
A: 100, Kifissou Street. Buses to Western
and Southern Greece and the Ionian
Islands. (Bus No. 051 every 10 minutes
from the corner of Zinonos &
Menandrou near Omonia. From 5am-
12midnight).
B: 260 Liossion Street (Closest to rail-
way stations). Buses to Northern and
Eastern Greece and Evia. (Bus No. 024
every 15 minutes from Amalias, in front
of the entrance to the National Gardens.
From 5am-12midnight. The nearest
Metro stop is Ag Nicholaos).

Railway Stations
Stathmos Peloponissou: for the
Peloponnese.
Stathmos Larissis: Northern Greece.
(Trolley Bus No #1 or Express Buses B
&B from in front of the Parliament
Building).

Metro
Piraeus to Kifissia. Runs from 5.30am-
12midnight.
Validate tickets in machines at barriers.
Journey times: Omonia - Piraeus 20
minutes. Omonia - Kifissia 30 minutes.
Stations: Piraeus (port) - Neo Faliro -
Moschato - Kallithea - Tavros - El.
Venizelos - Petralona - Thissio -
Monastiraki - Omonia - Victoria - Attiki
- Ag Nikolaos - Kato Patissia - Ag
Eleftherios - Patissia - Perissos -
Pefkakia - Nea Ionia - Iraklio - Irini -
Maroussi - K.A.T. - Kifissia

Hydrofoil (Flying Dolphins)
Tickets from office on quay at point of
departure or, in season, it is advisable to
book ahead in Athens. Enquire at EOT
for where to book. Buy return ticket on
arrival at destination. Daily service
direct to Aegina from Piraeus close by
Akti Tzelepi, 5-10 minutes walk from
the metro. Services to Poros, Hydra and
Spetses (Nafplion and Monemvasia in
season) depart from the Zea Marina, 20
minutes walk from metro.

Accommodation

HOTELS

There is no shortage of hotels and pensions in Athens from luxury (L) through to E class. The following list is just a small sample of what is on offer. Accommodation listed for Athens is close to Plaka and all listed below are open all year.

Hotel bookings can be made at the Hellenic Chamber of Hotels office at 2 Karegeorgis Servias Street. Syntagma, Athens (National Bank of Greece building) during opening hours. Also available from this address is a comprehensive list of hotels in Attica.

ATHENS: TELEPHONE PREFIX 01
Hotel Astir Palace (L)
Panepistimiou & Vas Sofias
106 71 Athens
☎ 3643112/9

Athens Hilton Hotel (L)
46 Vas Sofias
106 76 Athens
☎ 7220201/10

Grande Bretagne Hotel (L)
Syntagma Square
05 63 Athens
☎ 3230251/9, 3250701/9

Hotel Ledra Marriott (L)
113-115, Syngrou
117 45 Athens
☎ 9347711

Hotel Amalia (A)
10 Amalias
105 57 Athens
☎ 3237301/9

Hotel Electra Palace (A)
18 Nikodimou
105 57 Athens
☎ 3241401/7

Hotel Herodio (A)
4 Rovertou Galli
117 42 Athens
☎ 9236832/36

Olympic Palace (A)
16 Filellinon
105 57 Athens
☎ 3237611, 3237615

Hotel Ilissos (B)
72 Kallirois
117 45 Athens
☎ 9223523/9, 9223927/9

Hotel Omiros (B)
15 Apollonos
105 57 Athens
☎ 3235486/7

Hotel Aphrodite (C)
21 Apollonos
105 57 Athens
☎ 3234357/9, 3226047

Hotel Austria (C)
7 Mousiou
117 42 Athens
☎ 9235151/3, 9220777 (Reserv.)

Hotel Hermes (C)
19 Apollonos
105 57 Athens
☎ 3235514/6

Hotel Imperial (C)
46 Mitropoleos
105 63 Athens
☎ 3227617/6, 3227780

Hotel Nefeli (C)
16 Iperidou, Plaka
105 58 Athens
☎ 3228044/5

Hotel Niki (C)
27 Nikis
105 57 Athens
☎ 3220913/5, 3220886

PIRAEUS: TELEPHONE PREFIX 01
Hotel Noufara (B)
45 Iroon Politehniou
185 33 Piraeus
☎ 4115541/3

Hotel Savoy (B)
93 Iroon Politehniou
185 36 Piraeus
☎ 4131102/8

Hotel Triton (B)
8 Tsamadou
185 31 Piraeus
☎ 4173457/8

Hotel Anemoni (C)
65-67 Evripidou, 185 33 Piraeus
☎ 4111768, 4130091

Hotel Argo (C)
23 Notara
185 31 Piraeus
☎ 4121795/6, 4121918

Hotel Cavo (C)
79-81 Filonos 185 35 Piraeus
☎ 4116134/5, 4175290, 4110235

GLYFADA: TELEPHONE PREFIX 01
Congo Palace Hotel (A)
75 Possidonos
166 74 Glyfada
☎ 8946711/5

Palace Hotel (A)
4 Possidonos
166 75 Glyfada
☎ 8948361, 8946068, 8980847

Hotel Fenix (B)
1 Artemissiou
166 75 Glyfada
☎ 8981255/9

Hotel Golden Sun (B)
72 J. Metaxa
166 74 Glyfada
☎ 8981353/6, 8981974

Hotel Avra (C)
5 Lambraki
166 75 Glyfada
☎ 8947185, 8946452, 8946264, 8941111

Hotel Perla (C)
Possidono & 7 Hrissidos
166 75 Glyfada
☎ 8944212/4

VOULA: TELEPHONE PREFIX 01
Hotel Castello Beach (B)
8 Kerkiras & Aktis
166 73 Voula
☎ 8958985, 8959533

Hotel Plaza (B)
17 Alkionidon
166 73 Voula
☎ 8953575, 8990007

Hotel Minerva (C)
2 Metaxa & Vas Georgiou
166 73 Voula ☎ 8953186

VOULIAGMENI: TELEPHONE PREFIX 01
POST CODE 166 71
Nafsika Astir Palace Hotel (L)
☎ 8960211/9

Hotel Armonia (A)
1 Armonias
☎ 8960105, 8960030

Hotel Margi House (A)
11 Litous
☎ 8962061/5

Hotel Blue Spell (B)
1 Litous
☎ 8960676, 8960131/2, 8961868

SOUNION (SOUNIO): TELEPHONE PREFIX 0292
POST CODE 195 00
Hotel Egeon (A)
☎ 39200, 39234

Hotel Triton (B)
Athinon-Souniou
☎ 39103, 39316

Hotel Saron (C)
Lavriou-Souniou
☎ 39144

AEGINA TOWN: TELEPHONE PREFIX 0297
POST CODE 180 10
Hotel Nerina (B)
21 P. Eginitou
☎ 22795

Hotel Areti (C)
9 N. Kazantzaki
☎ 22806, 23917, 23593

Hotel Avra (C)
2 N. Kazantzaki
☎ 22303, 25036, 23917, 24493, 23968

YOUTH HOSTELS
The Greek Association of Youth Hostels
4 Dragatsaniou
Athens
☎ (01) 323 4107
Athens Youth Hostel (Ksenon Neotitos):
1 Aghiou Meletiou & Kypselis, Kipseli
(North of Areos Park) ☎ (01) 822 5860
International Youth Hostel: Peoniou 52
Stathmos Larissis ☎ (01) 883 2878

CAMPING
* = Open all year
There are four sites on the outskirts of
Athens offering on-site dining facilities,
bars and shops.

Athens Camping
198 Athinon
☎ (01) 5814101, 5820353

Daphni Camping
Daphni
☎ (01) 5811562/3

*Varkiza Beach Camping**
Faskomilia Varkiza
☎ (01) 8973613/4, 8970012

*Voula Camping (NTOG)**
A Alipedo Voulas
☎ (01) 8952712, 8953248

Sounio Beach Camping
Half-way between Sounion & Lavrion.
☎ (0292) 39358, 39718, (01) 7233910

Festivals

Athens
Herod Atticus Odeon
Performances during the summer at
8.30pm and at 9pm in September.
Tickets are sold at:
The Athens Festival Office, 4 Stadiou
☎ (01) 3221459/3223111-9 ext 137
Monday-Saturday 8.30am-2pm & 5pm-
7pm. Sunday 10am-1pm and The Herod
Atticus Odeon on performance days 5-
9pm.
☎ (01) 3232771 Advance sale of tickets
begins 15 days before each event.

Lycabettus Theatre
Performances during the summer at
9pm. Tickets sold at The Athens Festival
Office as above ☎ ext 240 and at the
Lycabettus Theatre on performance
days 7-9pm ☎ (01) 7227236. Advance
sale of tickets begins 10 days before
each event.

Sound & Light
Athens - Acropolis - Pnyx
April-October. Daily in English
9-9.45pm. Information and tickets from

The Athens Festival Office as above
☎ ext 127 and at the entrance to the show.
☎ (01) 9226210

Dora Stratou (Filopappou Hill)
Greek Folk Dance. End May-end
September. Daily 10.15pm. Wednesday
& Sunday 8.15 & 10.15pm.
Information ☎ (01) 3244395/9214650

Tourist Information Centres

Greek National Tourist Offices (EOT)
Information desks:

Athens
The East Airport
☎ 969 9500

2 Karageorgi Servias Street
Syntagma
Athens (National Bank of Greece building.)
☎ 322 2545

Syntagma Square & 1 Ermou Street
Athens
☎ 325 2267/8

Directorate of Tourism of East Mainland Greece and the Islands
Marina Zeas
Port of Piraeus
☎ 413 5716/413 5730/413 4709

EOT provide a very good street plan
free of Athens centre and Piraeus,
which includes transport information,
combined with a plan of the Arterial
routes in Athens and an Attica map.
Information sheets are available for:
Accommodation; Bus, Train and Air
Services; Bus Timetable; Ferry
Timetable; Car Storage Garages in
Athens & Piraeus.

2

THE PELOPONNESE: CORINTH AND THE ARGOLID

Greece is full of myths and legends. Every mountain, every rock, every stream and sometimes, it seems, every tree is the subject of some folklore or myth. Nowhere is this more true than in the Peloponnese. It starts with the name: the Greek word Peloponnissos translates into Pelops' Island. Pelops, the son of the mythical Tantalus of Mycenae, was sacrificed by his father and served as a meal for the gods. On discovering this sacrilege the gods were not pleased and devised a suitable punishment for Tantalus. He was left hanging from a tree over water which he could not quite reach and near fruit which forever rustled out of reach on the slightest breeze. He was 'tantalised' this way for an eternity. Pelops fared rather better. Restored to life by the gods he became consort to Zeus and eventually returned to earth as king of the Lydians and Phrygians. He fathered two sons, Atreus and Thyestes, who were rivals in the right to rule Mycena.

The Peloponnese, especially in the Middle Ages, was also known by the name of *Morea*. The mulberry tree figures in most explanations but comparisons to the shape of the leaf are unconvincing. More likely it is a reference to the cultivation of the mulberry tree and the growth of the silk trade.

Although the region is mostly regarded as distinct from mainland Greece with its own discrete character, Pelops' Island is not quite an island. It is a peninsula joined to the northern mainland by a narrow isthmus at Corinth, an isthmus which divides the Gulf of Corinth in the west from the Saronic Gulf in the east. The purists might argue that since the waters of the Corinth canal must be crossed to reach the Peloponnese it is technically an island.

Administratively, the Peloponnese is divided into seven regions or *nomes* with some regions like Corinth and Argolid better known than others. The regional names are often encountered, particularly in accommodation lists, so a quick reference map is very useful (see Introduction page 11).

Its central role in ancient history has left the region with a richness of historical sites second to none in their importance. Mycenae, Ancient Corinth, Epidaurus, Nestor's Palace at Pylos and Olympia are like honey pots to the present day tourists. As fascinating and evocative as these sites are, they are only a part of the Peloponnese and there is so much to discover. Two extraordinary Byzantine towns lie in wait, Mystra in ruins and Monemvasia under restoration. Add to this the castles of Nafplio, Methoni and Koroni, the wild and rugged Mani dotted with tower houses, resorts of character and style like Nafplio and Pylos, the fascinating hill villages of Karitena and Andritsena, the steepest rack and pinion railway in Greece at Kalavrita, scores of monasteries and an inspiring landscape of fierce mountain ranges, lush green valleys and gentle rolling forest and a more complete picture emerges of what lies in store.

Travelling by car is by far the most convenient way of exploring. The roads are mostly surfaced and are generally good with the usual provision that potholes may turn up anywhere, anytime on even the best of roads. Buses from Athens serve the major cities and, within the Peloponnese, each *nome* has a network of local buses radiating out from the main town. Somewhat slower is travelling by train. A diagram of the railway network in Greece is shown on page 266 of the Fact File. The Peloponnese is easily able to absorb as much time as you have to spare and still leave you wishing you could stay longer. Two weeks to complete the tours in chapters 2, 3 and 4 might leave you just a little breathless whilst weeks would feel quite leisurely.

Here in the Argolid, the heartland of the ancient Mycenaeans, lies the most remarkable record of human culture and achievement. Nowhere else in Greece is there such a concentration of archaeological sites all of which demand to be visited. Tiryns, Epidauros, Mycenae, Corinth, Acrocorinth and Ancient Nemea all lie within relatively close proximity. It may sound like an intensive culture trail but to make it feel more like a holiday there are some excellent coastal resorts on hand in Nafplio, Tolon and Paleo Epidauros, which make ideal bases for exploring the region. The Saronic Gulf islands of Poros, Hydra and Spetse are all within easy reach and they make a welcome diversion when cultural overload threatens.

Nafplio, at the southern end of the Argolid, crowned by the Palimidi fortress and graced by the Bourdzi fort on the offshore islet, has a lively air and plenty of character. If a beach is a priority then nearby Tolon scores highly. Primarily a fishing village, Tolon now ribbons its way along the coast. Many of the hotels are sandwiched between the road and the sea so that they open directly onto the beach at the rear. Justly popular, Tolon is crowded in high season. Paleo Epidauros is ideal for those seeking a little more peace. Beautifully situated in a picturesque bay, it retains all the character of a fishing village while coping with its role in tourism. The tours described here are based from Nafplio but they can be just as easily enjoyed from any of these bases.

THE PELOPONNESE
CORINTH & THE ARGOLID

Tour 1 • South To The Peloponnese (140km/87 miles)

Mainly over good roads, this journey is comfortably achieved in half a day leaving time to accommodate a visit to Mycenae, one of the few sites open for the full day. The road out of Athens passes by the Daphni Monastery and close to Elefsina providing a convenient opportunity to see them if they have not already been visited. Both are detailed in Chapter 1.

Escaping Athens is not especially easy but the road out to Corinth is signposted from Omonia Square. Suburbs seem to stretch on interminably and only after Elefsina, on 28km (17 miles), does it feel as though Athens has finally been left behind. Soon after Elefsina, toll booths announce the start of 'motorway.' Do not expect any significant road improvement and beware of the variable number of traffic lanes, sometimes down to one. The motorway ends with unused 'toll check' booths as

The walls of the Palimidi fortress crown the hill at Nafplio

The famous Lion Gate at Mycenae

Corinth is reached in 80km (50 miles). Keep to the left lane at the approach of the booths to be in position for crossing the almost insignificant bridge over the canal. A large parking area on the right with restaurant, shop and fast food caters for the passing tourists. A short walk back provides an opportunity to look along the 6km (4 mile) long canal. Started by the silver spade of Nero, it took longer than most projects and was eventually completed in 1890. It became instrumental in Piraeus developing into a major port but, at only 25m (82ft) wide, its usefulness soon became limited. One of the modern liners inching its way through is a spectacle which never fails to draw the crowds.

Follow Tripoli signs initially from Corinth but be careful to watch out for the Argos/Nafplio signs on reaching Acrocorinth. The road flirts with the railway, constantly bumpily crossing and recrossing. Rolling hills give way to the Argive plain with southerly progress, to shimmering silver green leaves of the olives and the scarlet splash of poppy fields. Mycenae (Mikines) is not too clearly signed so be alert for a left turn on reaching the village of Fychtia. The site, set on a hill with a mountain backdrop, is 2km (1 mile) further on through the village of **Mikines**.

It is generally thought the people who developed the Mycenaean culture around 1550BC were warrior-like Indo-Europeans who entered Greece from the Balkans or southern Russia. Their culture, inspired by the Minoans, flourished from 1550 to 1200BC and spread its influence throughout the Peloponnese, into the mainland and the Aegean. They built citadels with walls up to 6m (20ft) thick using huge rocks, 'cyclopean' walls as they were later called because the peasants believed that only Cyclops could have placed the stones in position. Within the citadels were built the Royal dwellings occupied by the king who was also the priest and general leader and by a hierarchy of officials. By 1500BC, towards the height of their domination, there were at least 320 citadels under their rule.

The search for knowledge of this golden age has more than a touch of romance about it. Apart from the archaeological work and pottery finds which tell much about the culture, later writings have also been significant. This is especially true of Homer's epic poems, *The Iliad* and *The Odyssey*, which were believed to have originated much later, around the ninth century or eighth century BC. Although rich in myth and legend, they seem to have a core of historical fact, *The Iliad* relates the tale of how King Agamemnon, overlord of Archaea (Greece), master of 'well-built Mycenae,' together with his brother Menelaus led their forces against King Priam of Troy. This was because Paris, one of Priam's sons had run away with the beautiful Helen of Argos, wife of Menelaus. After a protracted but victorious war, Agamemnon returned to find that his wife, Clytemnestra, had taken Aegisthos as a lover. Conspiring together, they brought Agamemnon to a rather undignified end, by murdering him whilst in his bath.

Mycenae passed into historical oblivion for centuries until Heinrich

Schliemann, an amateur archaeologist from Germany came onto the scene. Inspired by the Homeric tales, especially the references to 'Mycenae ... a town rich in gold,' Heinrich Schliemann started excavations in 1876. After only 6 weeks he discovered a grave circle crammed with golden objects including funeral masks. On 28 November 1876, Schliemann sent his now famous telegraph to King George I of the Hellenes in which he claimed 'I have gazed upon the face of Agamemnon.' The gold mask, which he believed to be Agamemnon and which is now housed in the National Museum in Athens, was later established as belonging to an earlier period. One of the irresistible pleasures of a visit to Mycenae lies in trying to fit the Homeric tales with what you see before you.

A violent earthquake around 1250BC, the time of its greatest prosperity, brought about some partial rebuilding only to be further devastated by fire some 50 years later. Further fires led to the decline and fall of the Mycenaean civilisation around 1100-1050BC. The main points of interest:

The Lion Gate: This famous gateway takes its name from the triangular-shaped sculpture above the door lintel depicting two lions either side of a Minoan column. This triangular symbol of power is believed to have a practical purpose in protecting the lintel from the weight of the wall. A relieving triangle is also seen at the entrance to the Treasury of Atreus. The Lion Gate forms the entrance to the site proper.

Grave Circle A: This is the Royal cemetery uncovered by Schliemann in 1876 were he found burial furnishings which proved to be the richest treasure in the history of Greek archaeology. Amongst the gold cups, gold crowns and inlaid swords were four gold death masks, one of which he believed belonged to Agamemnon. Now dated as sixteenth century with the last internment around fifteenth century BC, it is centuries earlier than the Trojan Wars and dispels Schliemann's unshakeable belief that he had discovered the grave of all those murdered by Aegisthos on their return from Ilium.

The circle is formed by a double ring of dressed slabs which are thought to have been filled with rubble while the top was covered by horizontal slabs. Within this six graves shafts were hewn down into the rock to various levels, five were discovered by Schliemann and the sixth was discovered more recently near the entrance.

The Palace: Located on the summit of the acropolis, there are now only foundations to help visualise the dimensions. The entrance from the north leads through two guard rooms to the Propylon were the column bases can be seen. Centrally situated is the Great Court. A porch and a vestibule led east into the Megaron, the central room of the palace. Centrally placed here is the sacred Hearth marked now by a ring of stones while the King's throne stood at the centre of the south wall. Still to be seen are the bases for the four wooden pillars which supported the roof. There are remains of a temple dedicated to Athena on the summit from a later period, around the sixth century BC.

Walking To Karathona Beach

The small Ellinikós Organismós Tourismoú (National Tourism Organisation of Greece or EOT) pay beach in Naplio becomes rather crowded at times. For those prepared to stretch a leg there is a large although narrow sandy beach about 3km (2 miles) away. A solitary taverna apart, do not expect facilities. It is a traffic free route although the odd rogue motor-cyclist can be expected.

Set out from the town beach heading south with the sea on your right. Follow the pedestrian track along the coast and watch out for some interesting flowers, especially where the hills on the left decline to scrubland. Spring walkers can expect to find wild orchids such as the mirror orchid (*Ophrys speculum*), the pyramidal orchid (*Anacamptis pyramidalis*) and the tongue orchid (*Serapias parviflora*). The beach is reached after some 40 to 45 minutes.

(opposite) The deep blue waters at Nafplio town beach

A panoramic view from inside the Palimidi Fortress, Nafplio

The Cult Centre: This is the name given to the group of buildings to the south of Grave Circle A which were built in the thirteenth century BC. Discoveries in these recent excavations suggest a temple and shrines where religious activity took place. The many finds include realistically modelled clay snakes which form a link with Minoan religious practice.

The Secret Cistern: This lies at the eastern side of the site. Steps lead down in total darkness to a deep underground spring. A good torch and considerable care is needed to see it.

The Treasury of Atreus (The Tomb of Agamemnon): This lies outside the main site alongside the approach road. It is one of the finest and best preserved Tholos tombs found in Greece, and one of the latest, built around 1350BC. The connection with Atreus, father of Agamemnon, or Agamemnon is speculative. Unlike the grave shafts, these tombs had all been plundered so less in known about their use but finds of skeletons in other tholoi indicate burial tombs.

There are several more tombs scattered around outside the acropolis site, none of which offer much to the casual visitor. The best known are Grave Circle B, to the right of the road opposite the parking area and the Tomb of Clytemnestra on the right of the approach to the Lion Gate. After returning to the main road, Nafplio lies only a further 25km (15½ miles) to the south with only Argos to negotiate.

✳ **Nafplio** (Nafplion), capital of the Argolid, is claimed by the locals to be the loveliest town in all Greece. Looking out over the fort of Bourdzi on the tiny offshore island and beyond into the Argolic Gulf, towered over by the Venetian fortress of Palimidi, its position alone gives credence to this belief. Add another castle complex in Acronafplio, a ramble of narrow, sometimes stepped streets, stuccoed houses, wooden balconies cascading with flowers, Turkish mosques, traditional tavernas in plenty and it is enough to convince visitors that it is quite incomparable.

Known from the Mycenaean era as a naval base for Argos, Nafplio has suffered a somewhat turbulent passage through time. Valuable as a trading post, it was twice in the hands of the Venetians, first time when it was bought in 1388 and the second time when it was recovered from the Turks in 1686 by Count Konigsmark, a lieutenant under the famous Morisini. The Palimidi Fortress, built 1711-14 by the Venetians and named after the mythical Palamedes, son of Poseidon and inventor of lighthouses and dice amongst other things, failed to keep the Turks at bay. Nafplio fell to them in 1715. Under the command of Kolokotronis, Greek forces besieged Nafplio in the War of Independence in 1821-1822 and brought the Turkish garrison to near starvation. Finally captured, Nafplio became the focal point of Greek opposition to the Turks.

From 1829 until 1834, Nafplio assumed the role of the first capital of the new Greek state and the Corfiot, John Kapodistrias, Greece's first regent. The fierce and sometimes violent factionalism was a major problem after the war and Kapodistrias fell a victim in his efforts to quell it. He was assassinated in Nafplio in 1831. Fear of civil war led the Great Powers to intervene. Believing the way forward was for Greece to become a monar-chy, Britain, France and Russia approached King Ludwig I of Bavaria who agreed for his son Otto to accept the crown. The monarchy was ratified in Nafplio's suburb of Pronoia in May 1832. Proud of its role in this period of history, the names of kings, queens, war heroes and political leaders are scattered freely amongst Nafplio's streets, avenues and platias.

Either the new road up to **Palimidi Fortress** is a well kept secret or people prefer the challenge of climbing the 900 or so steps to reach it. The pay box is at the top. Having expended the energy to climb up, none is dissuaded from entering on account of the small charge. This remarkably well preserved fortress is entered by a series of gates bearing the Lion of St Mark. There is still plenty of footwork to do if you plan to explore the three independent fortresses inside and enjoy the views from the 215m (705ft) summit, especially the bird's eye view down over Nafplio.

Exploration of Acronafplio, also known as Its Kale, is less demanding and, since it is now occupied by the Xenia hotel complex, less enticing. Its Kale is a corruption of the Turkish name 'UÇ Kale' meaning three castles (Greek, Frankish and Venetian). A fortress from ancient times, there has been successive rebuilding over the years. The lower castle, Castelo del Torrione, now housing the Xenia hotel, was designed by Gambello as was the castle standing on Bourdzi Isle. The luxury class Xenia's Palace now occupies the upper castle providing its residents with a superb view down over Bourdzi and the whole sweep of the bay.

Nafplio is not all chasing up hills, the lower town too is worthy of exploration. The main square, Platea Syndagmatos, bordered by three Turkish mosques, is a good starting point. One mosque is now a cinema, another has been reconsecrated and converted into a church, Ag Georgios, and the third, in the south-west corner, has the distinction of being the first parliament building for the newly independent Greece. The Archaeological Museum at the west end of the square houses many artefacts of the Mycenaean period including some intriguing jointed clay figures. The Folk Art Museum, tucked away in Ipsiladou street, is also worth a visit.

Tour 2 • Historic Argolid (195km/121 miles)

This tour, generally over good roads, fits comfortably into 2 days. It is not the distance which absorbs the time but the number of sites to accommo-date before the mid-afternoon closing time. Paleo Epidauros makes an ideal stop-over.

Only 4km (2 miles) outside Nafplio on the road to Argos, **Tiryns** is quickly reached. Masonry falls in the early spring of 1992 were serious enough for the authorities to judge that the site was unsafe for visitors until a survey and restorative work had been completed. Although assur-ances were given that it would re-open, they were unable to say how long

Larissa Castle is a prominent landmark overlooking Argos

One of the many archaeological remains to be seen at the ancient site of Corinth

it would remain closed.

Although its inland position on a small hummock seems insignificant, in Mycenaean times it stood as an impressive citadel by the seashore. This fortress-palace, in the style of Mycenae, is enclosed by huge, thick walls now far less than their estimated 20m (66ft) in height. 'Wall-girt Tiryns' was Homers description in *The Iliad* while the Roman travel writer Pausanias, second century AD, compared the walls of Tiryns with the pyramids of Egypt. Inhabited from the Bronze Age, the site was built to its present form during the thirteenth century BC but despite its size and wealth, it never reached the eminence of Mycenae. There is no need to leave your chariot outside because the steep entrance ramp is wide enough to take it but watch out for the nasty turn at the top. Inside, the whole palace complex is one of great architectural skill.

As with Mycenae, the Megaron (Great Hall), with its circular clay hearth, lies at the heart but its best known features are the vaulted galleries and secret passages. Many of the apartments were richly decorated with wall frescos and painted floors.

Larissa Castle at **Argos** is a prominent landmark seen long before Argos is entered. Reaching it is less easy. Head past the main square and look for the insignificant 'Kastro' sign indicating the road out to the north-west and a similar sign indicating a left turn further on. There is plenty of car parking space outside the castle entrance. It is an unattended site with no entry charge.

Archaeologists found evidence of Mycenaean occupation in excavations at Larissa Castle but it is the Byzantines, Franks, Venetians and Turks who have contributed to its present form. The extensive views from the castle take in the Argolic Gulf and much of the Argolid on a clear day.

Argos was important in ancient times but the prosperous modern town of Argos swamps the old site. The excavated remains, such as they are, are not too rewarding to the casual visitor. The best place to catch a glimpse of the past history is at the fine and airy museum located south-west of but close to the main square, attractive with its sidewalk cafés. Well displayed, the artefacts include bronze objects, pottery from the Mycenaean period and later work from the Roman period.

It is back to bumping over railway lines on the road north from Argos but is unlikely to distract from the heady scent of orange blossom which fills the lower plains throughout the early spring months. Once beyond Fychtia, watch out for the sign left to Nemea; the ancient site is before the village of the same name.

With so much to see in the Argolid, **Nemea** is not really part of the main tourist trail and it receives less attention than it would if it were in some other part of Greece. Located in a delightful valley famous for its red wine, Nemea has its special place in history. Near here Heracles (the Roman Hercules) slew the Nemean lion with his bare hands, the first of his twelve labours. Nemea was not an ancient city but, like Olympia, was a sanctuary with a temple dedicated to Zeus. It too held biennial panhellenic athletic games started, according to one legend, by Heracles after he had slain the lion. The prize to the victors was nothing more than a crown of wild parsley.

A visit to the excellent on site museum is strongly recommended before the site is explored. Apart from the various finds from this and nearby locations, there is a useful model which shows the layout of the site. The Temple of Nemean Zeus from 340-320BC, now with only three of its Doric columns standing, is the most obvious building but south of that are foundations of the treasury buildings and the bath house.

Return to the main road through the village of Kleoni and continue north through undulating hills to Ancient Corinth which is off left soon after joining the Corinth-Tripoli road.

Occupied from before Mycenaean times, **Ancient Corinth** did not rise to significance until around the eighth century BC. It was rebuilt by the Dorians to take advantage of its strategic position where a road allowed ships to be dragged on rollers between the Gulf of Corinth and the Saronic Gulf. From around 657BC for the next century, a succession of tyrant leaders, Kypselos, his son Periander and his nephew Psammetichos, threw their efforts into expanding trade and commerce. Corinth rapidly became a mercantile power spreading its influence throughout the Mediterranean, east and west. Its population rose as high as 30,000 in its most flourishing period as it enjoyed the prosperity gained from its unique trading position. A colonisation programme to relieve the problems of feeding such a vast population founded cities on Corfu (Korkyra) and Sicily (Syracuse) which themselves became influential.

In this climate of prosperity the Isthmian Games were started which achieved a prestige second only to the Olympics and the arts too flourished. The decline of Corinth started in the fifth century BC with Athens increasingly taking a share of their markets. Wars too had their effect and both the Peloponnesian War (431-404BC) and the Corinthian War (395-7BC) left them weaker. Prosperity returned again in a period of Macedonian rule which started in 338BC and ended in 224BC when the garrison was expelled. Corinth became the seat of the revised Achaean League and remained a lively trading centre until the arrival of the Romans.

The Corinthians were well known for their pursuit of pleasure. As worshippers of Aphrodite, the goddess of love, the licentious activities of these ancients reached new heights of profligacy. Prostitutes numbered in thousands rather than hundreds. All levels of society were catered for but the most illustrious of the courtesans, and history records Lois as one of the most sought after, were well educated and well schooled in all the necessary arts. A temple dedicated to Aphrodite was built on Acrocorinth, the prominent hill south of Ancient Corinth.

After the defeat of the Achaean League by the Romans in 146BC, the ancient city was razed to the ground by Mummius. It remained that way until Julius Caesar planted a colony there in 44BC. Rebuilt in Roman style, it quickly rose to importance as capital of the province of Greece. Wealth returned as did its reputation for prostitution which brought the Apostle Paul 'in fear and trembling' to convert the pagans.

It survived ravages by Herulian forces in AD267 and later by Alaric forces in AD395 but not the earthquakes of AD522 and AD551. It recovered something of its prosperity in the eleventh century only to suffer domination by a succession of captors. The earthquakes of 1858 again devastated the town and brought about relocation to its present position.

For one of the largest and most complex archaeological sites in Greece, Ancient Corinth disappoints from the poor on site information. Most of the remains on view are from the Roman period with just a touch of the original Greek city to be seen. After so many earthquakes it is not surprising that there is so little standing yet equally remarkable is that the foundations are so well preserved. The ruins are spread over a large area, not all of them within the enclosed site. The main points of interest:

The Odeon: This is outside the main site, just across the road from the entrance. It was constructed by the Romans to hold around 3,000 people.

The Theatre: Just north of the Odeon but not much to see. Built sometime in the fifth century BC and rebuilt by the Romans. Within the enclosure is:

The Museum: Exhibits include a good many artefacts from both the Greek and Roman periods.

The Temple of Apollo: With seven Doric columns still standing, this is one of the more prominent monuments on the site and undeniably Greek. Built in the sixth century BC when Corinth was growing in power and wealth, this is possibly one of the oldest temples in Greece.

The Agora: The market or meeting place. To the side were shops thought to be places of refreshment from the number of bones, both fish and animal, and cups found.

Fountain of Peirene: One of two natural springs, the other is on the acropolis. The water was stored in reservoirs hidden by a fountain house with a six-arched façade and fed into a sunken pool which is now dry.

Lechaion Street: Running to the northern port, part of this wide, paved road, flanked by colonnades backed by shops, has now been exposed.

For **Acrocorinth** continue past the site and take the signed road on the left. The fountain of Hadji Mustafa is passed on the final wind up the hill. There is plenty of parking space by the café. It is an unguarded site with no entry fee. Looking down on the main site from a height of 575m (1,886ft), the acropolis of Acrocorinth may tell little of its early Greek history but it does offer excellent views encompassing the Gulf of Corinth and the Saronic Gulf as well as a chance to look down over the ground plan of Ancient Corinth. Guarding the gateway to the Peloponnese, this important citadel has been captured and recaptured, built and rebuilt throughout the ages. The extensive towered walls guarding the hill top are Byzantine with contributions from the Franks, Venetians and the Turks. Three entrance gateways tell this story. The first is largely Turkish, the second Frankish rebuilt by the Venetians and the inner one originally

A colourful fishing boat moored at Paleo Epidauros harbour

The magnificent Epidauros theatre, famed for its splendid acoustics

fourth century BC. Once inside, pathways over rough ground lead through the herbage to the various points of interest. There are ruins of Turkish houses and Turkish barracks, Byzantine chapels and cisterns some seriously threatened by the undergrowth. The upper Peirene spring lies in the the south-east corner near the barracks but is not easily found. The highest summit housed the Temple of Aphrodite which was served in its day by a thousand religious prostitutes. It is hard to evoke memories of it now for this site has in turn been a church, a watch tower, a mosque and a paved viewpoint. It is the latter which makes it worth the climb.

Return to the main Athens road and, if the changed road priorities allow after current road-works, look to continue across to head for Examilia and the coast. Otherwise turn north and pick up the next road to Examilia. Slightly elevated, the scenic coastal road winds and twists its way south around hills cloaked in pine or through groves of almonds or olive occasionally yielding glimpses of the seashore. A sign warns of 'Continuous Dangerous Bents' (*sic*) but equally dangerous are the wandering goats and sheep. A left turn leads into Paleo Epidauros.

Strung thinly around an almost enclosed bay backed by pine clad mountains, a first glimpse of **Paleo Epidauros** suggests a slight air of neglect as if still awaiting discovery and not really expecting visitors. Once down amongst the colourful fishing boats watching the fishermen working on their nets, its divided role comes into perspective and the charm of its location overwhelms. The tavernas, like the hotels, mostly look out onto fishing boats dotted about on Homer's 'wine-dark sea.' The village is a staging post for ancient Epidauros and had the same role in antiquity. It sees a fair passing trade, especially throughout the festival of ancient Greek drama in summer when Athenians arrive on excursion boats from Piraeus, just a 2-hour sail away.

Paleo Epidauros has a recently discovered ancient theatre of its own which is quite a gem and not yet on the tourist map. It lies on the headland to the right and takes around 10 to 15 minutes walking to reach it. Follow the bay round onto the promontory until the track on the right opposite the church is reached. A sign on the eucalyptus tree directs to 'Cocktail, Playhouse Bar.' The track leads gently uphill through orange groves to reach a T-junction. Continue by turning right (a left turn takes you to some other excavations on the headland) and follow the track around to reach a shuttered stone house shaded by a palm tree. Go up the track on the left and the theatre is on the right, literally in the garden of the stone house. Easily visible through the wire fence, a good view is obtained by following around the perimeter to the rear of the theatre. Much of the tiered stone seating is still in place and particularly impressive is the well preserved inner circle of seats for the dignitaries.

Leave Paleo Epidauros to the south and follow the 'Galatas' sign left at the first junction. This new road reveals magnificent views as it winds and climbs away from Paleo Epidauros to join the main Epidauros road some 13km (8 miles) later; turn right. Once through the village of Adami, the mountain landscape imposes a fierce but transient beauty which is lost to a calm gentility before Epidauros is reached.

Epidauros was dedicated to Asklepios, the god of healing and ranked highly amongst the many such sanctuaries scattered throughout Greece. Originally, Apollo was worshipped here as the healing god but by the fourth century BC he had been replaced by his son Asklepios. According to myth, Asklepios, the son of Apollo and the earthling Kronos, was reared by the centaur Chiron who schooled him in the arts of healing. In turn he passed on his knowledge and skills to his daughters Panacaea and Hygeia who became part of the cult. Epidauros received pilgrims constantly and belief in the healing powers of this sanctuary lasted for almost a thousand years.

Although Epidauros is a fairly extensive site, much of it is only excavated foundations and a number of those roped off. The interest for most centres on the magnificent and well preserved theatre built to seat around 14,000. It is especially famed for its splendid acoustics and the visitor need only sit quietly somewhere on the upper seating and await the vocal demonstrations from the more extrovert tourists. Built in the fourth century BC, it seems to have had little restoration until modern times. Now it is used for the summer festival of ancient Greek drama.

The Temple of Asklepios lies just north of the Roman Odeon and the round building here, the Tholos, excites considerable curiosity and speculation. It was built over a labyrinth of concentric stone circles with access via a trap door. One theory amongst others is that it was used to house the sacred snakes. A model depicting how it might have looked is contained in the museum.

Perhaps the first port of call should be the museum which is located just inside the entrance to the site. Lygourio is the only village of any size passed on the route back to Nafplio but, unless fuel or refreshments are required, there seems no reason to stop. The remaining 24km (15 miles) is a peaceful run through quiet countryside.

Tour 3 • Off The Beaten Track Argolid (216km/134 miles)

Even allowing a couple of hours on the island of Poros, this tour through the countryside of the Argolid requires only one day. Further time is needed if Hydra and Spetse are to be included.

Tolon (Tolo) lies only 13km (8 miles) away from Nafplio and is well signposted. On the final approach, the road forks and both are signposted for Tolon centre but the right fork is the more direct. Follow the road as it winds endlessly through the village until the port area with space for parking is reached.

Bounded by low hills, Tolon fits comfortably around a long sweep of sandy bay looking onto a small island. A line of hotels with a scattering of tavernas front directly onto the narrow beach. The northern end of the beach, away from the port and the main town, has finer sand and is less public.

Return from Tolon to the Nafplio-Lygourio road and continue along mainly good roads towards Galatas. The route takes you through quiet countryside, past Epidauros and through Adami. Villages along the route are often nothing more than a cluster of houses and usually difficult to identify with the names on the map. Olives which are a near constant part of the modern landscape are known from Mycenaean times, carbonised traces of olives were found on Mycenaean palace sites, but the wide scale farming of olives is believed to have developed some centuries later. After a left turn at Traxia, the road winds and twists through undulating countryside revealing small areas of cultivated farmland snatched from the grip of the barren hills. The sight of Ano Fanari clinging to the rocky hillside signifies the start of a descent towards a scenic run along the coast. After leaving the coast, oranges and lemons in luxurious growth tell of a fertile region which was once Troizenia in ancient times. The modern village of Trizina is signposted off to the left and near the village, scattered over a wide area, are the remains of ancient Troizen. **Poros**, lying just offshore here, draws even closer as Galatas is reached.

Car ferries and water taxis ply back and forward frequently. The fare for passengers is cheap by any standards. Those intent on seeing the monastery of Zoodochou Pigis, a 6½ km (4 miles) drive out of town, might consider taking a car over otherwise it is barely necessary, Poros has only narrow streets and the island a limited road network. With its close proximity to Athens and regular ferry connection, weekends and high season sees the island fairly busy with local trade. Add to this a good dash of international tourism and it adds up to a busy scene. The waterfront with its cafés, tavernas and tourist shops is invariably bustling but the narrow streets which lead up the steep hill into the town provide a quick escape route for those who like to browse in peace. The clock tower is a good focal point to enjoy the views. It is only a short walk out of town to the east to reach the canal bridge which connects the small volcanic island of Sphaeria to the larger wooded Kalauria which together are Poros. The island is short on beaches but the best lies at Kanali, to the right after crossing the canal bridge.

Back on the mainland, **Galatas** has little to offer apart from waterside cafés looking over the narrow straits to Poros town. The route south-east out of Galatas passes shortly through the lemon forests of Limonodasos with its estimated 30,000 lemon trees although the carnations which are also grown commercially in the region are more eye-catching. The road, surfaced and wide enough for two way traffic, wends along the coastline passing through isolated clusters of housing which are difficult to identify with place names on a map. Lemon groves persist until the first significant village, Thermisia, just after the holiday enclosure of Porto Hydra. **Ermioni**, 11km (7 miles) further on, still remarkably free from tourist developments has ferry services to both Hydra and Spetse during the summer months but the more regular route to Spetse is from Kosta at the southern end of the peninsula. Pastoral scenery predominates through Kranidi to Didyma. Once beyond, the road winds and climbs through mountains until the outward route is rejoined at Traxia.

Spetse And Hydra

From early April onwards throughout the summer, excursion boats depart Tolon daily to the islands of Spetse and Hydra, usually as a combined trip. Hydra, reached after a 3-hour sail, has a picturesque and bustling harbour crowded with fishing boats and lined with waterside tavernas and pavement cafés. The island has no roads suitable for motor vehicles so transport is by mule and pack horse and they too are part of the harbour scene. It is a town of narrow streets, pastel coloured red-roofed houses tiered up the enclosing hills and donkey droppings. Once the town itself has been explored, it is easy to wander out into the hills along the many mule tracks.

It is perhaps a little unfortunate that Spetse is usually the second port of call since its harbour is less atmospheric than Hydra although it is not without its own charm. Normally it is a shorter stop leaving time only for a brief exploration of the fine old houses in the town. Like Hydra, there is no beach immediately to hand.

The island of Hydra has a picturesque harbour

Additional Information

Places to Visit

Ancient Corinth
Site and Museum
Open: 8.30am-2.45pm daily including Sundays and holidays.

Acrocorinth Castle
Unattended site and open at all times.

Argos
Museum
Open: daily 8.30am-3pm including Sundays and holidays but closed on Mondays.

Larissa Castle
Unattended site and open at all times.

Epidauros
Site and Museum
Open: 8am-5pm weekdays and 8.30am-3pm Saturday and Sunday.

Mycenae
Open: 8am-7pm weekdays and 8.30am-3pm on Saturday, Sunday and holidays.

Nafplio
Archaeological Museum
Open: daily 8.30am-3pm including weekends but closed on Monday.

Palamidi Fortress
Open: weekdays 8am-4pm and 8.30am-2.30pm on Saturday and Sunday.

Nemea
Site and Museum
Open: weekdays 8.45am-3pm and 9.30am-2.30pm on Sundays and holidays. Closed on Mondays.

Accommodation

HOTELS
* = Open all year
Hotels from luxury (L) down to C class are listed but rooms are also available, especially in the larger resorts like Nafplio.

NAFPLIO: TELEPHONE PREFIX 0752
Xenia Palace* (L)
Hotel and bungalows
Akronafplia ☎ 28981/3

Xenia*(A) Akronaplia ☎ 28991/3

Hotel Amphitryon* (A)
Staikopolou ☎ 27366

Hotel Agamemnon* (B)
Akti Miaouli ☎ 28021

Hotel Victoria* (C)
Staikopoulou ☎ 27420

Hotel Elena* (C)
Sid Merarchias ☎ 23217

Hotel Nafplia* (C)
Navarinou ☎ 28167

Hotel Park* (C)
Dervenakion ☎ 27428

TOLON: TELEPHONE PREFIX 0752
Hotel Dolphin* (B) ☎ 59162/220
Hotel Sofia (B) ☎ 59567/8
Hotel Aris (C) ☎ 59231/510
Hotel Artemis (C) ☎ 59458/125
Hotel Assini Beach (C) ☎ 59347
Hotel Christina (C) ☎ 59001
Hotel Elena's (C) ☎ 59158
Hotel Flisvos (C) ☎ 59223/437
Hotel Knossos (C) ☎ 59174
Hotel Minoa (C) ☎ 59207/146

PALEO EPIDAUROS: TELEPHONE PREFIX 0753
Marialena* (B) Furnished Apartments.
☎ 41090
Hotel Aegeon* (C) ☎ 41381
Hotel Aktis (C) ☎ 41407
Hotel Apollon (C) ☎ 41295
Hotel Christina* (C) ☎ 41451
Hotel Hellas(C) ☎ 41226
Hotel Maik* (C) ☎ 41213
Hotel Maronika (C) ☎ 41391/41491
Hotel Paola Beach (C) ☎ 41397
Hotel Plaza (C) ☎ 41395
Hotel Poseidon* (C) ☎ 41211
Hotel Rena (C) ☎ 41311
Hotel Saronis (C) ☎ 41514
Verdelis Inn (C) ☎ 41332

NEA EPIDAUROS: TELEPHONE PREFIX 0753
Hotel Epidauros* (C) ☎ 31209

Mykines: TELEPHONE PREFIX 0751
Hotel La Petite Planete* (B)
Hristou Tsounta ☎ 66240

Hotel Agamemnon* (C)
3 Hristou Tsounta ☎ 66222/32

ERMIONI: TELEPHONE PREFIX 0754
Hotel Lena-Mary (B) ☎ 31450/1

CAMPING
* = Open all year
There are some thirty-nine official camp
sites scattered around the Argolid. Most
offer on-site dining facilities, bars and
shops.

Kineta Corinthias
Assini*
☎ 0296 62005

Mycenae
Mycenae
☎ 0751 66247

Paleo Epidauros
Bekas Camping
☎ 0753 41333/394/583

Plaka Drepanou
Alkyon
☎ 0752 92336/01, 9815929

Nafplio
Lefka
☎ 0752 92394

Nea Epidauros
Diamantis
☎ 0753 31293/31240

Tolon
Avra
☎ 0752 59085/520

Lido I
☎ 0752 59489

Sunset
☎ 0752 59566

Sfakes Tolou
Lido II
☎ 0752 59396

Tourist Information Centre

Nafplio
Municipality Information Office
Iatrou Square
☎ 0752 24444
Hotel list available covering Nafplio,
Argos, Tolon and Drepano.
Local Transport: three buses daily
connect Nafplio to Mycenae and four to
Epidauros. Tolon is served by an hourly
service and there is a regular schedule
for Athens and Argos.

3

THE PELOPONNESE: LACONIA

Tucked away in the south-east corner of the Peloponnese, the province of Laconia is scenically enriched by two parallel mountain ranges. The Parnon which climbs to a mighty 1,935m (6,347ft) in the north of the province declines to a rumbling spine as it runs into the Laconian peninsula, the setting for Monemvasia. Further to the south-west, and topping 2,400m (7,872ft), the majestic Taygetos (Taigetos) runs down into the central peninsula, the Mani. Between the two ranges lies the fertile Eurotas plain, the garden of Sparta. Against this backdrop of snow-capped mountain peaks, precipitous rock faces, deep ravines and lush green forests is another distinct chapter of Greek history, written not in the intangible mists of the ancient past but in the more solid and recent medieval times. Mistra, sprawling against the foothills of the Taygetos and crowned by a castle, once a vibrant intellectual power in the Byzantine empire and rich on silk now lies dead and deserted. In such a picturesque setting and overrun with wild flowers, Mistra is one of the most exciting sites in the Peloponnese although the devotees of Monemvasia might take exception to praising it too highly. The old town of Monemvasia sits on a rocky peninsula, now an island since the isthmus was cut centuries ago to fortify its defences. Handily situated for sea contact with Constantinople, it was the home of the governor of the Peloponnese in Byzantine times until Mistra grew in power. Now it is an atmospheric old town accessible only on foot and steadily undergoing restoration in its original style.

There is still one more region which is equally compelling, the Mani. Dusty, dry, barren, rocky Mani occupies the central peninsula in the south of the Peloponnese and even though it shares the dwindling spine of the Taygetos, scenically it has little in common with the rest of the region. Without firm boundaries, the region south of Areopolis is often referred to as inner or deep Mani and the rest to outer Mani. The interest in the Mani lies in its architecture, villages of square, ruggedly built tower houses, its people and their interaction with a barren and hostile environ-

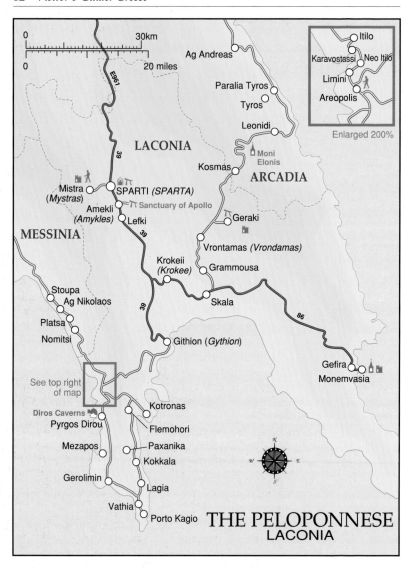

0   30km

0   20 miles

Ag Andreas

Paralia Tyros
Tyros
Leonidi

LACONIA

Itilo
Karavostassi Neo Itilo
Limini
Areopolis

Enlarged 200%

Moni Elonis
Kosmas

ARCADIA

Mistra
(*Mystras*)
SPARTI (*SPARTA*)
Amekli
(*Amykles*) Lefki
Sanctuary of Apollo

Geraki

MESSINIA

Vrontamas (*Vrondamas*)

Krokeii
(*Krokee*) Grammousa

Stoupa
Ag Nikolaos

Skala

Platsa
Nomitsi

Githion (*Gythion*)

Gefira
Monemvasia

See top right
of map

Diros Caverns
Pyrgos Dirou

Kotronas

Flemohori

Mezapos

Paxanika

Kokkala

Gerolimin

Lagia

Vathia

Porto Kagio

THE PELOPONNESE
LACONIA

ment. History relates how these proud and independent people indulged in insurrections against authority, lawlessness and almost perpetual feuding. A little knowledge of the character of these people turns a tour of deep Mani from a visual to an emotional experience.

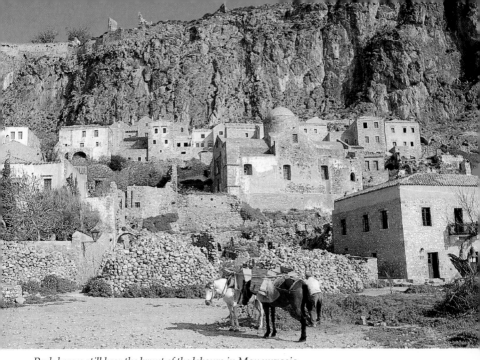

Pack-horses still bear the brunt of the labours in Monemvasia

The roof tops of Monemvasia, viewed from the castle above the town

Tour 1 • South To Monemvasia (200km/124 miles)

Despite crossing the Parnon range, the journey from Nafplio takes only around 5 hours which leaves time to loiter along the way. Although it is wise to start with a full tank, fuel is available at the larger villages along the route.

After following around the bay, the road south from Nafplio joins the main Argos-Tripoli road at Myli but only briefly. As the main road swings inland, turn left following signs to Astros. Hemmed in by mountains, the road has little option but to follow the coastline squeezing its way tightly between the mountains and the sea in places. The drab scrub covered hills are brightened considerably in spring by the yellow-flowered brooms. Both Astros and the larger Ag Andreas lie a little inland but once beyond the road returns to hug the scenic coastline.

Leonidi, a fairly large town on the estuary of the river Dafno with fuel, shops and telephones, makes absolutely no concession to the through traffic which is forced to thread itself through the narrow streets. Be warned, it can be slow if heavies are involved. Once through it is scenery of a quite different order as the road ascends a long, long gully up into the Parnon mountains. Above, to the left, Moni Elonis appears clinging impossibly to the rocks and, soon after it is spotted, the entrance is signed off left. Still on an upward wind, the highest point of 1,200m (3,936ft) is reached near the village of Kosmas. There are flowers on view for much of the summer at these altitudes and April may be rewarded with *Anemone blanda, Aubrieta gracilis, Muscari* and a small, yellow Gagea species.

The road narrows appreciably as you wind through **Kosmas**. At the heart of the village is a huge platia shaded by the inevitable Platanos trees and a restaurant to tempt the weary traveller. Beyond the village on the right lies a picnic area and viewpoint for those with their own food. From here its all down hill for a time , at least until **Geraki** is reached. The road does not enter the town but crosses a major road leading into it. Geraki is a fairly large town which does not normally attract visitors even though there are the remains of an acropolis to view with cyclopean walls dating back to Mycenaean times. Anyone wishing to explore medieval Geraki, which lies a few kilometres south-east of the town, should enquire in the village for directions. There are the remains of some fifteen medieval churches and a castle to explore.

Olive groves dominate the scenery again as the fertile plain is crossed to **Vrontamas** (Vrondamas) a large, sprawling farming community. Rolling hills and wooded valleys add a new texture to the landscape especially around Grammousa, another sprawling village. Turn left for Monemvasia (signposted 50km/31 miles) as the main road is reached and expect a little more traffic for the final leg of the journey. The road leads directly to the causeway and the bridge to Monemvasia. It is possible to drive a little further around the south side of the rock but vehicles cannot enter the old town and there is not too much parking space. The modern village of Gefira has sprung up to the west of the causeway with hotels, tavernas and all necessary facilities to cater for the passing tourist trade.

Monemvasia has made its own mark on history if only for its Malmsey wine which was well known throughout Europe in the Middle Ages. Do not look too hard for the vineyards because the wine was imported from Crete and the Aegean islands which tells something of its importance as a trading post in those times.

Situated on the southern side of a rocky promontory which is around 1 ½km (1 mile) long and 250m (820ft) high, it takes its name from the fact that there is only one entrance (*mone embasis*). Its significant history dates from the Middle Ages, from the time when the local Greeks took refuge there and fortified it against the invading Slavs. Its development into a sound fortress and important trading post made it a target for invaders. In 1147 it managed to repulse an attack from the Normans of Sicily but faired less well against William de Villehardouin, fourth in succession of the princes of Achaea, in 1249, although the siege had lasted 3 years. It was the same William who founded Mistra. After a mere 15 years, amidst the complexities of medieval history, William was forced to cede this fortress, and Mistra, to Michael Palaiologos as ransom payment. In this period of Byzantine rule, it became the seat of the governor of the Peloponnese, an important ecclesiastical centre and a flourishing port with special trading concessions. Its chequered history was not quite finished for in 1460 it came into the hands of the Pope and in 1464 the Venetians. For a time it became a major centre of their Levantine trade in the east but its prosperity declined in the sixteenth century when it passed into Turkish control.

Once through the impressive arched entrance to the old town, the view is of narrow cobbled streets crowded by buildings in warm stone. Continuing ahead leads past souvenir shops and cafés to the small main square. It is very difficult to get an overview of the town but there are vantage points from the castle above or the sea shore below. It is worth the climb to the castle, not just for the view, but to amble around the extensive remains and to look around the restored church of Ag Sophia perched on the cliff end. In the main town few of the original forty churches remain and the most important of these is the cathedral dedicated to Christ in Chains (Elkomenos Christos), the largest medieval church in Laconia.

Tour 2 • On To Deep Mani (185km/115 miles)

Mistra is easily worth half a day and there are some remains of ancient Sparta to inspect so the best option is to allow for an overnight stop in Mistra or nearby Sparti. Presently the one and only hotel in Mistra is the B class Byzantion (see Additional Information). There are a few rooms available around the village and a new hotel under construction. The first leg of the journey to Mistra is just over 100km (62 miles).

The magnificent view from the summit of Mistra

Mistra is surrounded by spectacular countryside

One of the numerous Byzantine churches to be seen at Mistra

Around Mistra wild flowers such as **Cyclamen repandum** *can be found*

It is a question of backtracking first from Monemvasia to Skala, passing the road to Geraki. As the road climbs towards Krokeii (Krokee) views of the Taygetos range open up and particularly towards the peak Profitis Ilias which remains snow capped well into early summer. At the junction just beyond Krokeii turn right for Sparti (24km/15 miles). The red terra rosa earth paints the rolling landscape like a colour wash from an artists palette. Red soil gives way to yellow soil and to the left the Taygetos mountains rise abruptly from the Eurotas valley. Watered by streams from the Taygetos, this fertile plain produces endless crops between the groves of oranges and olives. Maize, wheat, barley and vegetables chase each other in endless succession.

The Sanctuary of Apollo at **Amekli** (Amykles), just 8km (5 miles) before Sparti, makes an interesting diversion. There is little now to see at the sanctuary but it does make a pleasant picnic spot situated on a hillock with magnificent views over the plains and mountains. Turn off right at Amekli and follow the signs. Do not worry when the road surface runs out since the location is only $1\frac{1}{2}$ km (1 mile) from the road.

Steadily increasing tractor traffic announces Sparti. Continue ahead to the centre and turn left for Mistra following the signs. Mistra lies 6km (4 miles) outside the town.

The new village of **Mistra**, situated around a road junction, is quite small. Unchanged by tourism, perhaps because it has little accommodation, the atmosphere is of an old Greek village with some really interesting tavernas run by the old folk. They are worth trying if only for the local rosé wine. The site of medieval Mistra (lower gate) lies 2km (1 mile) to the right as you enter the village. The site occupies a hillside position and has a top entrance, served by an outer road, in addition to the lower one.

Modern Sparti, the capital of Laconia, is a busy agricultural centre. Built as recently as 1834 on the site of the ancient city, it has a grid structure of straight streets lined with orange trees. There is little to entice the present tourist except that it has a number of hotels convenient for Mistra and, of course, the museum. Tucked away to the north of the city are some remains of ancient Sparti which are worth seeking out if only to enjoy the solitude of the location and the superb views of the Taygetos. To find it head for the stadium and keep going around and beyond onto a narrow cobbled road which rises up onto a wooded knoll with space to park.

Ancient Sparti was formed as early as 1000BC when invading Dorians subjugated a number of villages. Their place in history is assured by the harsh regimes practised and their military approach to life. Strict rules governed all aspects of life and determined the physical training both men and women should endure. Boys from the age of 7, provided that they had survived earlier tests of endurance, were trained under harsh supervision. Tough living conditions, deliberately inadequate food and physical endurance tests were all part of the course. The accent was strongly on the physical with total disregard to intellectual development. To add to their mystique, doors were closed to outsiders. Gradually the Spartans exerted their power over the whole of the Peloponnese except Argos. Whenever wars were around the Spartans had a role; the Persian Wars, the Messenian War and the Peloponnesian War (431-404BC). A succession of defeats followed which saw the gradual decline of the Spartans as a power until they were forced to join the Achaian League in 221BC.

Their physical approach to life left no room for pursuing the arts or fine architecture which characterised other civilisations throughout Greece. It seems contradictory that Homer should depict Helen, the most beautiful woman in the world, as a Spartan, a race that eschewed art, grace and beauty. Helen, wife of Agamemnon's younger brother Menelaus, was abducted by Paris son of King Priam of Troy. According to Homer's *The Iliad*, this was the cause of the Trojan War.

Thucydides, an Athenian historian, said of Sparta that if the town were laid waste and there remained only temples and foundations of their buildings, it would be hard to believe that the power of the town corresponded to its fame. Now you can see for yourself.

The site is open with free access. Nothing is marked which makes it difficult to identify many of the locations with certainty. The theatre, south-west side of the Acropolis hill, is the most obvious. It has been excavated to some extent and a few rows of seats are exposed. Acropolis hill itself is distinguished by the remains of two Byzantine churches. To the south lies the Agora well sprinkled with olive trees and still to the south are the remains of a building which is believed to be a Sanctuary to Leonidas.

Mistra (Mystras) lies on the east face of one of the foothills of the Taygetos. The lower entrance gate lies at an altitude of around 350m (1,148ft) while the castle on the summit tops 600m (1968ft). Footpaths weave all over. In practical terms it means there is a lot of walking and climbing involved; wear sensible shoes and allow plenty of time. An alternative for those not comfortable with uphill walking is to taxi to the upper entrance by the castle and wander down through the site. The walk described in the feature box starts at the top entrance and provides a quite spectacular return route for those who enjoy countryside walking.

Unlike other ancient sites in Greece and probably because of its size, Mistra is not subject to an annual treatment with weedkiller. Goats too are excluded. The consequence is that the site provides an exhibition of wild flowers throughout the spring months, including wild orchids, and all can be seen from the footpaths. Some of the species spotted in early April include the tall purple perennial honesty (*Lunaria rediviva*), the beautiful red anemone (*A. pavonina*), the ubiquitous yellow *Alyssum saxatile* growing on every rock, the delicate white flowered *Saxifraga chrysosplenifolia*, the dark blue *Muscari commutatum*, purple toadflaxa (*Cymbalaria microcalyx*) and at least three orchids; the yellow bee orchid (*Ophrys lutea*), the somewhat rarer bee orchid (*Ophrys spruneri*) and the giant orchid (*Barlia robertiana*). The list could be extended to include *Onosma frutescens* which droops its reddish yellow bells from rock crevice, yellow

Euphorbias, tall spiky Asphodels, yellow and white daises in abundance and perhaps the greatest glory of all, the purple Judas tree, *Cercis siliquastrum* , but it still only represents a fraction of the species present. Mistra did not emerge through the mists of time, it crystallised in 1249. William II de Villehardouin decided to build a castle on the hill, known then as Mesythra, in order to protect the fertile Eurotas valley. Under this Frankish influence, the name soon corrupted to Mistra. A few years later William was captured by Michael Palaiologos and, in 1262, after 3 years imprisonment, he was forced to cede his three fortresses, Mistra, Monemvasia and Maina (in the Mani), to Byzantium to gain his freedom. Mistra became the centre of resistance for the next 50 years until the Greeks had recovered most of the Morea, as the Peloponnese was then called. The seat of government moved from Monemvasia to Mistra and, ruled by despots, descendants of the emperor, it enjoyed a long period of prosperity. It attracted intellectuals, scholars, theologians and artists who thrived in the blossoming Byzantine culture. The Ottoman Turks brought the beginning of the end when they captured the city in 1460. It remained prosperous on silk trade for a time and thrived again for a spell under Venetian rule (1687-1715) but it rapidly declined when the Turks returned. It was destroyed by the Albanians in 1790 and was abandoned completely when Sparti was rebuilt in 1834.

Apart from the beauty of the site and the pleasure of rambling its many footpaths, the numerous Byzantine churches and the Frankish castle on the summit are the main points of interest. The Monemvasia gate divides the upper town where the privileged classes lived apart from the lower town. The oldest churches are found in the lower town. The Mitropolis, the church of Dimitrios built in 1309, lies to the right from the lower entrance and adjoining is a small museum. Further along lies the monastic complex of Vrontochion which was the burial place of the despots. The only occupied building is the Pantanassa Convent, part way up the hill, but the nuns welcome visitors and the opportunity to display their handicrafts. Through the Monemvasia gate, little can be seen of the Palace of the Despots since this is currently under restoration. The Frankish castle on the very summit is worth the climb if only for the magnificent views of the Taygetos. Although built by the Franks, the castle was significantly rebuilt by the Turks.

The onward route from Mistra to Areopolis (80km/50 miles) demands little in the way of navigational skills. The first part of the journey offers the opportunity to review the landscape from a different perspective as the outward route is retraced as far as Hania. Distant vistas shrink as the road winds through the foothills of the Taygetos. New road sections cut many twists and turns off the old route and hasten the arrival at Githion.

Githion (Gythion), the port of both ancient and modern Sparti, is an attractive base for exploring the Mani. Neo-classical houses built in tiers up the hillside look over a summer trade of tour boats disgorging passengers for Mistra. Offshore is the islet of Marathonisi now connected to the

A Mistra Circuit On Foot

There is a spectacular countryside return route from the top gate at Mistra which emerges eventually on the road between the village and the bottom gate. It requires about 45 minutes on foot and is only recommended for experienced walkers since navigation skills are required from the point where an obvious track finishes and another path is located. Sensible shoes are an absolute necessity.

Ignore the road to the right on leaving the top gate at Mistra and turn left instead. Pass beneath the archway and bear right a little to join a wide track which starts into immediate descent. Goat bells, snow capped peaks on the towering mountains and flower filled meadows instantly bring an alpine feel to the walk. After around 10 minutes walking the track ends at gates into a small holding and this is where some self-navigation is required. The tactic is to work around the fenced enclosure to pick up a path on the far side, a slightly longer diversion than first imagined. From just before the gates take a small path right, heading back uphill, broadly following the perimeter of the fence on the left. The path gradually leads around to the left and down into a

wooded depression; find the way left, downhill through the woods, to join a distinct path almost immediately. Turn left downhill with a valley to the right. Continue ahead as the path runs into another and becomes stronger.

Many of the wild flowers are the same as those seen in Mistra but there are more besides like the blue iris (*I. unguicularis*), the delicate anemone so popular in gardens (*A. blanda*) and, towards the end of the walk, two small colonies of *Cyclamen repandum*.

A goat pen on the left is passed after about 20 minutes and from here it is possible to see Sparti in the distance. The well trodden path winds down the valley to a small river which is crossed easily on available stones. Once over, turn left to take the lesser of two paths (the other goes ahead and up) and it is a scramble over rocks for a few minutes until a beautiful old cobbled trail is joined. Follow this into narrow jaws as the gorge closes around only to emerge with startling suddenness onto the plain and back into Mistra. At the outskirts of the village, fork left towards the church to arrive at the top of the one-way system between the site and the village. Left returns in 20 minutes to the lower gate and right to the village.

mainland by a causeway. For the romantics, Marathonisi is believed to be the ancient Kranai where Paris took refuge with Helen on his way back to Troy.

Beyond Githion, the countryside remains pastoral with valleys filled with broad-leaved trees and there is no hint yet of Mani terrain. It changes once the turn off to Vlahos is passed. Suddenly the countryside takes on a barren look where even the olive trees crouch against the wind. A filling station greets your arrival at Areopolis where the town lies off the main road to the right.

Tour 3 • Deep Mani (110km/68 miles)

This route around the Mani is a pleasure to drive, surfaces are mostly good but care is needed in the most southerly section beyond Vathia. Care is needed too through the villages where the road often narrows appreciably. The circuit described traces the scenic east coast first to catch the morning sunlight lighting up the hillsides. Reaching the caves before they close at 3pm can be a problem for early season visitors and they may opt to reverse the route. It is no problem in high season when the caves remain open until 7pm. Do not expect too much from the villages, Areopolis is the largest and the others considerably smaller but are worth visiting for their tower houses, delightful location or old-world atmosphere. Some are fairly basic but others may have a shop or taverna.

The Mani is for the curious, for those fascinated by a peep into a private and very unruly past. There is beauty enough in the barren, treeless hills and rocky coastline but as an environment to prosper in it offers no encouragement. Every scrap of land brought into cultivation has to be fought for against the unyielding, rocky and stony terrain. Terracing clings impossibly to mountain faces defying nature in a search for crop space. Even the olive trees in the stony meadows are small and wind cut. Geographically isolated and with such a harsh environment it is a place to seek refuge rather than a place to settle. Wherever the refugees arrived from, and certainly some were from Sparta, they proved to be as hard and tough as their surroundings. Hostile to outside interference, they managed to remain independent from the Venetians, Franks and Turks. Their isolation went deeper. The villages too lived in isolation and were ruled by local chieftains in an atmosphere of constant friction and warring between the clans. The Maniots were notorious too for feuding between themselves and indulged in vendettas which were long and bitter, protracted over generations. Square built tower houses rising to several stories were built for safety, many of which still stand grouped on the hillsides. Their fighting qualities were respected in the War of Independence in 1821 when many of their generals distinguished themselves but the pressure for the Mani to join the new state following the end of the war was not welcomed. One consequence of the continuing dispute was the

From Areopolis To Ag Sotiras On Foot

This is only a short walk taking 30 to 40 minutes in total. Ag Sotiras, or Kouscouri as it was once called, is a partly deserted village lying just east of Areopolis.

Set off from the large square in Areopolis to cross the main road and enter a narrow road opposite. Already Ag Sotiras can be seen on the hillside ahead. As the surfaced road swings away left, keep ahead to join a cobbled trail which becomes stepped just below the village. The lower village is mostly deserted but there are more signs of life in the upper part. The large open area in front of the church provides fine elevated views of the surrounding area. Return to Areopolis the same way.

assassination by a Maniot of John Kapodistras, the first elected leader of the new independent Greece. Eventually, in 1834, Mani reluctantly agreed to join the independent state.

Feuding is now a thing of the past and visitors are welcomed by the Maniots with a full measure of the usual Greek hospitality. A local comment suggested that the young men have not lost their aggression but now channel it into serving in the armed forces. Many of the tower houses are still around and some are being converted by the EOT (Greek National Tourist Office) for tourist accommodation.

Areopolis is the capital of the Mani. Its spacious platia, which serves as a bus terminus and where the best tavernas are located, seems like something of an after thought. It is appended to a tangle of narrow streets crowded with grey stone houses. In the midst of these lies the church of the Taxiarchis built in 1798 which shows a Byzantine eagle above the main door. One of the EOT guest houses nearby has a private museum of Maniot weapons, small canons, daggers, swords and rifles, which are displayed in a window for outside viewing. The Saturday market adds colour to the town. On a practical note, Areopolis has the only bank in the region and this is part time, opening Tuesday and Thursday mornings only.

Leave Areopolis heading south but shortly watch for the left turn signposted Kotronas and Kokkala. The road climbs over the spine of the Mani. Slender cypress trees, like exclamation marks slashed on the landscape, are even more noticeable in this environment. The left turn down to Kotronas starts a short scenic run which offers beautiful coastal views. **Kotronas** itself is a mixture of sombre grey towers and bright white houses. It has a taverna and a shop. Retrace the route back to the main road and continue south. The very next village, **Flemohori**, is worth a stop to see the exceptionally tall tower house there. Further south, the cluster of tower houses sprawling down the hillside is the village of Paxanika. That

The shingle beach and shore line at Kokkala

One of the many tiny tower house hamlets on the way to the southern tip of the Mani peninsula

too has some tall towers. **Kokkala**, the next stop en route, is a picturesque village on the sea front with a bakery and tavernas. The broad sweep of shingle beach leads the eye to a church located right on the shore line.

Small villages slip by with southerly progress, most with tower houses and some totally deserted. After the tower house village of Lagia, the road takes a new course across the tail of the peninsula to meet the western coast road. Turn left here for **Vathia**. The small, tight cluster of tower houses perched on a hillock overlooking the sea is Vathia. It is worth a stop to wander around amidst these buildings which are in various stages of restoration to tourist accommodation. The final section of the southern journey re-crosses the peninsula to the east coast village of **Porto Kagio**, the end of the road. This tiny port with its modern cube style houses is located on a beautiful bay and boasts what is probably the most southerly

Flowers Of The Mani

Orchis papilionacea
(pink butterfly orchid)

In spite of the barren and hostile appearance of the landscape for much of the year, spring time is very colourful. The hillsides support pink and white cistus bushes and masses of spiny brooms, spanish broom and euphorbias all which splash yellow about very freely. Against this background the occasional purple Judas trees in bloom really shines out. Cultivated ground swarms with white daisies, yellow crucifers, pink geraniums, purple echiums and wild gladioli. Amongst these are a surprising number of wild orchids like the pink butterfly (*Orchis papilionacea*), the purple *Orchis mascula* and the pink pyramidal orchid (*Anacamptis pyramidalis*). The bee orchids might be harder to spot but they are present in numbers including the yellow bee (*Ophrys lutea*), the saw-fly orchid (*O. tenthredinifera*) and *O. spruneri*. One other fascinating orchid is the pink-flowered *Orchis Italica*, the naked man orchid, in which the individual flowers are man-shaped. It takes its common name from the small appendage between the 'legs.'

taverna in mainland Greece. It is possible to walk further south to the very tip of the peninsula.

Retrace the route through Vathia to start the west coast leg of the tour. **Gerolimin** is hard to miss at the moment, the road plunges you into its very narrow streets. There is a wide by-pass road not far from completion so it may soon be necessary to turn off to visit. Set in a barren wilderness, it is another village of mixed old tower houses and modern cubes around a shingle bay but not without character. Not only does it boast a taverna and a post office but it also has a hotel and rooms. A narrow coastal plain ribbons along the west coast keeping the road off the mountain side and some of the visual impact is lost. The tiny fishing village of **Mezapos** lies just over 2km (1 mile) from the main road but the route down to it is on a concrete track just wide enough for one car. It is famed locally for its deep water harbour and its fish taverna.

Next stop is the spectacular **Diros Caverns** (Pyrgos Dirou), just 7km (4 miles) short of Areopolis. These caves are very much on the tourist route so expect queues in summer. The trip round the caves, which takes around 25 minutes, takes place in small boats which glide noiselessly through 1km ($1\frac{1}{2}$ mile) of illuminated passages and caverns. It is an entirely visual experience with no commentary on the various rock formations. Head room is tight in some passages. There are occasions, and the wind is a factor, when the water levels are too low for the caves to open.

Additional Information

Places to Visit

Mistra
Open: daily 8.30am-3pm but the museum inside is closed on Monday.

Sparti
Museum
Open: 8.30am-3pm. Closed on Monday.

Accommodation

HOTELS
* = Open all year

AREOPOLIS: TELEPHONE PREFIX 0733
Hotel Mani* (C)
12 Agiou Petrou Square
☎ 51269/51397

Pension Londas (A) ☎ 51360
Pension Pyrgos Kapetanakou* (A)
☎ 51233

Pension Tsimoba (Traditional House)
☎ 51301

GITHION: TELEPHONE PREFIX 0733
Hotel Githion* (A)
☎ 23523/23452/23777

Hotel Belle Helene (B)
Vathi Ageranou
☎ 22867/9

Hotel Laryssion* (C)
71 I. Grigoraki
☎ 22021/6

Hotel Milton* (C)
Mavrovouni
☎ 22091/22914/5

Hotel Pantheon*(C)
33 Vas Pavlou
☎ 22284/89

MISTRA: TELEPHONE PREFIX 0731
Hotel Byzantion (B but expect E stand-

ard), Vas Sophias ☎ 93309
Best accommodation is in nearby Sparti.

MONEMVASIA: TELEPHONE PREFIX 0732
*Hotel Minoa** (C)
14 Spartis
☎ 61209/61224

*Pension Ano Malvasia** (A)
☎ 61323/61113

*Pension Malvasia II** (A) ☎ 61323
Pension Castro (A) ☎ 61413/4
*Pension Malvasia** (B) ☎ 61323/61435
*Pension Monemvassia** (B) ☎ 62381
Furnished Apartments Panos (B) ☎ 61480

SPARTI: TELEPHONE PREFIX 0731
*Hotel Lida**(B)
☎ 23601/2

*Hotel Menelaion**(B)
91 K. Paleologou
☎ 22161/5

*Hotel Apollo**(C)
14 Thermopilon
☎ 22491/3

*Hotel Dioscouri**(C)
94 Likourgou & Atreidon
☎ 28484/28666

*Hotel Laconia**(C)
61 K. Paleologou
☎ 28951/2

*Hotel Maniatis**(C)
72 K. Paleologou
☎ 22665/9

*Hotel Sparti Inn**(C)
105 Thermopilon
☎ 21021/6 & 22021

Traditional Settlements run by the EOT
Kastro Monemvasias:
Xenonas Kellia (12 rooms) ☎ 0732 61520

VATHIA (MANI): TELEPHONE PREFIX 0733
Pirgos Exarhakou (4 rooms) ☎ 54229
Pirgos Giannoakakou (2 rooms) ☎ 54229
Pirgos Keramida (3 rooms) ☎ 54229
Pirgos Mitsakou (3 rooms) ☎ 54229
Pirgos Papadongona ☎ 54229
Pirgos Tselepi ☎ 54229

CAMPING
* = Open all year

Agadeika
Gythion Beach Hellenic Camping
☎ 0733 23441

Gythion
Meltemi
☎ 0733 22833/23260

Mavrovouni
Mani Beach
☎ 0733 23450/1, 01 8931810

Mistra
Castle View
☎ 0731 93384, 01 3212812

Monemvasia
Capsis
☎ 0732 611123

Neochori
Porto Ageranos
☎ 0733 22039

Skala Glykovryssis
Lykourgos
☎ 0735 91580/2, 01 3611496

Slaviki, Mistra
*Mistras**
☎ 0731 22724

Vathi
Kronos
☎ 0733 24124, 01 6468453

Transport

Public Transport
By Bus: Around 7 buses a day run
between Athens and Sparti, a journey of
around 4½ hours. From Sparti buses run
to Mistra, Monemvasia and Areopolis.
One bus daily travels Athens-
Monemvasia (7 hours).
Gythion, for Mani, is served by four
buses daily from Athens (5½ hours)
Within Mani, local buses are limited to
two per day down the west coast and
one down the east.
By Boat: there is a summer hydrofoil
service Piraeus/Monevasia from Zea
Marina in Piraeus.

4

THE WESTERN PELOPONNESE

This tour, which completes the circuit of the Peloponnese, visits the remaining four provinces. First is Messinia, the garden of Greece, a region tucked away in the south-west corner which attracts perhaps fewer visitors than other provinces. The reasons can only be geographical but with an ever improving road system it must be set to change for it has much to interest the traveller. It is another *nome* which has a strong vein of historical interest from the ancient through to medieval. Homer addicts revel in Nestor's Palace where one archaeological find was a bathtub which has been brilliantly restored and placed in its original location. *The Odyssey* relates how Telemachus, son of Odysseus, visits King Nestor seeking news of his father. Whilst there, the beautiful Polycaste, youngest daughter of the king, gives Telemachus a bath and rubs him with olive oil so he emerges looking like a king. Like many other visitors, you can stand, look at the bathtub and wonder! The whole site is evocative but so too is the site of ancient Messini (Ithomi) situated some 24km (15 miles) north of the modern capital. It is a natural stronghold and a splendid setting for an ancient site. Down on the Messinian peninsula are two fine examples of medieval fortifications, the twin citadels of Methoni and Koroni both of which are visited in Tour 2 from Pylos. Pylos, standing at the southern end of Navarino Bay, is the most attractive resort in the region and a convenient base for exploration. Kalamata, the largest city of the southern Peloponnese suffered a massive earthquake in 1986 which killed twenty people and destroyed thousands of homes. Today it has largely recovered from that disaster but it remains a bustling industrial and market town which has a Frankish castle, a museum and some Byzantine churches to explore but the motorist can expect to tangle with congested traffic and find difficulty in parking.

The remaining three provinces are less extensively explored, particularly Arkadia which is entered only to visit the mountain village of Karitena to admire the castle and the old bridge featured on the 5,000 *drachma* note. Ilia, the *nome* immediately north of Messinia, has a site of antiquity known throughout the world; Olympia, home of the Olympic

THE WESTERN
PELOPONNESE
STOUPA TO OLYMPIA

games. Like Delphi, it is one of Greece's major tourist attractions but, in spite of that, the commercialisation is still relatively low key. Heading north-east from Olympia, the final leg of the Peloponnese tour cuts through the province of Achaia to visit Kalavrita and the famous rack and pinion railway which descends from there through the spectacular Vouraikos Gorge to Diakopto.

Tour 1 • Outer Mani (140km/87 miles)

Improvements to sections of the coastal road from Areopolis to Kalamata are in progress. There may be dusty stretches to face in these parts but otherwise the road is asphalted and generally good. Taken leisurely, and both the winding nature of the road and the dramatic scenery demand that it is taken leisurely, the full journey takes around 5 hours. Stoupa and Messini offer alternative stopping points if time is short.

Heading north from Areopolis, the coast road signposted Kalamata is soon reached. Scenic interest starts almost immediately as the road by-passes **Limini** which lies by the sea shore in an attractive bay. At the north end of the bay is Karavostasi, a tiny port serving **Itylo**, a village teeming with tower houses which has the distinction of being a former capital of the Mani. Sandwiched between the slopes of the Taygetos mountains and the sea, northerly progress along the route is punctuated with cameo views around every bend. Wandering coastlines, tower houses, olive groves, grazing sheep, slender cypress trees, steep mountain slopes, Byzantine churches and tiny villages chase each other in endless procession. Good beaches run north from above the small fishing village of Ag Nikolaos. **Stoupa**, with its delightful bays, has the best of the beaches, undoubtedly the best in the Mani region. Tourist developments are slowly turning Stoupa into a resort area but for the moment it remains an acceptable blend of new whitewashed villas and old mellow houses with pensions and tavernas. **Kardamili**, further north, claims to be the top resort and it certainly has more sophistication if that is measured in tourist shops and fast food places. Its small harbour looks onto a fortified offshore island. The beach there is pebbly but good for swimmers. Good area for walking.

While the character of the Mani may wain with progress beyond Kardamili, this is not true of the scenery. The road winds into the tree clad mountains and is breathtakingly scenic near Stavropigio where the road plunges to cross a gorge and climbs away back into the hills. Traffic density increases as Kalamata nears but the main road by-passes the town centre and flirts only with the outskirts. **Messini** is adequately signed and fairly soon reached. Again the main road is kept away from the town centre and once beyond it is back into pastoral countryside. Olive groves, vineyards and white farm houses hide amongst the low rolling hills. There are tantalising glimpses of the harbour on the descent into Pylos where the main road leads down to the waterfront. There is some parking around the platia by the harbour and more on the road which continues past the harbour along the sea front.

Pylos, earlier known as Navarino, sits looking out into Navarino Bay. It is a small town with some elegance and style with its arcaded streets and large shady platia. It has its own place in history on account of the famous naval battle which took place in the bay on 20 October 1827 and which proved to be a turning point in Greece's struggle for independence from Turkish rule. In the Treaty of London 1827, it was agreed that Britain,

Messinia, The Garden Of Greece

The extraordinary luxuriance and fertility of the region has been recognised since ancient times and it is not without justification that Messinia has been labelled Graecia Felix, the Garden of Greece. Somehow the geography and climate have conspired to produce growing conditions found nowhere else in the country. Mountains shelter the plains from the cold northern winds and provide the water for irrigation while the southern sun and warm winds from Africa turn it into a hothouse. Currant vines are an important commercial crop and one product for which the region is locally famous is its currant brandy. Kalamata too claims to grow the tastiest olives in the whole of Greece and Kalamata olive oil is recognised as the finest available. It is without a doubt the best buy to take home but look for virgin oil which is obtained from the first pressings. This is the very highest quality, superb for salad dressing and usually available in 5 litre sealed tins.

Everything grows well but figs are another fruit which are economically important. Petalidi, visited in Tour 2, claims to grow the best in Greece. The list is extensive but the other product worthy of mention is the mulberry tree. From the time the Chinese silk worm was brought to Europe, the mulberry proliferated and it grew especially well in Messinia. The silk trade it produced passed through the port of Methoni in medieval times. First the Turks destroyed the trees during the War of Independence and then disease decimated the silk worm to all but destroy the industry. In spite of these difficulties, the silk trade still survives and silk handkerchiefs and scarves are a speciality of the region.

France and Russia should guarantee the autonomy of Greece and send a joint fleet to enforce an armistice on the warring parties. In spite of orders not to engage in battle, the fleet sailed into the bay as a show of force when the Turks had refused an armistice. Shots fired by an Egyptian ship on the Turkish side started a fierce battle in which 26 men-of-war of the allies faced up to 82 warships of the Turko-Egyptian fleet. Within the space of a few hours the Turkish fleet lost 63 ships and was almost annihilated without the loss of a single allied vessel.

From the time the French troops arrived under the command of General Maison to rebuild the town, it slowly abandoned its name of Navarino in favour of Pylos but it should not be confused with the classical site of Pylos, the home of King Nestor, which lies some 17km (10 miles) away at the north end of the bay.

Just south of the town, 10 minutes on foot from the harbour, is the Turko-Venetian fortress of **Neokastro** which was rebuilt by the French in

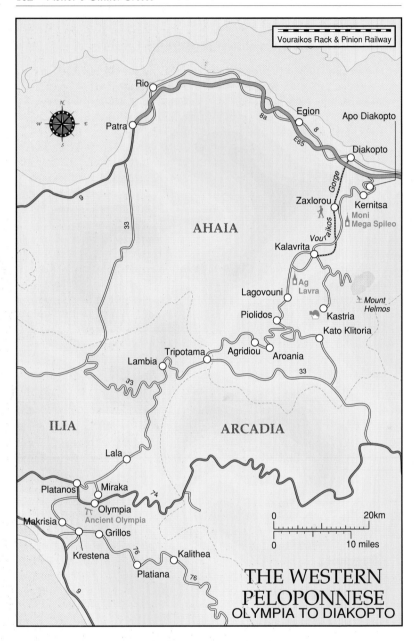

Vouraikos Rack & Pinion Railway

AHAIA

ILIA

ARCADIA

THE WESTERN
PELOPONNESE
OLYMPIA TO DIAKOPTO

1829 and later used as a prison. The extensive boundary walls enclose a defended area wherein lies a church converted from a domed mosque. Some landscaping is in progress which includes a picnic area and, whilst opening hours are observed, access to the fortress is free.

A small Byzantine church within the fortress at Koroni

Tour 2 • The Peninsula Tour (150km/93 miles)

With the twin medieval castles of Methoni and Koroni to visit and Nestor's Palace, this tour happily fills out a day. If there is a problem with the timing, it is the restriction imposed by the mid-afternoon closing times of the sites visited en route. At least they all have early opening hours. The unclassified roads used to cross the southern end of the peninsula, between Methoni and Koroni, were all well surfaced and presented only the usual pothole hazard.

Leaving Pylos on the Messini road, take the left turn, signposted Pyrgos, less than 3km (2 miles) outside the town. Nestor's Palace is only signposted as it is reached, just before the village of Hora.

π   **Nestor's Palace** is beautifully situated on a hill overlooking Navarino Bay. First explored in 1939 by Carl Blegen, World War II intervened and it was only fully excavated in 1952. Little stands above foundation height but the complex ground plan is clearly defined and the rooms are all labelled with good on site information. The museum housing many of the artefacts is in the nearby village of Hora.

Although the site was occupied from around 2000BC, the royal palace was not developed until Mycenaean times, around 1300BC. Two storied buildings were built with the extensive use of wood in columns, half timbered walls, roofs and ceilings. Its final destruction was by fire around 1200BC and, with so much wood involved, little remains of the upper story apart from objects.

King Nestor, son of Neleus, was a contemporary of Agamemnon of Mycenae. His kingdom was rich, flourishing on the agricultural wealth of the region. He fought alongside Agamemnon in the protracted Trojan Wars when, in the 'catalogue of ships' he was credited with supplying ninety vessels, second in numbers only to Agamemnon. Nestor features strongly in Homer's *The Iliad* and *The Odyssey* depicted as a wise elder statesman whom Agamemnon valued as a trusted councillor. It was to Nestor that Telemachus turned for guidance when his father, Odysseus, failed to return from the Trojan Wars.

Apart from the rich Homeric associations, there is another story to relate which is romantic in a different sense. In the search for the site of Nestor's Palace and encouraged by the number of tholos tombs around, Blegen chose to start excavations on the hill known as Epano Englianos. Hundreds of inscribed clay tablets were unearthed within hours on the very first day of digging. Unfortunately on that same day, following Italy's invasion of Albania, Greece was drawn into World War II and the tablets were removed to Athens for storage in a bank vault until after the war. It was not until 1952 that work was able to start again when more of the tablets were found. Experts agreed that these were different from the Linear A script used by the Minoans and were designated Linear B but Blegen and other scholars like Sir Arthur Evans were convinced that the language was Minoan. The break through in translating this script came not from an historian or archaeologist but from an architect, Michael Ventris. He believed Linear B to be an archaic form of Greek and progressed by assigning values to the frequently recurring signs until a breakthrough was achieved with the word 'tripod.'

From Nestor's Palace continue ahead towards the village of **Hora** and pick up signs for the museum. This is located by the junction with the Kalamata road. The museum adds significantly to a visit to the palace and shows some of the Linear B clay tablets found there as well as frescos and pottery.

Take the Kalamata road from Hora through Metamorphosis and Vlachopoulo to rejoin the Pylos/Messini road. Still heading towards Messini and Kalamata, look, as the road narrows to pass through the village of Rizomilo, for the right turn to Koroni. This route meets up with the coast at **Petalidi**, a large village with an attractive platia situated in the grand sweep of a sandy bay. Yellow blossom of broom and the purple of the Judas trees light the way along the fast coastal road down to Koroni.

The fortified village of **Koroni** with its narrow, sometimes stepped streets, wrought iron balconies and white houses is one of those towns which is unmistakably Greek. The harbour front is lined with fish tavernas and all that is missing is a beach although there is one some 2km (1 mile) south of the town. From the parking area on the sea front, the castle is reached by walking inland a block then following the narrow stepped streets to the south. The fortress, built by the Byzantines, enlarged by the Franks and added to by the Turks is now largely walls. Although the ruins may not be as impressive as Methoni, its position on the headland looking towards Mani and the Taygetos is superb. The area inside the walls is given over to houses and gardens but there is also the nunnery of Timiou Prodromou and a small Byzantine church nearby.

Leave Koroni by the same route but watch out for a left turn on a bend just 5km (3 miles) from the harbour front. This is the road through **Finikounda** which cuts across the southern tip of the peninsula. It is a scenic run winding through the valleys giving a view of Lamia slumbering on a low hilltop. The approach to Finikounda provides a spectacular view just as the road starts a descent into it. It is a small picturesque resort enjoying a fine position looking onto a sandy bay. Blankets draped from balconies of the whitewashed houses suggest this is more of a residential village than a resort but it is popular with the Greeks in summer. Farmland cultivation dominates the scenery increasingly and an array of polythene greenhouses announces **Methoni**. The town is entered by a very narrow bridge.

The fortress at Methoni is as impressive as any in Greece. Its massive walls and bastions are lapped on three sides by the sea and isolated by a moat. Such is its domination that the modern town is swamped by it but the facilities offered to tourists by way of hotels and beaches do not go unnoticed.

Once called Pedasos, Methoni is known from antiquity and was re-

The impressive fortress at Methoni

(opposite) The azure blue sea at Finikounda

ferred to by Homer as 'rich in vines.' It was not until the Middle Ages that it became commercially important under Venetian control as did Koroni. Apart from trading in silk and vines, it was used as a port of call for pilgrims en route to the Holy Land. Whatever fortifications there might have been, they were strengthened by the Venetians and the walls on the west side defended by five towers are part of their construction. It fell to the Turks in 1500 and was recovered by the Venetians in 1686 but fell again to the Turks in 1715. It remained in Turkish hands until liberated by French troops under General Maison in 1826 following the battle of Navarino Bay. All these occupations have left an imprint on the construction of the fortress which throughout these times sheltered a sizeable town. The long narrow bridge leading to the Venetian arched entrance was rebuilt by the French in 1828 who actually pulled down the medieval town in the centre and rebuilt it in its present position on the mainland. The road north from Methoni leads fairly quickly to Pylos, a distance of some 12km (7 miles).

Tour 3 • North To Olympia (255km/158 miles)

This may not be the obvious way to Olympia but it is a scenically spectacular route taking in the ancient site of Messini and calling in at the mountain villages of Karitena and Andritsena along the way. Karitena offers a castle and a beautiful old bridge and Andritsena just good mountain ambience. Both villages offer accommodation for an overnight stop but expect to find only rooms in Karitena. The short diversion to see the remarkably well preserved temple at Bassae is from Andritsena. It is not a journey to be taken quickly, winding mountain roads restrict speed and there is too much to be savoured. An overnight stop at one of the two mountain villages is recommended.

Follow the road from Pylos as far as Messini and turn left off the by-pass road to enter the main square in the centre. Look for the sign to Meligalas and head north up this road, turning left at the unsigned T-junction shortly encountered. Olive groves and Judas trees predominate as small farming communities follow one after another. Turn left at Lambena to follow signs to Ithomi, which, incidentally, lies close to the village of Mavromati. The plains are left behind as the encroaching hills of Mount Ithomi draw ever nearer and a gentle ascent starts before the village of Arsinoi where old ladies in black dominate the population.

The hills get steeper as Mavromati is reached. The modern town is built part way up Mount Ithomi, above is the acropolis perched on the very crown of the hill and below, on the valley bottom, is the most important part of the ruins of **Ancient Messini (Ithomi)**. A signpost at the centre of the village indicates directions to the various parts of the ancient city. New roads are being cut down to the main site but access is by a steep, narrow concrete track which forks down to the left just about 100m (328ft) beyond the signpost. As with many of the ancient sites, it occupies a position of great natural beauty.

Protected by the 800m (2,624ft) high Mount Ithomi, Epameinondas chose this site in 371BC to build a stronghold to defend Messinia from the Spartans and allow the return of the Messinians to their country. This new fortified city formed a link with other strongholds stretching across Arcadia, including Megalopolis, Mantineia (Mandinia) and Argos, all ranged against Sparti. Diodorus claimed, somewhat extravagantly, the city was built in 85 days but considering that the circuit of walls alone was some 9km (6 miles) long, 4m (13ft) high and 2½m (8ft) thick, it would have been a mighty feat. The walls were strengthened by square or semicircular towers at intervals along its length.

On the valley bottom lies a square building thought to be an agora but possibly a Sanctuary of Asklepios. A small temple occupies the central position and to the outside is a colonnade. Nearby is a small theatre and to the west of the agora amongst the olive groves is a stadium. Much of the stone seating is roughly in position and the seating for the dignitaries has been reset. The main theatre, lying to the north of the stadium, is well overgrown and all that remains is the analemma wall.

Those with the time and energy to explore the acropolis can reach it by a path from the village or an alternative path via the Laconian Gate. On top of the mountain there is the abandoned sixteenth-century Monastery of Vourkano standing on the site of the Sanctuary of Zeus Ithomatas which

Horta

Outside the village of Arsinoi, one or two of the women were seen in the fields assiduously collecting leaves of a dandelion species to use as a vegetable. This is not especially a local habit, it can be seen all over Greece. Collectors are easily recognised, usually they have a knife in one hand and a polythene carrier bag bursting with green leaves in the other and eyes down searching the ground.

The leaves are first boiled in water, like cabbage and then well coated with oil and lemon and served as *horta*. It is often available in tavernas in season, which is throughout winter and spring, but not always on the menu. One reason is the translation problem and it is sometimes erroneously listed as spinach. Worth asking for if it is hot and freshly cooked but less appetising when cold and soaked too long in oil. High mountains produce the best *horta*.

is said to have witnessed human sacrifice. Myth claims that Zeus was born by a spring on the mountain and taken to the top by the nymphs Neda and Ithomi. Even today, Mavromati celebrates an annual festival which is believed to survive from the ancient feast to Zeus.

Leave Mavromati by continuing through the village to the Arcadian Gate from where fine stretches of the old city walls can be seen, particularly to the west. Turn right here to pass through the gate onto what may appear to be nothing more than a track but, fear not, the road is asphalted almost immediately beyond. It continues as a good road through some fine mountain scenery passing occasional small villages like Neohorion where the road may narrow and become rough as it often does through villages. **Meligalas** is a fairly large town with a road system which is not well signed. Turn right at the T-junction as the village is reached then left on meeting the major road in the centre to head out north, soon to run alongside the railway on the right. Once through the village of Zevgolatio, follow signs to Kalamata which means turning right at the complex road junction, before passing beneath the road bridge, to join the main road. Turn left at the next major junction following signs to Tripoli but only as far as **Megalopoli**, reached after a long wind up into the hills.

For Andritsena (44km/27 miles) follow around the platia in Megalopoli to the left. Just over 1km (½ mile) along this road there is the opportunity to detour left, just before the power station, to see the ancient theatre which has survived from around the fourth century BC when Megalopolis was founded as the capital of the federated states of Arcadia. Much of this ancient site has now disappeared and the theatre is all that remains of significance. Pausanias described it as the largest theatre in Greece built with seating for more than 20,000. Built against the north side of a hill, there is not so much to see now, only the front rows of seats are

The terracotta tiled roof top of the Byzantine church at Karitena

The Odeon at Ancient Messina, occupying a position of natural beauty

The old bridge at Karitena is featured on the 5,000 drachma note

Removals by donkey are a speciality in Greece!

well preserved. The large power station nearby is rather dominant and adds nothing to the ambience.

Although the mountains are not far away, the road stays on the plain of Megalopolis for a time yet weaving its way through cultivated countryside. Shortly, where the castle on the pinnacle announces Karitena; stay ahead at the junction as the major road to Andritsena bends away to the left. Drive up into the village as far as possible and park in the large platia.

With stone built, red-roofed houses clustering around the base of a castle crowned hill, **Karitena** is nothing if not picturesque. A steep path to the castle is signposted out of the platia and it takes around 15 minutes on foot. At the fork part way up turn sharp right for the castle. Built by Hugh de Bruyeres in 1254, the walls are the best preserved part but there are the remains of a vaulted hall inside and a number of cisterns. The superb views alone make the climb worthwhile. Apart from the eleventh century church of Panagia, the other point of interest in Karitena is the old bridge which is featured on the 5,000 *drachma* note. The easiest way to see it is to stop on the main road as you drive along by it shortly after rejoining the Andritsena road but it is possible to walk footpaths down from the platia.

Leave Karitena by the same road and follow signs to **Andritsena**. To view the old bridge at close quarters, stop just after crossing the new bridge and find a small footpath down to the left. For a time scrub covered mountains dominate the scenery but distant vistas open up as the road winds up into the mountains and to Andritsena (765m/2,509ft). It is hard to tell now that it was once a major town throughout the years of Turkish occupation, except perhaps from the wooden houses which still remain. On a walk down the main street, crowded out with shops and houses with overhanging balconies, it is possible to see women weaving away making the woollen rugs which are sold locally. Andritsena is an attractive base from which to visit the temple at nearby Bassae but it is still not blessed with too many hotels. The superbly situated B class Xenia Hotel, just by the entrance to the village, is comfortable if somewhat austere although breakfast scored no points while the D class Hotel Pan in the centre of the village looks perhaps more homely.

Once through the crowded main street, turn left for the Temple of Apollo Epikourios at **Bassae (Vassae)**. It is only a 14km (9 mile) drive but the route is scenically spectacular. The modern, asphalted road climbs up into the mountains and follows along ledges and skims in and around the peaks, always comfortably wide but with possible hazards from fallen rocks and edge subsidence.

Bassae means ravines which is an appropriate description for the site of this magnificent temple built on a terrace at an elevation of 1,131m (3,710ft) overlooking a deep ravine. The ancients built temples in locations appropriate to their dedication. A temple to Poseidon, like the one at Sounion in Attica, would be found near the sea and here, so close to the sun, it is no surprise to find the temple is dedicated to Apollo but this time he is attributed with another epithet, Epikourios (the saviour). Pausanias

A 5,000 Drachma Walk

The return walk from Karitena Castle takes around 1 hour and, while it is easy enough going down, remember the return is all uphill. The footpaths are stony too so that stout shoes or trainers are needed.

Leave the platia as for the castle but stay ahead immediately ignoring the castle route to the left. Follow the stony track which stays close to the castle hill on the left to emerge on a loop of the surfaced road. Leave the road straight away to continue downhill on a trail starting between two shrines which shortly crosses a track. Keep heading down until another track is reached then turn right to continue down in the direction of the new bridge; the old bridge lies alongside. About half of this medieval bridge remains in good order but the view through its arches back to the village, as shown on the 5,000 *drachma* note, is now masked by the new bridge.

Return by the same route as far as the two shrines on the surfaced road and now enter the track used on the downward leg. Almost immediately, take a narrow path off right to weave your way through the narrow village walkways back to the platia.

relates that it was built as a thanksgiving to Apollo for sparing them the plague which ravished much of the area during the Peloponnesian War. Constructed in the dark grey local marble, scholars still argue whether the temple was built before or after the Parthenon but generally agree on somewhere between 450 and 420BC.

Probably because nobody wanted the stone for other building purposes in this inhospitable part of the world, and because of its isolation, the temple has survived in a remarkable state of preservation. Its location was rediscovered by the Frenchman Jaochim Bocher in 1765 who was murdered by bandits on his return a year later. The British and Germans braved the lawlessness in 1811 and persuaded the Turks to sell pieces of the cella frieze which ended up in the British Museum. The temple now is protected by a huge tent, a remarkable structure in its own right, and it does add atmosphere once inside. It is the best preserved temple in Greece and most of the doric columns are still standing.

Return by the same route to Andritsena and from there follow the signs left to Kalithea (17km/10 miles) and Pyrgos. The appearance of pines brings a softness to the barren landscape as the road gradually descends out of the mountains. **Kalithea** with its wooden balconied, stone houses, some colourfully festooned in washing, is a village large enough for tavernas but without a bread shop. Olive trees appear after further descent and the hills give way to a rolling undulating landscape dotted with farms. **Krestena** is the biggest village en route with Hotel Athena and a restaurant but is no more than a ribbon development. Turn right through here following signs to Olympia and be prepared to weave through the narrow streets of the next village, Makrisia, before crossing the intensively cultivated plain to Olympia.

Olympia is a small modern village which has grown in response to the influx of tourism. Hotels and tourist shops dominate but, in spite of the commercialism, it is a pleasant enough place for a short stay to visit the site. It is perhaps busiest throughout the day when the coach trippers are allowed their regulated free time to wander but by evening everything quietens down very appreciably. Parking is permitted along one side of the road only and this alternates according to the month as indicated by the signs with either a single or a double vertical bar. For further information refer to the Travelling in Greece (Driving in Greece) section in the Fact File at the end of this guide.

It is famed throughout the world as the birthplace of the panhellenic Olympic games which took place here every 4 years from 776BC to AD393. Unlike other great cultural centres of the period, Olympia was never a great city. It was a sanctuary built in the middle of a fertile plain by a spring at the foot of Mount Kronos, around 2000BC, for the worship of Kronos, the father of Zeus, and the earth-goddess Rhea. The origin of the games is lost in a jumble of myths and legends. It may have started from a chariot race organised by King Oinomaos of Pisa who did not wish to lose his beautiful daughter Hippodameia by marriage. Suitors were invited to race their chariot against his to win his daughter but the penalty for losing was death. King Oinomaos was full of tricks to prevent being beaten but he was eventually outsmarted by Pelops. The linchpins in the King's chariot were replaced with some made of clay which held only long enough for the race to get underway. The King was killed in the accident and Pelops claimed his daughter. Alternatively, the origins may have been simpler. It is said that Heracles, son of the great Zeus who lived on Mount Olympos, marked out a sacred grove, the Altis, and introduced games in honour of his Olympian father.

In early Bronze Age religions, women and female deities were much in control and there is evidence to suggest that the early games involved women and remained that way until the worship of Zeus intruded. Myths and legends apart, the games were restarted in 776BC and the winners then and thereafter recorded. Pausanias claims that the prize first of all was for a footrace which was won in the first games by Koroibos of Elis. The race was over the distance of one stadion (192m/630ft). At the fourteenth Olympics, according to Pausanias, a two lap race was added and in the eighteenth the pentathlon (foot race, long jump, wrestling, javelin and discus) and wrestling. Eventually the games built up with the further introductions of boxing and equestrian events, including the very prestigious four horse chariot race and even races in armour. When the games became too large to be completed by dusk they were extended into the following days and they were truly panhellenic, open to all whose native tongue was Greek. So that all could attend, and there was virtually

Olympia station stirs only at the arrival of a train

The Judas trees paint Olympia purple in spring

continuous warring in the various regions, a truce was strictly enforced and observed for the period of the games. It was clearly obeyed because the games continued with the utmost regularity. Male competitors only were allowed in the stadium and they, and their trainers, were obliged to demonstrate their sex by competing in the nude.

The prize for success at the games was nothing more than a garland of wild olive but it immortalised the victor and his family. Such was the prestige of the games that the wealth of the sanctuaries steadily accumulated and treasuries were built to accept the votive offerings from the various Greek states. The Romans were eventually accepted and admitted to the games which, after reaching new heights of professionalism, ended under the ban of Emperor Theodosius in AD393.

Excavation of the site by the Germans started in 1875 and lasted for a period of 6 years but there have been further excavations since, notably 1936-41 and 1952. All the finds are located in the excellent museum in the town. A consequence of the excavations was the eventual revival of the games; the first modern Olympiad being held in Athens in 1896.

Within a few minutes walk from the centre of the village, the site lies in a silvan setting below Mount Kronos. In mid April, it takes on a haze of purple brilliance under the blossom of the Judas trees which flourish there. Things to see are:

The Palaistra: This square building from the third century BC, on the left after entering, was of uncertain purpose. It was either for wrestling and boxing or simply a meeting place. Some of its Doric columns have been restored but originally there were colonnades on all four sides.

The Temple of Hera: Both this temple and the Temple of Zeus lie within the Altis, a sacred area reserved for gods. It is a square area bounded on three sides by walls whose lines only can now be traced. The Doric Temple of Hera is the oldest temple on the site built around 600BC on foundations which are even earlier. The earlier wooden columns were replaced by stone in various styles. Four columns have been restored and there are several partial columns in place.

The Temple of Zeus: Built by Libon of Elis and completed around 457BC, this Doric style temple was one of the largest in Greece. In spite of the sixth-century earthquake, the foundations and many of the column bases and capitals survived allowing some restoration. Similarities with the Parthenon in Athens suggest that the same architect, Pheidias, may have been involved with the design.

Nymphaion Fountain: This semicircular fountain, close to the Temple of Hera, was built by the Athenian Herodes Atticus around AD160.

Treasuries: Lying adjacent to the fountain towards the stadium and built on a terrace overlooking the Altis, the treasuries were in effect small temples built by various cities to house their votive offerings.

The Stadium: In spite of all that is fine on the site, this is the biggest attraction to many visitors. The stadium as it is presently seen is the result of excavations and restoration by the German Archaeological Society in

1961-2 to its fourth-century form. There was no seating, only earth embankments to seat some forty thousand spectators and the starting and finishing lines can still be seen.

The **Archaeological Museum** is housed in a modern building at the far end of the car park which is opposite the archaeological site. A prior visit to this excellent museum is worthwhile if only to see the scale model of the site which helps with locating the various buildings and visualising Olympia as it was in a late stage of its development. The excavations unearthed a treasure of finds from helmets and shields through to votive offerings, most of which are now housed in chronological order in the museum. Amongst many fine exhibits, one highlight is the sculptures from the Temple of Zeus in the central hall. The sculpture from the east pediment is thought to commemorate the chariot race between King Oinomaos and Pelops.

A history of the olympic games in memorabilia is in the Museum of Olympic Games located to the rear of the village on the west side.

Tour 4 • The Scenic Inland Route To The North Coast (105km/65 miles)

This drive through the mountains is as scenic and as varied as any in the Peloponnese. At the end awaits one of the great little train journeys of the world; the Kalavrita-Diakopto rack and pinion railway. Road surfaces are generally good and the section from Tripotama through Aroania, a non-classified road, is asphalted and good although some widening work is in progress in parts. Even taken slowly, the journey is easily accomplished in half a day.

Leave Olympia by heading east past the archaeological site in the direction of Tripoli. Just over a kilometre past the site entrance turn left following signs to Lambia (40km/25 miles) which leads straight away through the village of Miraka. A slow and steady climb leads through pine filled hollows and hillocks towards the distant mountains.

Beyond the village of Lala, which ribbons its way along the main road, pear trees dot the fertile plains and deciduous oak takes over from the pine. At the T-junction turn right towards Lambia and Tripoli. Scrubland dominates the hills with steadily decreasing height and, as trees seek refuge in the sheltered valleys, the terrain looks increasingly barren. **Lambia**, scattered around and down the hillside, has the charm of old wrought iron balconied houses and flocks of long haired woolley sheep. Kalavrita (50km/31 miles) appears on the signpost as a left turn at the next village, **Tripotama**, and from here the road follows through a long, broad river valley which is lush and green with crops of maize, wheat and vines. The tree-lined village of **Aroania**, festooned over the mountainside, marks the end of the valley and from here the road climbs into the mountains and to an open vista of distant mountain tops. Go left on

The Spectacular Vouraikos Railway

The rack and pinion railway which descends from **Kalavrita** through the spectacular Vouraikos Gorge down to **Diakopto** is not to be missed. The fact that a railway exists at all can only be attributed to a remarkable feat of engineering. The small train wends and twists through tunnels and over rocky ledges squeezing through the narrowest parts with only the river as close companion and descends the steepest gradients (1 in 7) with

Zaxlorou village and station on the Kalavrita line

Travel by rail through the Vouraikos Gorge

the help of its rack and pinion system. There are around four trains a day in each direction and while the 22km (14 mile) journey through the gorge is spectacular at any time, trips made close to noon have the advantage of better lighting from an overhead sun. The train has only two coaches, one in front of and one to the rear of the diesel engine, providing good viewing for all passengers. It is still worth booking a first class (single or return) for the opportunity to sit in the small compartments at the extreme front or rear for this 1 hour journey. With a first class return fare costing barely more than the cost of a beer in Europe, this journey has to be the best value in Greece.

Kalavrita Railway Timetable Daily	
dep. Kalavrita	09.06; 13.35; 16.26; 17.35
dep. Zaxlorou	09.28; 13.57; 16.48; 17.57
arr. Diakopto	10.15; 14.45; 17.35; 18.44
dep. Diakopto	07.45; 10.42; 12.15; 15.08
dep. Zaxlorou	08.30; 11.30; 13.03; 15.56
arr. Kalavrita	08.54; 11.51; 13.24; 16.17

The Vouraikos Railway meanders through tunnels and over rocky ledges

meeting the main road to follow a pastoral route between the hills. An avenue of trees finally announces Kalavrita.

Situated at the foot of the Mount Helmos range at an altitude of 750m (2,460ft), **Kalavrita** is favoured by cool mountain air which keeps it fresh throughout spring and pleasant in the summer months. It has a reasonable amount of accommodation in the way of hotels and rooms largely to serve the nearby ski resort on Mount Helmos. If the town has a modern look then it is largely on account of one particular day fixed indelibly in the town's history, 13 December 1943. On this day the occupying German troops massacred 1,436 males over 15 and burnt the town. The clock on the Metropolitan church stands permanently at 2.34pm, the time of the massacre. Expect remembrance but do not expect too much sadness. The town has come to terms with it in its own way, by wearing it openly and sharing it with all its visitors. The large white cross just outside the town, on the road up to the ski resort, is part of a simple but poignant memorial to those who died.

Just 6km (4 miles) to the south-west lies **Ag Lavra**, perhaps the most famous monastery in Greece. It was here on 21 March 1821 that Germanos, the Archbishop of Patras, raised the standard of revolt against the Turks which launched the War of Independence. It was destroyed by fire in 1943 at the hands of the Nazis but rebuilt later.

Skiing at the Mount Helmos ski resort comes to a close sometime in late March or early April. The peaks on the Aroania range are mighty, reaching as high as 2,341m (7,678ft), so the snow hangs around the tops until well into early into summer. If the road starts off without much promise, it is immediately wider and better surfaced beyond the village. Turn left for the ski resort at the junction reached about half way up. The whole of the 15km (9 mile) drive is scenic but the real rewards are at the top with superb alpine views and a host of rare alpine flowers. The road ahead at the junction mentioned leads on to caves at the village of **Kastria**. Commercialisation of the caves is a recent development and road construction should now allow access. According to tourist office information, a narrow passage leads first into a small cave which broadens into an enormous cavern fully 2km (1 mile) long with fifteen miniature lakes formed by natural rock formations and attended by impressive displays of stalactites and stalagmites.

Moni Mega Spileo, the Monastery of the Great Cave, lies 6½km (4 miles) north of Kalavrita by the road down to Diakopto and can just as easily be visited by car as on foot. The monastery, built against a near vertical rock face utilising a cave, has early beginnings but it has suffered serious fires on a number of occasions. The last time was in 1934 when it was blown up by a barrel of gunpowder left over from the War of Independence. Its reconstruction in modern style is not so endearing. Once an important place of pilgrimage throughout the Middle Ages, it became one of the richest monasteries in Greece and possesses many old ikons. Visitors are usually shown around by a monk.

The Pine Processionary Caterpillar

The nests seen dripping from pine trees both here and along many of the Mediterranean coasts in Greece are full of the Pine Processionary Caterpillar (*Thaumetopoea pityocampa*). They live in these communal nests through the winter and come out to feed only when the weather is warm enough. Their communal behaviour persists even on leaving the nest and they move in procession, each one in contact nose to tail with the next to form chains extending to several metres in length. When fully grown, which is usually by late spring or early summer, they pupate in cocoons below ground and emerge as moths later in the summer. Eggs are laid in large numbers around the pine needles and are covered by scales from the body of the female. The reproductive cycle is completed in the course of one year.

A word of warning; these dark brown caterpillars are covered in hairs which are highly irritant and will cause a painful rash if they come into contact with the skin.

Tour 5 • Back To Athens

There are choices to make for the return to Athens. The first route is the most direct whilst the second takes advantage of the ferry between Rio and Andirio to cross the Gulf of Corinth and include Delphi in the itinerary.

Route 1 : Kalavrita • Diakopto • Corinth • Athens (205km/127 miles)

The first stage descends to the coast at Diakopto and then there is a choice of either joining the fast road, which passes as motorway, or continuing along the old coast road as far as Corinth. The latter is easily the most scenic run and fairly free flowing although some heavies still use the route. For the final leg from Corinth to Athens, the toll road is the better option.

Route 2 : Kalavrita • Diakopto • Rio • Andirio • Delphi (198km/123 miles) • Levadia • Thiva • Athens (364km/226 miles)

For travellers with time in hand, this route offers the opportunity to see Delphi on the return without too much extra mileage. Details of Delphi and other places of interest en route back to Athens are included in Chapter 5. This is also a convenient route for those who might wish to join in the tours into the northern region of the mainland (Chapter 5 onwards).

Zaxlorou To Moni Mega Spileo On Foot

Apart from a halt just outside Kalavrita, Zaxlorou is the one and only station on the line down to Diakopto and the journey time is around 25 minutes. From the tiny and isolated village Zaxlorou which seems only a taverna and a clutch of houses bigger than the station, there is an old trail which leads up to join the main road just below the Monastery of Mega Spileo. The way is constantly uphill and the footpaths are often very stony. It takes around 45 minutes to reach the monastery from the station and much the same to return.

The Anemone blanda *found by the wayside*

Alight at Zaxlorou and walk past the front of the hotel and taverna to join the path which continues alongside the gorge rising steadily. Very shortly there are good views looking backwards to the station but, soon afterwards, the path starts to wind to the left, up the side of the gorge and away from the railway line. The slow, steady uphill pace at least leaves time to appreciate the wild flowers by the wayside which in April includes the dwarf iris-like flowers (*Hermodactylus tuberosus*) and the *Anemone blanda*. The road is reached in around 30 minutes and the monastery can now be clearly seen up to the left. From here the route to it follows along the road.

Road conditions are good throughout and the ferry crossings are frequent, inexpensive and require only 20 minutes sea time. After descending from Kalavrita to Diakopto, the coastal road westwards to Rio is pleasing to drive and rewarding for its fine scenery over the gulf. A good, fast road from Andirio skims along the coast for much of the way revealing occasional glimpses of attractive little bays. One such bay, at Skalana, just after Nafpaktos, makes an ideal picnic spot.

Additional Information

Places to Visit

Arcadia
Castle
The castle is unguarded with free access.

Methoni
Castle
Open: daily, including Sundays and holidays, 9pm-3pm.

Nestor's Palace
Site and Museum (at Hora)
Open: daily, iencluding Sundays and holidays, 8.30pm-3pm. Closed on Monday.

Olympia
Site
Open: 8am-7pm Monday to Friday and 8.30am-3pm on Saturday and Sunday.

Olympia Museum
Open: 11.30am-6pm on Monday 8am-7pm Tuesday to Friday and 8am-3pm on Saturday and Sunday.

Olympic Games Museum
Open: 8pm-3.30pm Monday to Saturday and 9am-4.30pm on Sunday.

Pylos
Neokastro
Open: daily 8.30pm-3pm. Closed on Monday.

Accommodation

HOTELS
* = Open all year

ANDRITSENA: TELEPHONE PREFIX 0626
Hotel Theoxenia (B)
☎ 22219/35/70

Hotel Pan (D)

Arcadia
Karitena has no hotel but there are private rooms available.

Finikounda: TELEPHONE PREFIX 0723
Hotel Finikounda* (C)
☎ 71208/71308/71408

Hotel Porto Finissia* (C)
☎ 71358/71457/71458

KALAMATA: TELEPHONE PREFIX 0721
Hotel Elite* (A)
2 Navarinou ☎ 25015/22434/85303

Hotel Rex* (B)
26 Aristomenous
☎ 22334/23291-4

Hotel Flisvos* (C)
135 Navarinou
☎ 82282/82177

Hotel Valassis* (C)
95 Navarinou
☎ 23849/25751

KALAVRITA: TELEPHONE PREFIX 0692
Hotel Filoxenia* (B)
☎ 22422/22290/22493

Hotel Helmos (B)
Eletherias Square
☎ 22217

Villa Kalavrita
Rooms and suites
☎ 22712/22845

KARDAMILI: TELEPHONE PREFIX 0721
Hotel Kalamitsi (B) ☎ 73131

Karamili Beach*
Hotel & Bungalows (C)
☎ 73180/84

Hotel Pariarcheas (C) ☎ 73366

KORONI: TELEPHONE PREFIX 0725
Auberge de la Plage, pension (B)
☎ 0725 22401

MESSINI: TELEPHONE PREFIX 0722
Hotel Messini* (C)
Pilou Ave
☎ 23002/3

Hotel Drossia* (C)
20 Dariotou
☎ 23248/22457

Hotel Lyssandros* (C)
☎ 22921/24336

METHONI: TELEPHONE PREFIX 0723
*Hotel Odysseas** (B) ☎ 31600
*Hotel Alex** (C) ☎ 31219/31245
*Pension Methoni Beach**(B) ☎ 31544/5

OLYMPIA: TELEPHONE PREFIX 0624
*Hotel Amalia** (A) ☎ 22190/1
*Hotel Antonios** (A) ☎ 22348/9
Hotel Altis (B) ☎ 23101/2

Hotel Apollon (B)
13 Douma ☎ 22522/22513

*Hotel Neda** (B)
1 K. Karamanli ☎ 22563/22692

Hotel New Olympia (B) ☎ 22547/22506
Hotel Artemis (C) 2 Tsoureka ☎ 22255
*Hotel Hercules** (C) ☎ 22696/22532
*Hotel Inomaos** (C) ☎ 22056
*Hotel Pelops** (C) 2 Varela ☎ 22543

PYLOS: TELEPHONE PREFIX 0723
*Hotel Miramare** (B) ☎ 22226/22751

*Hotel Karalis** (C)
26 Kalamatas ☎ 22960/22980

*Hotel Galaxy** (C)
Trion Navaron Square
☎ 22780/22784

*Pension Karalis Beach** (B) ☎ 23021/2

STOUPA: TELEPHONE PREFIX 0721
Hotel Halikoura Beach (C) ☎ 54303
Hotel Lefktro (C) ☎ 54322
Hotel Stoupa (C) ☎ 54308

CAMPING
* = Open all year
The sites listed here open April/May through until September/October.

Finikounda
Ammos ☎ 0723 71262/71333

Kardamili
Melitzina ☎ 0721 73461 or Athens 01 6513420

Koroni
Koroni Camping ☎ 0725 22119

Memi Beach
☎ 0725 22130 or Athens 01 2523406

Methoni
Camping ☎ 0723 31228

Olympia
Alfios, Drouva Arch ☎ 0624 22950/2
Diana (open all year)
Ancient Olympia ☎ 0624 22314/22425
Olympia Beach ☎ 0624 22738/22745

Pylos
Navarino
Gialova ☎ 0273 22761

Petalidi
Petalidi Beach ☎ 0722 31154

Sun Beach
Petalidi ☎ 0722 31200/31110 or Athens 01 8171406

Stoupa
Kalogria ☎ 0721 54319/54327

Transport

MESSINIA: Kalamata, as capital of the region, is well connected to Athens. There are daily flights from the airport which lies just outside Kalamata towards Messini as well as bus and train services. The trains, around 5 daily, run via Kiparissia and Patra for a journey time of 7½ hours. The buses, some 10 daily, use a more direct route which takes about 4½ hours.

Locally, there are fairly frequent bus services out of Kalamata to destinations such as Messini, Pylos, Olympia, Gythio and Areopolis. From Pylos connections to Athens are limited, two buses daily, but there is a better service to Methoni.

ILIA: Olympia is well served by bus to Athens and to many centres in the Peloponnese including Tripoli, Argos, Sparti, Megalopolis, Karitena, Andritsena, Kalamata and Nafplio. In addition is has also a rail service with daily trains to Patras, Corinth Athens, Piraeus, Pirgos, Kalamata and Argos.

Tourist Information Centres

Ilia
Municipality Information Office
Praxitelous Kondili
Olympia ☎ 0624 231125/23100/23173

Messinia
Municipality Information Office
221 Kalamata 24100
☎ 0721 22059/21959

5

CENTRAL GREECE

The five *nomes* which make up central Greece are, since becoming firmly established as part of the newly independent Greek state in 1821, referred to collectively as Sterea Ellada (Sterea Ellas). They cover the region below a line roughly drawn across from Arta in the west to the east coast opposite Evia down to the Gulf of Corinth and Attica. A region of mountains, fertile plains and numerous coves it is still known by the older and more popular name of Roumeli, the Land of Rome, which survives from Roman times. It is believed the word 'Greek' originated when colonists from Graia, a town in Viotia, one of the *nomes*, came in contact with the Romans in southern Italy and Latinised Graia to *Graeci*.

Mount Parnassos and lesser mountains, at the southern end of the Pindos range, dominate the interior of the region whilst a sprinkling of ancient fortresses and medieval castles guard the fertile plain areas at their feet. An amalgam of the wild and the beautiful where small villages hide amongst the mountains and fishing hamlets cluster along the convoluted coastline. In this setting Oedipus answered the riddle of the Sphinx and acted out the tragedy of his life but it is Delphi which draws the crowds. Today the Oracle is silenced but the evocative site has regained its ancient reputation as being one of the best known in Greece.

There is something to satisfy all tastes on this tour. Besides the obvious draw of Delphi there are many more archaeological sites especially around the less mountainous area to the east. Unfortunately, nothing much is left of many of these remaining sites except relics in museums but the fortresses of Aigosthena, Eleutherai and Gla are worth a visit. For those more interested in things Byzantine and medieval there are castles, especially the one at Levadia, and the not to be missed monastery of Osios Loukas with its famous mosaics. Parnassos itself provides a diversity of interest, with skiing in winter, walking in summer and a mass display of wild flowers in the spring, but bird lovers may be tempted to head for one of the inland lakes or the swampy coast around Messolongi. Small resorts and fishing hamlets dot the coastline from where it is inviting to swim in the clear water. Island buffs can bag yet another, without even having to get onto a ferry, as Lefkas (Lefkada) is connected by bridge to the mainland. This pretty, green island attracts water sports and sailing enthusiasts.

If a fast run to Delphi is the first consideration, there is a choice of two routes. One is north, via the motorway, as far as the turn off for Thiva, then continuing on the old route. The other uses the motorway south via Corinth towards Patra, crossing over to the northern mainland on the ferry at Rio, then driving the good coastal road back towards Athens and Delphi. Visitors driving up from the Peloponnese can join in the latter route at Rio if they are heading for Delphi. The more interesting and atmospheric route, described below, follows closely the ancient road from Athens to Delphi and can easily be covered in a few hours driving. The roads are good overall and, for those wishing to travel at a more leisurely pace, Levadia is an interesting place for an overnight stop.

Tour 1 • West To Delphi (190km/118 miles)

Leave Athens along Iera Odos (the Sacred Way) off Pireos which passes through sprawling suburbs and industrial wastelands. It joins the main Athens-Corinth road at Daphni and continues to Elefsina (site of ancient

Eleusis) in 24km (15 miles). Turn right at Elefsina, just before the motor-way toll booths, to Mandra and Thiva, immediately heading into more pleasant hill country. If time is not of the essence, a left turn, 3km (2 miles) after passing through the village of Inoi, to Vilia and Egosthena (Porto Germeno) leads in 23km (14 miles) to the substantial remains of the fortress of **Aigosthena**. On the right, continuing just past the same junc-tion on the Thiva road, are the remains of Eleutherai the best preserved fort on the Viotian border.

Despite a well chronicled past steeped in myth and, more recently, importance as a silk centre there is little now to persuade the traveller to remain long in Thiva. Ancient **Thiva** lies buried beneath modern build-ings but recent excavations have revealed walls belonging to the Mycenaean stronghold of Kadmeia. Finds have included Linear B tablets and also cuneiform texts which add weight to the myth that Kadmos, who built the stronghold in about 1500BC, came from Phoenicia in search of his sister Europa who had been carried off by Zeus. The invention of the Greek alphabet is also attributed to this same city of Kadmos. If there is not time to seek out the locations of the seven gates of the ancient city the interesting Archaeological Museum is worth a visit. It can be found beneath the one surviving thirteenth century-tower in the walls of what remains of the castle. Exhibits include painted Mycenaean sarcophagi

The Oedipus Myth

Laius and Jocasta, having been warned by the Oracle at Delphi that their baby son would grow up to kill his father, pinned the child by the foot on Mount Kithairon and left him to die. Rescued by a shepherd, Oedipus grew up believing the shepherd and his wife to be his real parents. After a visit to consult the Oracle at Delphi, where he learned that he would kill his father and marry his mother, he came into conflict with a charioteer who tried to whip him to one side at the Triple Way. In the fracas which followed Oedipus killed the charioteer who was in fact none other than his real father Laius. As he continued on his way through the countryside he was stopped by a Sphinx who terrorised travellers with a riddle which wrongly answered meant death. 'What being has sometimes two feet, sometimes three and sometimes four, and is weakest when it has the most?'. Such was the Sphinx' rage when Oedipus replied correctly that the being was a man, who walked on all fours as a child, on two as a man and with a staff in his old age, she threw herself off Mount Springion. Still the innocent victim of events, on his return to Thebes, he was given Jocasta for a wife and made king by a grateful people who, although saddened by the loss of Laius, rejoiced in the death of the Sphinx. Thus, unbeknown to Oedipus, the prophesy came true. Some years later, when the truth about their relationship was revealed to them by the seer Tiresius, Jocasta killed herself and Oedipus put out his own eyes and left Thebes.

which are unique examples of this type to be found on the mainland. Heracles, of the wondrous feats of strength, was born in Thiva but it is better remembered for its association with the tragic tale of Oedipus.

The road onwards from Thiva to Levadia skirts the plain of Kopais with sight of Parnassos in the distance ahead. To the north is forbidding Mount Fagas, or Mount Springion, off which the Sphinx hurled herself to her death. Kopais was once the largest lake in Greece until it was drained at the end of the last century. The area is now a large fertile plain on which is grown cereal crops, tomatoes, water-melons and cotton.

Levadia, the capital of Viotia, is a busy modern town on the edge Kopais plain and renowned for its colourful textiles. The impressive medieval castle still dominates the town due in no small measure to the period of Turkish occupancy between 1460-1829 when it prospered and became wealthy. A Turkish bridge spans the Erkina (Herkyna) river below the Spring of Trophonios which is fed by a group of springs including the two known in antiquity as Lethe (forgetfulness) and Mnemosyne (remembrance). They played an important part in the function of the Oracle of Trophonios, located on a hilltop close by. Trips out from Levadia can

The Oracle Of Trophonios

Oracles, the relayed voices of gods, are as old as religion and before the pantheon of Greek gods and goddesses was recognised. It was Gaea, the Earth Mother who spoke. This particular Oracle was established as a reward for Trophonios. He and his twin brother had been told by the Delphic Oracle to enjoy themselves for six days and on the seventh they would achieve their heart's desire. As they were both found dead on the seventh day it was assumed their heart's desire had been to die for their god.

Most oracular consultations took place above ground, where the 'truth' was revealed to them by a priestess, but at Levadia one had to 'enter the Underworld' to see and hear the 'truth' for oneself as Pausanias recounts. Before pilgrims were even considered fit to consult the Oracle they had to subject themselves to a purifying ritual which took place over a few days. This involved making sacrifices to various gods, eating only sacrificed meat and foregoing hot baths in favour of bathing in the river Erkina (ancient Herkyna). When the priest pronounced them fit to consult the oracle pilgrims were once more led to the river Erkina where they were ritualistically bathed and anointed. They then drank from the springs of Lethe to forget the past and the Mnemosyne to remember what would be heard and seen in the 'Underworld'. The whole uncomfortable procedure seems to have involved being almost sucked into some kind of underground pit, whilst clutching honey cakes, being subjected to echoing whispers transmitting visions of the future, then being unceremoniously deposited feet first back in the real world. What exactly transpired is not clear but it is not surprising to learn that initiates returned in a state of terror.

easily be made to three other ancient sites: to Heronia, about 12km (7 miles) 𝕽 along the road to Lamia, to see the Lion of Heronia monument which stands guard over Thebans who were slain in battle by Alexander's cavalry and to Orhomenos and Gla, 12km (7 miles) and 30km (19 miles) respectively from Levadia. They can be reached by turning right about 6km (4 miles) along the Lamia road in the direction of Orhomenos, famed for trout and melons. Located at Orhomenos is the Treasury of Minyas besides which are the remains of a fourth-century BC theatre and the ninth-century Byzantine church of the Dormition of the Virgin. Further along the same road across the national highway (E75) from the village of **Kastro**, is the Mycenaean Citadel of Gla about which little is known (follow sign to Larimna). It is an 𝕽 amazing and extensive site not on the tourist trail.

Leaving Levadia the scenery becomes more dramatic as the road leads closer to Delphi and Parnassos. Around 21km (13 miles), close to the

The carpet shop at Arachova shows off many of its colourful designs

Mount Parnassos provides the backdrop for this church near Distomo

Arachova is clustered on the shoulder of Mount Parnassos

Moni Osios Loukas, one of the most beautiful Byzantine monasteries in Greece

location of the Triple Way in the Oedipus myth, turn left for Distomo and Osios Loukas. Keep ahead into the centre of Distomo where the road to Osios Loukas goes off left. The road winds round the hillsides to end at the isolated spot where **Moni Osios Loukas** perches on the side of Mount Helikon.

Justifiably one of the most beautiful Byzantine monasteries in Greece it was dedicated to the hermit Osios Loukas, St Luke of Stiri (Osios meaning Holy). Born in AD896 at Kastoria (Kastri), the village built on the site of ancient Delphi, he became famous throughout the Byzantine world for his intellectual gifts and prophecies. His prophesy that the island of Crete would be recaptured from the Saracens by the Emperor Romanos Lekapenos was fulfilled in AD961, 8 years after his death, and attracted the attention of the Byzantine court. Fame brought a flood of wealth to the monastery which was being built around a chapel on the site of Osios Loukas' hermitage.

Visitors enter the monastery across a pleasant shaded platia from which there are superb views out over the valley below. It is a wonderful place to picnic and where it is possible to buy refreshments and souvenirs. There is also a small restaurant and limited accommodation but these facilities are only available in season. Proper dress is required to visit the two churches which means no shorts for either sex and no trousers for women. The principal church, built in the eleventh century, is dedicated to St Luke and built over the original chapel dedicated to St Barbara which is now the crypt. This larger church houses the sarcophagus of St Luke in its crypt and is where the famous mosaics are to be found. Dedicated to Theotokos (Mother of God), the smaller church is an earlier construction from the late tenth century. Its simple architectural form matches a plainly decorated interior but it does have some interesting frescos and a lovely pavement consisting of large mosaic slabs. A peaceful haven today, especially away from the main holiday season, it is difficult to detect the restoration work which went on for 10 years from 1953 to repair war damage.

Returning to the main road via Distomo, turn left to continue to Delphi. Driving between barren, scrubby hills with evidence of bauxite mining in places, the vista suddenly opens up and **Arachova** can be seen ahead. Clustered on a shoulder of Mount Parnassos it clings tenaciously to its perch above the olive swathed valley below. The main road narrows appreciably as it passes through this picturesque town and it is easier to stop and park before reaching the centre. A health resort and also a busy ski centre in winter it makes an alternative place to stay if visiting Delphi only 12km (7 miles) away. Either way it merits a stop if only to wander its narrow streets and stairways and admire the hand-woven carpets (*flokates*), for which it is famed. A festival takes place here every St George's Day, 23 April, when villagers dress in traditional costume and dance in the main square whilst lambs roast on spits. If this date falls before Easter the festivities are postponed until immediately afterwards.

A pastoral pocket, where Judas trees splash the landscape with purple in spring, heralds the arrival of the beautiful yet dramatic site of **Delphi** (Delfi). Of the modern village there is no sign but it is only a stone's throw away conveniently out of sight just beyond a ridge. The old village of Kastri (now modern Delphi), which was built over the ancient site, was relocated in 1892 to allow excavation by French archaeologists. Modern Delphi is a small compact town hanging precariously on the mountainside and its inhabitants are solely dependent on the tourists, who visit the site, for their living. Having said that, it is pleasant and interesting enough for a short stay despite its being a tourist centre. Food and accommodation are not over expensive and it is possible to discover some good places to eat. There is a wide range of hotels and accommodation from which to choose. Many hotels have good views down the narrow valley of the Pleistos river where myriad olive trees spill out onto the plain below and reach as far as the coast. An ancient route brought the many pilgrims who arrived by sea up this same valley to the site. The two main streets in the village form a one-way system, the upper, by forking up right on entering from Arachova, and the lower straight ahead when approaching from Itea. One advantage of staying in Delphi is that it is easy to walk the 1km (½ mile) or less to the site. It can become more crowded in June for the Delphic Festival when Classical drama performances take place in the ancient theatre.

There are opportunities for walking on Mount Parnassos. One, which affords good views across the Gulf of Corinth, leads up from behind the town of Delphi by following the perimeter fence of the site to join a cobbled trail.

Delphi is regarded as one of the most important sites of Classical Greece, sitting on a terraced semicircular slope beneath the overhanging rocks of Phaedriades, 'shining rocks', on the southern slope of Mount Parnassos. Evidence points to cult activity on the site as far back as prehistoric times and to when Delphi was a Mycenaean village in the second millennium BC. The combination of its isolated dramatic setting and reputation as the centre of the world helped ensure the development of Delphi into the most influential oracular site in Greece. Men came here in search of the self knowledge required to be at harmony with themselves and their gods. It suffered a gradual decline over many years, when many of its treasures were plundered, and finally sank into oblivion with the establishment of Christianity in the fourth century.

The site is spread over both sides of the road and it is a steep climb up through the Sacred Precinct to the Stadium. Sensible footwear is essential and, if possible, avoid the middle of the day in high summer when it can get very hot. A prior visit to the museum helps recreate some of the ancient mystical atmosphere before exploring the site. From the entrance to the main site, a paved path leads further down the road to the Kastalian Spring. Across the road, adjacent to a café, steps lead down to a lower and more level part of the site where a path leads through the Gymnasium and

The Sanctuary Of Pythian Apollo At Delphi

Legend relates how Zeus defined and marked the centre, or naval of the world, with a sacred stone after two eagles he released to the east and west met at Delphi. Thus began the rise to power and fame of the Delphic Oracle. In these early days the monster Python guarded the shrine of the Earth Mother who, assisted by the sibyls, uttered prophesies from a cave.

Apollo appeared on the scene after slaying the Python and purifying himself in the river at the Vale of Tembi. He usurped the Earth Mother to become the new deity, Pythian Apollo, and the old name for the site, Pytho, was replaced by Delphi. To appease the Earth Mother, the Pythian games were instigated and held every 8 years but this was eventually reduced to 4 years to alternate with the Olympic Games. Legend attributes the origin of the name Delphi to the cult of Apollo Delphinios from Crete where the deity was worshipped in the form of a dolphin (Delphoi). Only men were allowed to consult the Oracle. Before being allowed to present their question on a leaden tablet they had to make an acceptable votive offering, wash their hair in the Kastalian Spring and make an animal sacrifice. Prophesies were now uttered by a priestess, the Pythia. She would purify herself before consultations in the Kastalian Spring then, sitting on a sacred tripod stool and chewing laurel (bay) leaves, inhaled vapours from a cleft in the ground which sent her into a trance. Her incoherent mutterings were translated and relayed by priests in hexameter verse. The priests at Delphi were highly organised and a widespread network of informants, keeping them up to date with happenings outside, helped them give reasoned answers to questions related to affairs of state.

(opposite) Tholos of Marmaria at Delphi

The scenery surrounding the Theatre at Delphi is breathtaking

olive groves to the Marmaria or Sanctuary of Athena Pronaia. To avoid walking along the narrow main road return by the same route.

The **museum** is well laid out and full of fascinating finds from the site. Exhibits are labelled in Greek and French but guide book translations, available at the entrance, cover a selection of what is on view. In the entrance hall is a copy of the marble Omphalos which marked the reputed centre of the world as decreed by Zeus. Fragments, friezes, grave stele, sculptures, bronzes and pottery add colour to the former glory of the oracular site but the main attraction is without doubt the magnificent Bronze Charioteer whose proud demeanour epitomises the Greek ideal of the time.

The **Sacred Precinct** is entered along the Sacred Way which leads from the Roman Agora. It passes at first between a succession of votive monuments and treasuries which belonged to the richest Greek cities. Monuments were usually erected in celebration of a victory and treasuries were mini temples built by various city states as a gift to Apollo. The reconstructed Treasury of the Athenians gives some perspective to these treasuries which were used to store and display the wealth of a city state. Behind the Athenian Treasury are the remains of a small Asklepion dedicated to Asklepios the son of Apollo.

Continuing up the Sacred Way, on the left stands the Rock of the Sibyl, in the oldest part of the sacred precinct, from where the earliest prophesies were dispensed. Next to this is the Rock of Leto where she is said to have instructed her son Apollo on how to kill the Python and behind, the foundation stone of the Sphinx of the Naxians (Oedipus fable) now in the museum. Further along was a circular threshing or dancing floor (*halos*) where, every 8 years, a ritual purification of the Oracle drama was performed.

The grandeur setting of the **Temple of Apollo** compensates for the scant remains of the building now reduced to foundations and six reconstructed columns. Here, in an inner sanctum or adyton, the Pythia sat on a tripod placed next to the omphalos and uttered her prophesies.

The **Theatre** was first used for the singing of hymns and musical contests in honour of Apollo, and later developed by the Romans for the presentation of plays and musical performances. The musical contests were the early form of the Pythion Games before they became athletic contests.

The **Stadium** is hidden away higher up the hillside on a specially flattened area amongst the pines. It was constructed at a time when the Pythion Games were transformed into an athletic contest and completed in its present form by the Romans. During quiet interludes these are possibly the most evocative remains on the whole site.

The **Kastalian Spring** was dedicated to the nymph of the sacred waters Kastalia, who drowned herself in the spring rather than submit to the unwanted attentions of Apollo. There are actually two springs in the ravine between the Phaedriades; close to the road is the older Archaic

Spring and, further in, the Hellenistic Spring.

The site of the **Gymnasium** is at present being excavated and its lay-out is better seen from above. The upper level consisted of covered and open air tracks for the athletes and lower down was a circular cold bath and hot baths.

There is evidence that the site of **Marmaria** or **Sanctuary of Athena Pronaia** (Guardian of the Sanctuary) was occupied in Neolithic times and later by the Mycenaeans. At this time it was associated with the Earth Mother cult before transferring to Athena. The first Temple of Athena was one of the earliest major temples in Greece but it is the much photographed Tholos which holds centre stage today.

Tour 2 • Mountain Of The Gods (76km/47 miles)

Mount Parnassos dominates the landscape around Delphi and is now a major ski resort which makes access into the heart of the mountain available to all. In ancient Greek times it was important as a religious and spiritual centre associated with the cult of Apollo and Dionysos. The drive up, along a good road, is especially beautiful in springtime when snow still softens the bare summit and there is an abundance of exciting botanical finds on its wooded slopes.

Leave Delphi by heading back to Arachova. On entering the town turn left up the road signposted Xionidromiko (snow road), which is kept clear throughout winter, keeping right at the fork soon afterwards. The road rises up and around the mountain to cross the Livadi plateau. A misty haze of blue speedwell in spring brightens the austere landscape at this point. Once through the scattered houses and tavernas of nondescript Kalivia, a signposted right turn to the ski centre leads along a road winding up through the trees. *Anemone blanda* and crocus form carpets of colour whilst searches in the woodland reveal *Corydalis densiflora* and *Scilla bifolia* with clumps of *Helleborus cyclophyllus* close to the road. The first junction right leads to the Kellaria ski station and the next one, also to the right, leads to the station of Fterolaka.

Return via the same route and maybe sample the local red wine in Arachova. An alternative circular tour requires a right after returning 15km (9 miles) down from the ski centre instead of left to cross the plateau. This much longer route goes via Lilea, Gravia and back through Amfissa, noted for its olives and where there are the remains of a medieval castle.

Mount Parnassos dominates the landscape around Delphi

Tour 3 • Byron Country (280km/174 miles)

Never far from the shore, the road skirts the mountains and winds its way along some lovely unspoilt coastline to Lefkas. Except for the occasional pot-hole and short stretch of bumpy surface between Messolongi and Vonitsa, the road is well surfaced and overall presents no problems.

From Delphi the road loops down to the plain below to cut a swathe through the olive trees to the port of **Itea**. Cruise ships bringing passengers to visit Delphi dock here but the village of Kira further to the east was the ancient port. Skirting Itea to the right, avert the eyes from the bauxite mining scars to look for the pretty seaside resort of **Galaxidi**; a picturesque town with imposing nineteenth century mansions which were built as homes for shipping magnates when it was an important trading and shipbuilding centre. Artefacts connected with its past importance can be seen in the small maritime museum. Sleepy Galaxidi is a pleasant alternative stop from which to visit Delphi if a seaside location is preferred. The glistening yellow of tree euphorbia brightens the barren hillsides as the route twists along the convoluted coast close to the sea. In season, a ferry boat plies between Ag Nikolaos and Egion in the Peloponnese which cuts out a lot of driving if heading for Kalavrita or Corinth and links in to earlier tours in this book.

Road priorities can appear strange at times in Greece and one such is encountered just before Nafpaktos. The major coastal road suddenly loses priority and a stop is necessary at the minor road which joins from the right. Continue into **Nafpaktos** with its interesting walled harbour and attractive well preserved Venetian fortress. Known as *Lepanto* in medieval times it was the scene of a famous naval battle of the same name in 1571. For those heading into the Peloponnese or returning to Athens via the Corinth motorway route, turn left into Andirio for the frequent year round ferry to Rio on the Peloponnese. Keep ahead for Messolongi where the road now heads up and squeezes round the mountain before heading inland to weave through valleys.

Messolongi, the capital of the *nomos* of Etolia-Akarnania, stands on a lagoon. A busy though not very visually interesting town it became famous through its association with the English poet Byron. His untimely death, only 3 months after arriving in January 1824 to consolidate the Greeks into an effective fighting force, has ensured its place on the map for modern day pilgrims. His name is still revered throughout Greece, despite his unsuccessful mission to assist them in their struggle against the Turks during the War of Independence, and almost every town has its Byron Street. Little remains of the old town which was mostly destroyed in 1826 when the Turks laid siege and 9,000 Greeks attempted to break through the Turkish lines. Only about 2,000 succeeded and those who were left behind blew themselves up by setting fire to the magazine. There is a statue of Byron, by the memorial to those who lost their lives in the war, and a museum in the town hall containing paintings and Byron memorabilia.

Bird watchers may wish to linger in Messolongi to explore the lagoon and salt marshes which are a wildfowl sanctuary. A long causeway runs

The quiet waterfront at Mitikas

out to the open sea and local fishermen use flat-bottomed boats to get around in the shallow waters of the lagoon. If a stop here is not on the agenda go round to the right alongside the old town wall to continue to Etolikon. Gypsy tents by the roadside add splashes of colour to an otherwise fairly drab landscape. The route lies across the causeway to the left, which connects the intriguing island of Etolikon with the mainland, then right along a promenade in the direction of Astakos. Follow the sign left to Neohorion and, once through the village, cross a long narrow bridge. The scenery becomes more rural now as the salt marshes are left behind. Traffic is diverted to the right round the village of Katochi and once this is negotiated the route becomes more straightforward again. There is hardly time to notice the charcoal burners before the road passes through a swampy valley decorated with Tamarisk trees and the tall *Arunda donax* reed then sweeps up into the rolling hills. Astakos comes into view across the bay and is soon reached.

❋   A fishing village, **Astakos** is also a small Greek resort and it is worth diverting off the through road to park on the quay for a break. Boats leave from here to Kefalonia and Ithaki (Ithaka). A hotel on the quay side, with views out over the bay, is a pleasant place for an overnight stop. The bakery on the main road sells the tastiest *spanakopita* in Greece and there are cafés and tavernas along the sea front. Between here and Mitikas the road hugs the coastline and there are superb offshore views. Strawberry trees (*Arbutus unedo*), holly oak and cistus cloak the hillsides whilst the sea sparkles its many hues of blue and green. Leave the main road to the left
❋   for the village of **Mitikas** and park in the large square opposite the church. This is a delightful spot with waterfront tavernas and wooden jetties strung out along the shore. The enticingly clear sea is ideal for swimming even early in the season. Old Mitikas, with its tumble of fishermens' cottages and flowers in painted tin cans, is out on a point at the far end of the village from where it is almost possible to reach out and touch the mountainous island of Kalamos. The whole exudes a traditional Greek atmosphere which is unfortunately becoming more difficult to find.

Return to the junction on the main road and turn left to Paleros passing more lovely bays on the way. Once through Paleros the scenic interest
▟   reduces as the road heads inland towards **Vonitsa**. A medieval castle on a hill ahead heralds the approach to Vonitsa but the road goes off left to Lefkas (Lefkada) on the outskirts of the town. After passing through Ag Nikolaos, and the road which goes to Preveza via the ferry, the sea comes into sight again. Interesting sand spits stretch their fingers out into the sea and a causeway, guarded by castles either end, crosses a lagoon to where a clanking swing bridge, over the Lefkas canal, gives access onto the island. Remains of the original Turkish aqueduct, used as an earlier causeway and destroyed in an eighteenth century earthquake, can be seen in the lagoon to the north of the present causeway. Turn left and keep ahead to park outside the town close to hotels and the pedestrianised main shopping street.

Tour 4 • Lefkas (Lefkada) 80km/50 miles ❄

Limestone mountains dominate the centre of this beautiful island and shed their water down the eastern side making it green and fertile. This pretty side of the island is where the majority of the resorts are located but there are many secluded beaches along its wilder and less populated western coast. Despite increased tourist development, especially after Aristotle Onassis bought the offshore island of Skorpios, the resorts remain quite small and compact. Lefkas attracts the sailing fraternity who are lured by the many smaller islands within easy sailing distance. Only recently has the infrastructure received more attention and the road round the island is now properly surfaced albeit narrow in parts on the western side.

Lefkada town has little on offer for a long stay but has a good selection of hotels. It is interesting to wander the long main shopping street and there is a cathedral and small museum of ikons and antiquities to visit but no beach. A two week Arts Festival in August livens up the town with folk concerts and theatrical performances. Leave Lefkada by following the inland coastline to Nidri. Most of the filling stations can be found along this road on the outskirts of Lefkada town. The road wends its way southwards past the site of ancient Lefkas and small hamlets which are developing as holiday resorts. Mountains, olive groves, thickly wooded islands and a sparkling sea all help to create a picture of scenic beauty. **Nidri**, the main resort on the island, must have indeed been an idyllic spot when it was a small fishing village. Small scale development has no doubt helped Nidri to retain some of its charm aided by the fact that the quay is away from the main through road. Although it is a busy yachting centre and local ferry departure point there are no large hotels as yet. Tavernas line the quayside and accommodation is mainly in rooms, usually with private facilities, some of which are located inland behind the town. The archaeologist Wilhelm Dorpfeld lived and is buried close to the small white church at the tip of the Vliho peninsula across the bay. He spent years trying to prove that Lefkas was the home of Odysseus and not Ithaka. The closest he got was to uncover some Early Bronze Age circular tombs close to the town but nothing Mycenaean which would have been nearer the mark. Nidri is a good place to stay out of season but does become very crowded in summer.

A short drive to the south of Nidri is the small and quieter village of **Vliho** facing across the gulf of the same name, a sheltered anchorage for yachts. Quiet for most of the year, it becomes a lively place in summer when bouzouki festivals are a regular feature. Just past the village a narrow potholed road to **Ag Kiriaki**, signposted Desimi and Geni, forks off left. This becomes stabilised track after 4km (2 miles) for the final short stretch as far as a turning space. From here it is a 10-minute walk along a path to the church with a good view of Nidri on the opposite shore. The peninsula is a beautiful place to wander amongst the trees in search of

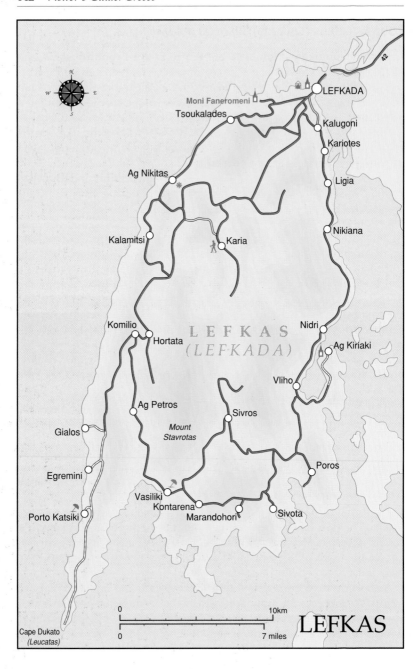

LEFKAS

Nidri's marina is a busy yachting centre

Easter Sunday celebrations in full swing with the spit roasting of a lamb, a scene repeated all over Greece; Vliho, Lefkas

wild flowers, especially orchids, and maybe even visit the taverna opposite Vliho village. Silvery olive groves, multifarious greens and the purple haze of sage blossom create a silvan setting, where Cypress trees stand out like exclamation marks, as the road moves inland away from the coast. Detours can be made to the villages of Poros, Sivros in the mountains or Sivota on the coast en route to the village of Vasiliki. Pass through the villages of Marandohori where there is a filling station and Kontarena whose old village lies in ruins on the hillside. Heading over to the western side of the island the landscape becomes noticeably more barren.

In stark contrast with leafy Nidri, the picturesque fishing village of **Vasiliki**, shelters at the head of a bay amidst rugged terrain. In the shadow of Mount Stavrotas (1,145m/3,756ft), the island's highest peak, it is fast developing as a windsurfers paradise. The harbour-side tavernas offer a tranquil ambience to linger over a meal and watch the world go by. There is accommodation here but most of it is closed away from the main season. The stark scenery takes on a remoteness and beauty all its own as the route passes through Ag Petros and heads for Hortata. Thyme dominates the vegetation in this arid spot so it is not surprising to find Thyme honey as a local speciality. Life still goes on much as it has always done in these, until quite recently less accessible, villages. The women of the island wear brown rather than the more usual traditional black found in other parts of Greece. At Komilio a road goes off left down to the islands' most southerly tip at **Cape Dukato** (Leucatas) but becomes a rough track for a great deal of the way. There are some beautiful but remote beaches on the west side of the track especially at Porto Katsiki. The name Lefkas originates from the white cliffs at the Cape where there was once a Temple to Apollo and from where the lovesick poetess Sappho allegedly flung herself into the sea.

The landscape is almost denuded of vegetation except for shrunken olive trees and the vines which produce the red Santa Maura wine, a name by which the island was once sometimes known, and the Lefkas white. About 4km (2 miles) after Hortata turn left to snake down the mountainside to **Kalamitsi** with its faded yellow ochre tiled houses. Straight ahead at the previous junction provides an alternative route back to Lefkada, via the mountain village of Karia. Noted for its needlework, **Karia** is also a good starting point for walks in the mountains. Every 11 and 12 August there is a folk song and dance festival held here in honour of St Spiridon. Once through Kalamitsi, the road follows the coast to the very pretty fishing village of **Ag Nikitas**. The barren face of Lefkas is left behind as thriving olive groves and increased vegetation again cast their green mantle over the mountain slopes. Where the main road swings to the right, on arrival at Ag Nikitas, keep ahead to park on the edge of the village near a modern but unobtrusive hotel. There are rooms to let in season and tavernas but the village retains an air of intimacy due no doubt to its enclosed position which restricts modern development. Popular with the Greeks, this village is definitely worth a stop. Leaving Ag Nikitas, the road passes a lovely sandy bay before rising up the cliffside to Tsoukalades. This elevated area provides an alternative for those not wishing to stay by the sea and accommodation can be found dispersed amongst the olive groves. The sea is not too far away though and is accessible by a track which leads from the village down to the coast. One final stop before returning to Lefkada is to sidetrack left to visit **Moni Faneromeni** from where there are good views down over the town.

Additional Information

Places to Visit

Daphni Monastery and (Eleusis) Elefsina
See Chapter 1 for opening times.

Delphi
Museum and Archaeological Site
Open: Monday-Friday 8am-6pm
Saturday. Sunday & Holidays 8.30am-3pm.

Haironia
Museum
Open daily: 8.30am-3pm. Closed Monday.

Kellaria-Fterolaka
Parnassos Ski Centre
☎ (0234) 22689. 22693/5
Arachova
☎ (0267) 31630/31692

Parnassos
Mountain Shelter
Sarantari (1,900m/6,232ft)
☎ (0234) 22640

Thiva
Archaeological Museum
Open: daily 8.30am-3pm. Closed Monday.

Accommodation

HOTELS
* = Open all year

**AMFISSA: TELEPHONE PREFIX 0265
POST CODE 33000**
Hotel Amfissaeum (C)
18 Gidogiannou
☎ 22161/2

Hotel Stallion (C) 3 Thoandos
☎ 28330/29135

ARACHOVA: TELEPHONE PREFIX 0267
Hotel Anemolia (B) ☎ 31640/4
Maria Pension (B) ☎ 31803
Xenia Pension (B) ☎ 31230/4

Villa Filoxenia Furnished Apartments (C)
Souvalaki
☎ 31024/31046

ASTAKOS: TELEPHONE PREFIX 0646
Hotel Stratos (B) ☎ 41911/12

**DELPHI: TELEPHONE PREFIX 0265
Post Code 33054**
Hotel Amalia (A)
Apollonos
☎ 82101

Hotel Apollo (A)
Vas Pavlou & 59B, Friderikis
☎ 82580

Hotel Vouzas (A)
1 Vas Pavlou & Friderikis
☎ 82232/4

Hotel Xenia (A)
☎ 82151/2, 299607

Hotel Kastalia (B)
13 Vas Pavlou & Friderikis
☎ 82205/8

Hotel King Iniohos (B)
☎ 82701/3, 82444

Hotel Orfeas (B)
☎ 82077/82462

Hotel Aeolos (C)
Vas Pavlou & 23 Friderikis
☎ 82632/82213

*Hotel Hermes** (C)
29 Vas Pavlou & Friderikis
☎ 82318/82163

*Hotel Pan** (C)
53 Vas Pavlou & Friderikis
☎ 82294

*Hotel Pythia** (C)
Vas Pavlou & 6 Friderikis
☎ 82328/82320

*Hotel Stadion** (C)
21 Apollonos
☎ 82251

*Hotel Varonos** (C)
27 Vas Pavlou & Friderikis
☎ 82345

Delphi **(Youth Hostel)**
31 Apollonos
☎ (0265) 82268

GALAXIDI: TELEPHONE PREFIX 0265
*Hotel Akroyali** (C) ☎ 61204

Papalopoulos Furnished Apartments (C)
☎ 61247/9

ITEA: TELEPHONE PREFIX 0265
Post Code 33200
*Hotel Galini** (B)
57 Possidonos
☎ 33890

*Hotel Panorama** (B)
153 Possidonos
☎ 33161/2

*Xenia Motel** (B) ☎ 32262/3

LEFKAS ISLAND (LEFKADA): TELEPHONE
PREFIX 0645

Ag Nikitas
Hotel Odyssia (C)
Ag Nikitas
☎ 99366

Lefkada Town
*Hotel Lekas** (B)
2 Panagou, Lefkada
☎ 23916/8

*Hotel Niricos** (C)
Ag Mavra
☎ 24132/3

*Hotel Santa Mavra** (C)
2 Sp. Vlanti, Lefkada
☎ 22342/22552

Hotel Xenia Lefkas (B)
Lefkada
☎ 24762/3

Nidri
Nydrio Akti Pension (B)
☎ 92400/1

VASILIKI
Hotel Ponti Beach (B)
☎ 31572/5

Hotel Lefkatas (C)
☎ 31229, 31132/4

LEVADIA: TELEPHONE PREFIX 0261
*Hotel Levadia** (B)
4 L. Katsoni Platia
☎ 23611/7

*Hotel Helikon** (C)
Georgiou A. Platia
☎ 23911/28520

*Hotel Philippos** (C)
Athinon
☎ 24931/2, 22121

MESSOLONGI: TELEPHONE PREFIX 0631
*Hotel Liberty** (B)
49 Thissias
☎ 28050/24560

*Hotel Theoxenia** (B)
At the port
☎ 28098/23303/22493

Mitikas: TELEPHONE PREFIX 0646
*Hotel Simos** (C)
☎ 81380/2

NAFPAKTOS: TELEPHONE PREFIX 0634
*Hotel Lepanto Beach** (B)
Gribovo
☎ 27798/28763

*Hotel Lido** (B)
15 Menehmou Psani
☎ 22501/4

*Hotel Akti** (C)
Gribovo
☎ 28464/5

THIVA: TELEPHONE PREFIX **0262**
Hotel Dionyssion Melathron* (B)
7 I. Metaxa & Kadmou
☎ 27855/22255

Hotel Meletiou* (C)
56-58 Epaminonda
☎ 27333/22111

Hotel Niobe* (C)
63 Epaminonda
☎ 27949/29888

CAMPING
* = Open all year
All sites listed have on-site facilities for
food and drink or available close by.

Delphi
Apollon* ☎ (0265) 82750/82762
Delphi ☎ (0265) 28944/82363/82745

Itea-Kirra on the coast near Delphi
Ayannis ☎ (0265) 32555/32948
Beach Camp* ☎ (0265) 32305/32475
Kapareli* ☎ (0265) 32330/32990

Galaxidi on the coast near Delphi
Galaxidi Camping ☎ (0265) 41530/32523

Lefkads
Kariotes Beach
Spasmeni - Vrissi near Lefkada town
☎ (0645) 23594

Episkopos Beach
Between Lefkada & Nidri
☎ (0645) 92410/23043

Desimi Beach
Vliho near Nidri
☎ (0645) 95225/95374

Poros Beach
Aspros Gialos
☎ (0645) 95452/23203

Vassiliki Beach
Vassiliki
☎ (0645) 31308/31335

Nafpaktos
Dounis Beach
Antirio Nafpaktos
☎ (0634) 31565/31665

Platanitis Beach
K. Plataniti - Nafpaktos
☎ (0634) 31555/31200

Transport

Delphi: There are daily buses to Athens
and also to Lefkas via **Astakos**. Local
buses also connect the main towns and
villages.
Levadia: The nearest railway station for
trains to Athens.
Lefkas: Buses penetrate most parts of
the island round the main circuit.
Excursions to Cephalonia, Ithaka and
other small local islands run from
Lefkas, Nidri and Vassiliki mainly in
season. Yachts can be chartered in
Lefkada.

Tourist Information Centre

Delphi
Municipal Information Office
Vassileos Pavlou
☎ (0265) 82900

6
EPIRUS

Epirus covers the region north of Preveza to the Albanian border with the Ionian sea to the west and the Pindos mountains forming a barrier to the east. Its isolation ensured independent development under a succession of rulers. Traces of their occupation can still be found in architecture and traditional crafts, none more so than from the long period of Turkish rule.

The region was united under King Pyrrhus of 'Pyrric victory' fame, conquered by the Romans and came under Byzantian influence before falling to the Turks in 1431. Except for occasional incursions by the Venetians in the fifteenth and sixteenth centuries, the Epirots enjoyed a long period of autonomy under the Turks during which their economy and culture flourished. The fruits of this growth can be seen in the old mansions, churches, bridges and fine craft work especially in gold, silver and wood. The Greek War of Independence passed the region by and it was 1913 before the Turks were finally ousted and Epirus became part of the Greek state.

It is an area of outstanding natural beauty. The long, and for the most part, undeveloped coastline edges an interior of soaring rocky peaks and rushing rivers where villages, fashioned out of the same stone, blend anonymously into the wild terrain. Here can be found two of the most ancient oracles in Greece, the Nekromantion at Ephyra and Dodona, and the prettiest coastal resort on the mainland, Parga. On the shores of Lake Pamvotis lies Ioannina, the capital of the region, from where spectacular Katara Pass crosses the Pindos range to the high mountain village of Metsovo and the aerial monasteries of Meteora in Thessaly. This is a delightful area to tour in late spring when the snow has almost gone from the mountain tops and the roads are still relatively quiet.

The best way to explore the region is by car and on foot. Ease of movement has been greatly enhanced by massive road improvements and places mentioned in the text are accessible along surfaced roads. Despite its winding twisting nature, the Katara Pass has a new wide road easy to drive without any sense of danger. Earlier accounts, in other literature, of negotiating this pass may once have filled travellers with fear and trepidation but this is no longer the case today.

Tour 1 • The Unspoilt Coast (145km/90 miles)

This is a relaxing route along a scenic coast with the mountains never far away and history a constant companion.

Leave Lefkas along the road to Vonitsa but turn left at Ag Nikolaos for **Aktion** (Actium) and the ferry to Preveza. Never out of sight of the sea for long, the route skims through a semirural landscape to pass the airport then leads out onto the headland at Aktion. It was here at the Battle of Actium (31BC) that Mark Antony and Cleopatra, Queen of Egypt, suffered an historical defeat at the hands of Octavian who became Emperor

Ancient Nikopolis

Built by Octavian to celebrate his victory over Mark, Antony and Cleopatra at the Battle of Actium, Nikopolis turned out to be something of a white elephant. Although it was sited strategically, close to the entrance to the gulf, it was in all probability founded on an emotional rather than a practical ideal. Built on unstable land and with no immediate water supply it is little wonder coercion had to be employed to populate the new city. In spite of these drawbacks it enjoyed a short period of prosperity before plundering and neglect hastened its decline.

Turn right at the crossroads 5km (3 miles) outside Preveza then left on meeting the road from Preveza to Arta. Look for a small museum and parking area on the left. The museum contains a miscellany of Roman sculptures but does not appear to open regularly out of season. Despite rather grand remains of some walls, there is not a great deal to see on this widespread site except a small restored Odeon and fine floor mosaics in the Basilica of Doumetios. If the museum is closed access to the Odeon can be gained by walking along the road and turning left on to a track. The Theatre commands a prominent position less than 2km (1 mile) further along the road to Arta. Close to here is the Stadium whilst the commemorative Monument erected by Octavian after the battle of Actium on the site where his tent had been pitched is sited above the nearby village.

Return in the direction of Preveza to the right turn back towards the Parga road where, almost immediately on the left, are some ruined baths. Rejoin the E55 to Parga and turn right.

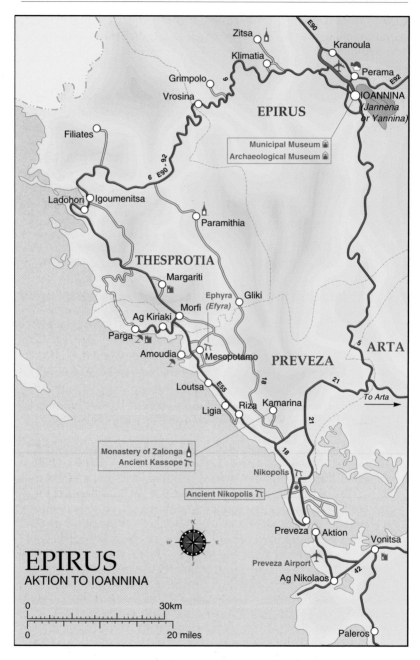

EPIRUS
AKTION TO IOANNINA

Augustus. A frequent ferry service takes 8 minutes to cross the narrow strait at the entrance to the Amvrakikos Kolpos (Ambracian Gulf). Plans to construct a bridge across the strait have been mooted but current local knowledge refutes this in the certainty that a tunnel is planned.

Preveza does not offer much incentive to linger although besides being a port it is a seaside resort. There are hotels, rooms to let and camping sites on the west coast. On leaving the ferry boat take the road along the coast to Parga.

A return detour from Preveza to Arta to see the famous seveteenth-century Turkish packhorse bridge, reputedly the oldest in Greece, will add around 80km (50 miles) to the tour. Arta also boasts a number of interesting Byzantine churches.

Continuing up the west coast road, which widens on leaving the confines of Preveza, reach crossroads in 5km (3 miles) where the right turn is signposted Ancient Nikopolis (see feature box). This is a short detour and rejoins the main route a few kilometres further up the coast.

In a further 7km (4 miles) a road goes off right signposted Athens and Igoumenitsa. The route of this tour keeps ahead along the coast but a 28km (17 mile) return detour from this point can include a visit to ancient Kassope and the Monastery of Zalonga (see feature box).

Good progress can be made along the wide coast road from Preveza. So much so that there is hardly time to take in the wonderful views along the natural coastline with its superb strands of sandy beach. The road rises up above the coast. On approaching Riza it is possible to stay ahead to cross the high level bridge and follow the new Ligia by-pass. The old route is much more romantic so, if time is not pressing, turn left at 10km (6 miles) after the Athens junction and wind down towards the seashore. At shore level the pace slows to meander past enticing beaches, which are ideal for

---

Ancient Kassope And The Monastery Of Zalonga

Turn right towards Athens but turn left in about 2km (1 mile) in the direction of Paramithia and Igoumenitsa. After 5km (3 miles) take a right turning, signposted Zalonga, to the village of Kamarina. Follow signs to Kassope. The monastery is a half kilometre further up the mountain.

Built on a south facing plateau in the fourth century BC on the site of an earlier Bronze Age settlement, Kassope enjoyed a relatively short life before being burnt by the Romans in 167BC and was finally abandoned when the population was forced to move to Nikopolis. It was a centre for the worship of Aphrodite and is among the best preserved ancient towns. The compact geometrically laid-out ruins, protected by a polygonal wall, were only discovered 40 years ago. The Monastery of Zalonga is the scene of a more recent drama when Suliots, a tribe of Christian Epirots, sought refuge there in 1802 from attack by Ali Pasha. High above the monastery is a memorial, in the form of a sculpture, to the women and children who escaped capture by flinging themselves over the precipice.

The Nekromantion Of Ephyra

Situated on a hill above the confluence of the rivers Kokytos and Acheron, a branch of the mythical river Styx, lie the remains of the Sanctuary to Hades and Persephone. In ancient times the site was believed to be the entrance to the Underworld (Hades). The myth relating to this Oracle tells how Hermes would bring the souls of the dead to the shores of Lake Aherousia where, on payment of an *obolos* (farthing), Charon would row them across to Hades. The fourth-century BC Nekromantion was built over a much earlier settlement which followed the same cult. The Oracle of the Dead developed around a belief that the souls of the dead could tell the future of the living. Homer relates in his *Odyssey* how Odysseus himself visited the Oracle to consult with the dead and this was a few centuries before the present sanctuary was constructed. Besides undergoing the usual purification rituals associated with oracular consultations, evidence also suggests the use of hallucinatory drugs. This supports the theory that petitioners were induced into a highly emotional state before being allowed into the shrine. Disorientation was further heightened as the unfortunate victim had to negotiate a dark labyrinth to reach the inner sanctum. Here, further chicanery was enacted with the use of a windlass (remains in the museum at Ioannina) which was in all probability used to embellish the charade by winding figures up from below.

At the entrance to the site is an excellent plan carved in stone which helps to identify the layout of the ruins. The remains are remarkable in that many walls are still intact. In an inner room, an iron ladder leads down through a hole in the floor to an underground room.

picnic and swim stops, and where spiny broom colours the surrounding scrub a brilliant yellow. Wend through the village of **Ligia** where there are rooms and tavernas and ascend once more to rejoin the high level route. Soon after a turn off to Loutsa the road suddenly descends onto a fertile plain and the site of ancient Ephyra (Efyra) and the Nekromantion or Oracle of the Dead (see feature box). Today, the modern village of **π Mesopotamo**, on the right of the road, straddles the site of ancient Ephyra which was on the edge of the ancient Aherousia Lake, now dry. Turn off the main road into the small village and, at the crossroads in the centre, turn uphill for the few hundred yards to the car park at the entrance to the Nekromantion.

Return to the crossroads in the village, turn right and in under 1km (½ mile) turn left again back to the main road to continue the tour to Parga.

If time allows, a side trip to **Amoudia** on the coast can be accomplished fairly quickly by keeping ahead at the crossroads in Mesopotamo towards the coast. A 5km (3 mile) drive, along a tree lined avenue across the plain, leads to the small, isolated, purpose built resort of Amoudia where the Acheron river flows into the sea. It boasts a magnificent sandy beach, hotels, rooms and tavernas but nothing much moves outside peak holiday times. Return by the same route to Mesopotamo and back to the Parga road.

Occasional splashes of the purple Judas tree lighten the phrygana as the scenery becomes more mountainous. After passing a viewpoint with picnic tables on the left, head down to Parga at the well marked junction. In June, when the oleanders are in blossom, the roadside is a blaze of colour on the approach to the village of **Ag Kiriaki** which has rooms and fuel. A couple of kilometres outside Parga there are two routes down to sandy Lichnos beach. The first, by a restaurant, is a track for general access and the second, shortly afterwards, is a surfaced road down to the Lichnos Beach Hotel which is part of a private complex. Dip down to enter **Parga** and meet a fork in the road. Taking the lower fork leads very shortly to the seafront, where traffic is banned from going any further into the village, and parking is very limited. The upper fork leads up and round the back of the village. There is much more room to park up there and some conveniently situated hotels. A wander round the village reveals an abundance of good accommodation on offer, mainly in rooms and apartments, but the demands of tour operators limits this supply over the summer.

The old fishing village of Parga nestles intimately into the curve of a small bay adjacent to a Venetian castle sat atop a green fingered promontory. Set amidst olive groves against a mountain backdrop with a sprinkling of tiny white churches, sandy beaches and offshore islands, which take on an ethereal quality in an early morning mist, Parga has all the magical ingredients for a holiday spot. Olive groves are a feature of the area and the small black olives are grown for their oil. Although still fairly isolated from other habitation, improved roads have led to an inevitable increase in tourism. It is one of the few places where Greek tourism possibly still exceeds international tourism. Development is small scale and much of the old character retained amongst its narrow streets and alleyways. It is not the sort of place to leave in a hurry and an overnight stop usually results in a stay of a few days. Like many places throughout Greece though, it can become very crowded during the peak holiday season.

First impressions are that beach space is very limited but a walk up to the castle reveals the magnificent crescent of sandy Valtos Beach to the west. Still relatively unspoilt, facilities which include water sports are low key and merge into the pine and olive trees fringing the shore. The beach is easily accessible along a wide paved path which leads down from the castle. To drive to the beach, follow the road which skirts round the back of Parga taking a signposted left turn down to the shore.

A Climb To The White Church

Most people are intrigued by the small white church high on the headland to the east of Parga and wonder about the route up. It is a fairly steep climb in parts, and good footwear is advisable, but the views on the way up and panorama at the top are well worth the effort. The time taken to reach the top is about 45 minutes or as long as it takes.

Leave the quay at Parga by following the road out east. Keep round right to follow close to the shore where the exit road goes up left. Continue ahead to pass between hotels, rooms and tavernas and, in around 10 minutes, reach a large supermarket on the right. Turn right immediately afterwards onto a fenced-in path initially which soon leads steeply up through the olive groves. The path eventually runs into track and continues up. Take care not to miss the path up right to the church, partially hidden by olive trees, just before the track begins to descend over the hill.

The steep climb to the church is rewarded with panoramic views

The Lion of St Mark, the symbol of Venice can still be seen on the Norman-Venetian castle, testament to 400 years of Venetian rule. Ali Pasha bought Parga from the British in 1817 after they had acquired it from the French who in turn had only enjoyed a brief period of rule. There is no charge to explore the castle ruins which are amazingly extensive. The harbour is still used for fishing boats, their numbers swelled in summer when boats call in from Corfu and there are regular trips across to Paxi.

Parga is connected with the main coastal road by a 10km (6 mile) spur which means returning along the same route to the main road and turning

By Ferry To Corfu

Ferries to Corfu run hourly in season from early morning until late evening and, at other times of the year, every 2 hours in a shorter working day. The journey takes 1 hour 40 minutes. A selection of agencies sell tickets for specific boats and if in doubt which to use for the next boat ask the Port Police who have an office on the quayside. In Corfu Town, ferries mainly sail from the new port. Ticket office on the quay. There is plenty of accommodation, especially outside the main season.

Once on the island Corfu Town itself holds a great deal of interest in its older part with castles, museums, churches, market and lively narrow streets. A Tourist Information Office on Rizospatsen in the town will provide a map of the town and island as well as hotel information. For a quick escape turn right and keep heading along the coast to join in the road north and then across to the west coast and the best beaches. The mountainous northern half of the is-

land around Pantokrator holds more appeal than the flatter southern end. Tourist development has swamped most of the

A Corfiot woman, instantly recognised by her national costume

east coast and threatens the west coast to a degree but a car allows for forays off the beaten track. Best of all is to leave the car and walk. That is the only way to recapture something of the essence of Corfu before tourism.

left to continue to Igoumenitsa. The lush vegetation around Parga gives way to swamps and barren hillsides covered in yellow Jerusalem Sage. At **Margariti**, once imposing Venetian castles, now derelict, still keep a windswept watch over the high level road as it wends between the hills. Rounding a sharp bend, shortly after regaining sight of the sea, Igoumenitsa comes into view across a very picturesque bay. A picnic and children's play area on the left provides a good place to stop to soak up the view. Soon down at sea level again pass through Ladohori on the outskirts of Igoumenitsa where the centre is round to the left. On reaching the sea front turn left for the Corfu ferry boat or right to continue on to Ioannina. **Igoumenitsa**, although a busy port and not very large, is a rather nondescript town albeit in a pretty setting. There are hotels but if time is not desperate move on.

Tour 2 • Inland to Lakeside Ioannina (92km/57 miles)

A good road switchbacks through fine mountain scenery to Ioannina, the stronghold of despotic Ali Pasha, on the shores of Lake Pamvotis. It is possible to make fairly rapid progress through the mountains, despite having to negotiate some easy hairpin bends.

The road from Igoumenitsa to Ioannina exits up the coast before swinging inland on the outskirts of the port to head across the plain to the mountains. Off the route to the left is the village of **Filiates** with its several old mansions and the 1285 Monastery of Giromeriou. Ahead serried ranks of mountains appear as cardboard cut-outs which fade into the distance. The picturesque township of **Paramithia**, with castle ruins and the Byzantine church of Kimissis Theotokou, lies down the road on the right signposted Paramithia and Parga. Hairpin bends, sheep and goat chewed terrain and crouching vegetation do not create a spectacular mountain image but this improves rapidly on entry into the Prefecture of Ioannina. **Vrosina** offers cafés and fuel. Oak, poplar and Judas trees soften the landscape with distant snow-capped mountains adding a touch of drama. Approaching Ioannina, a road goes left to the village of **Zitsa**, famous for its sparkling wine, and the Monastery of Profitis Ilias with fine frescos.

Keep ahead into **Ioannina** (Jannena or Yannina) then eventually follow signs left to the centre (*kentro*) to meet the main north-south road in Platia Pirrou by the Town Hall (*Nomarxia*). The Tourist Office is close by on Napoleontos Zerva but parking can be a problem. A left turn leads down Averof to the old town and lakeside. There is accommodation close to the centre and out at Perama which, although out of the town is not particularly inspiring, also on the island in the lake. The most interesting places to eat are to be found on the island.

Ioannina sits comfortably on the shore of Lake Pamvotis at a height of 500m (1,640ft) enclosed by a ring of mountains. It is thought to have been founded by the Emperor Justinian in the sixth century and named after the monastery of Ag Ioannis which stood near the lake. Captured by the Turks in the fifteenth century it was not until the rule of Ali Pasha in the eighteenth century and nineteenth century that it became the most important province in the Ottoman Empire. Although a spark for the Greek War of Independence it remained isolated despite being ceded to Greece under the Treaty of Berlin in 1878 and it remained under Turkish rule until 1913. Today, Ioannina is still an important Epirot centre of culture and commerce.

Ali Pasha, of Tepeleni in Albania, is inextricably bound up in the more recent history of Ioannina. His self-interest and burning ambition for

The Perama Caves

Take the Metsovo road out of Ioannina to the village of Perama (4km/2 miles). Follow the signs to the cave which is located on the main street. Regular guided tours take around 30 to 45 minutes, depending on the size of the party, but some degree of fitness is required for the constant climbing up and down steps and the final 163 steps to exit. The temperature within the cave remains a constant 17°C (63°F).

Considered one of the best horizontal caves in the Balkans, it was discovered in 1940. Imaginatively illuminated stalactite and stalagmite formations decorate its many galleries which penetrate for more than a kilometre into the hill. It was here also that the bones and teeth of a cave bear were found for the first time in Greece. Exit further round the hillside and return the ½km along a high level concrete footpath, from where there are excellent views over the countryside, back to the entrance.

power found fruition when he was made Pasha of Trikala for assisting the Sultan in the war against Austria. He soon made Ioannina his capital, paying only lip service to the Sultan, and, by a combination of savagery and cunning, built up his own power base within the Ottoman Empire. Under his tyrannical rule he turned the town into a major political and cultural centre and Epirus became the most important province in the Ottoman Empire. In an over confident move Ali Pasha declared Epirus an independent state which prompted the Turks to take action against him. As Turkish troops laid siege to Ioannina in 1820 he set fire to the town and retreated to the castle. Eventually, he was forced to seek refuge on the island on the lake where he was finally betrayed and assassinated in 1822.

Turkish influence is still very evident today around the old bazaar and within the walls of the fortress (*Frourion*) which survived the nineteenth- century siege. Inside the fort, the seventeenth-century Aslan Pasha Mosque houses the Municipal Museum of Epirot costumes and jewellery. A visit to the museum, enhanced by the superb views from its terrace across the lake to Mount Mitsikeli, is definitely worthwhile. In another corner of the fort, the tomb of Ali Pasha lies close to the once neglected Fetiye Mosque. Some of the old Turkish houses survive within these walls which provide a surprising retreat from the bustle outside. On the other hand, venture into the bazaar outside the walls to shop for local craftware, especially silver on which the city's economy was once based, and sample the local speciality *bougatza* the delicious vanilla custard pie.

A visit to the excellent Archaeological Museum is a must, especially if visiting Dodona. Varied exhibits include the remains of the winching

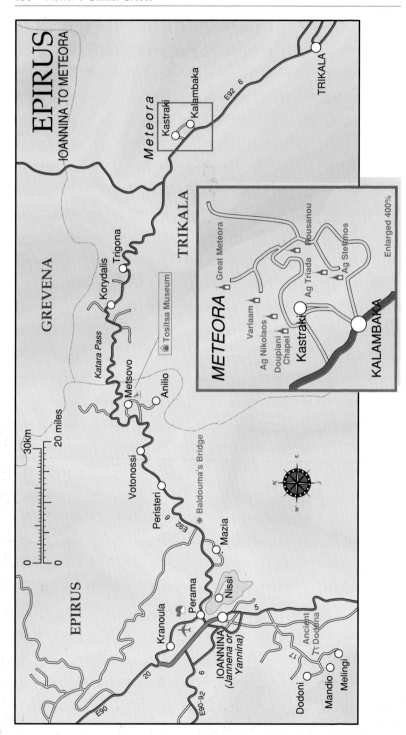

EPIRUS
IOANNINA TO METEORA

Meteora

Kastraki
Kalambaka

E92 6

TRIKALA

TRIKALA

GREVENA

Korydalis
Trigona

Katara Pass

Metsovo
Anilio

🏛 Tositsa Museum

30km

20 miles

Votonossi

Peristeri

✳ Baldouma's Bridge

Mazia

EPIRUS

Kranoula
Perama
Nissi

IOANNINA
(Jannena or
Yannina)

5

Ancient
Dodona

E90

E90-92 6

17

Dodoni
Mandio
Melingi

20

METEORA

Great Meteora

Rousanou

Ag Triada
Ag Stefanos

Varlaam

Ag Nikolaos
Doupiani
Chapel

Kastraki

KALAMBAKA

Enlarged 400%

system from the Nekromantion at Ephyra and range from prehistoric times through to Roman and after with a good collection of coins, weapons and helmets. Most fascinating of all though are the small lead tablets on which questions for the Oracle of Dodona were written. Questions which would not be out of place today, for example, 'Am I her children's father?' fourth century BC; 'Shall I be successful in my craft if I migrate?' fifth BC century and 'Shall I take another wife?'

The island of Nissi, populated by refugees from the Mani in the sixteenth century, is 10 minutes away by regular ferry service. Viewed directly across the water from Ioannina, **Nissi** tends to merge with the far shore of the lake and the small village only comes into view moments before actual arrival. A frequent ferry service from the quayside at the bottom of K. Karamanli makes eating out at one of the restaurants along the quay a pleasant alternative to the town. Frogs legs are a speciality and if these hold little appeal there is a choice of fish, displayed for selection in huge tanks, from the polluted lake. The grills suddenly seem more appetising. The narrow cobbled street from the quay leads round east to the Monastery of Pantelimon where, in an annexe, Ali Pasha was shot from below through the floorboards whilst hiding in an upstairs room. This building became a museum but suffered partial destruction on the morning of 7 May 1992 when a branch of a huge plane tree snapped off during a gale. Continue along a wide path, which circumvents the island, making a pleasant and leisurely 40 minutes lakeside walk with ever

Ali Pasha museum on the island of Nissi has been restored after damage by a gale in May 1992

The Oracle At Dodona

When the Oracle was actually founded is lost in antiquity but it is regarded as the most ancient in Greece. During this earlier period, the site was sacred to an earth-goddess called Dione, after whom the site was named, whose prophesies were thought to have been relayed through the rustling leaves of a sacred oak tree. Sometime during the second millennium BC Dione was usurped in favour of Zeus and became his consort. Despite its importance, the sanctuary retained much of its earlier mystical atmosphere by remaining close to nature. It consisted simply of the sacred oak tree of Zeus, in which he was believed to live, surrounded by a grove of oaks. The prophetic rustlings of the tree were interpreted and delivered by priests and, later, priestesses who never washed their feet and slept on the floor with their ears close to the ground to keep in contact with the god.

The rise of the Delphic Oracle spurred development of the site at Dodona in the fourth century BC but its isolated position was against its ever equalling Delphi's supremacy. Delphi was more accessible to the masses and its priests in a better position to gather information on which to interpret prophesies. It therefore built up a reputation as being more reliable, especially in matters of state, so Dodona declined in importance and became more associated with the mundane concerns of everyday life.

changing panoramic views. Gently waving reed beds line the shore and shady pine woods provide an ideal spot for picnics but the lake itself is none too savoury for swimming. Before completing the circuit, three more monasteries lie close together on the hillside and are open to visitors. The ferry service to the island is sometimes suspended during extreme weather and high winds.

Dodona (Dodoni) lies 22km (14 miles) south-west of Ioannina in a secluded narrow valley beneath the peaks of the Mount Tomaros range. To reach it, leave Ioannina on the main route south to Arta as far as the signposted turning on the right after around 7km (4 miles). Keep ahead on this road which wends its way over a ridge and down into the valley on the far side to arrive at the large car park for ancient Dodona. A seasonal pension with restaurant and café stand near the entrance to the site.

This wild and remote setting must have been even more so in the days when the Oracle was at the height of its importance. The most impressive remains now, however, are those of the Theatre which distracts attention from the partially excavated remains of the Stadium closer to the entrance. Originally constructed in the third century BC and remodelled later by the Romans for more gory pursuits than Classical drama, the Theatre is abutted by the foundations of the Bouleuterion (Council Chamber) and above lie the largely unexcavated remains of the Acropolis. A recently planted oak tree, standing amongst the ruins, marks the Sanctuary of Zeus which was the site of the ancient Oracle. Between the Theatre and sanctuary was a Temple of Aphrodite and on the far side, close to a fifth-century Christian basilica, Temples to Dione and Herakles.

Tour 3 • Over Katara Pass (132km/82 miles)

The road may have been considerably improved but that has not stretched to bridge building as yet. This in no way detracts from the exhilarating drive over this memorable pass and the solid single width iron and wood bridges add to the experience.

The road leaving Ioannina en route to Metsovo and Trikala skirts the north-west corner of the lake. Snow ploughs usually keep Katara Pass clear during the winter months but a roadside sign, soon after Perama, indicates whether or not it is open. The steady climb into the mountains on the far side of the lake affords some of the best views down over the lake and across to Ioannina. Majestic scenery dominates as the route undulates and weaves steadily upwards and deeper into the Pindos mountains. Just short of reaching the summit of the Katara Pass a right turn leads down into the platia at Metsovo. The garage here supplies diesel, super and unleaded fuel.

Metsovo is a winter ski resort which lies at an altitude of 1,160m (3,804ft). Traditional houses cling tenaciously to the sides of a steep ravine in this wild and inhospitable setting. Its people are descended from the Vlachs, who were nomadic shepherds, and remained a close knit and isolated community despite being on a strategic route through the Pindos mountains. Better road communication and increased tourism have released Metsovo from its cocoon and its older, slower pace of life is fast disappearing.

A combination of long years of independence from Turkish rule and the beneficence of the Tositsa and Averof families has ensured the continuance of local traditions. The eighteenth-century mansion of the Tositsa family has been restored as an excellent museum which shows how a wealthy family lived. Carved wood and wall mosaics are the main features in the church of Ag Paraskevi and the Monastery of Ag Nikolaos has some seventeenth-century frescos.

Local traditions are very much alive and Metsovo is the place to buy wood carvings, especially walking sticks, brightly coloured woven rugs and copper and brass ware. Food specialities are sheep and goat's milk cheeses including a smoked variety and *Hylopites*, a type of pitta with cheese, ham, egg or chicken.

Accommodation is plentiful especially away from the ski season and main holidays and there is a choice of restaurants. The ski run lies above the village and the lifts operate during the summer months. There are also opportunities for walking and a cobbled trail leads from the lower end of the village down into the ravine and across to the village of Anilio offering a different view of Metsovo. Local costume was normal dress until quite recently but there has been a decline in the numbers wearing it everyday. Tradition is still very much alive though at weddings and festivals such as Easter when colourful costumes are worn and there is dancing in the square.

Leaving Metsovo continue climbing up amongst alpine meadows and forest where, at the beginning of May, early alpine flowers such as *Primula veris*, *Scilla bifolia* and *Helleborus odorus* are in bloom. The Pass reaches a height of 1,690m (5,543ft) before descending a greener and less stark side of the mountain range where the orchid *Dactylorhiza sambucina* lurks on the edge of the forest. At Korydalis there is fuel and the village of Trigona, 27km (17 miles) from Meteora, has hotels and restaurants. The thrusting rock turrets of Meteora dominate the approach to **Kalambaka** which is a small town dedicated to the demands of tourism. There are plenty of hotels, rooms and tavernas which make it a good base for touring the monasteries. Most of the town was destroyed during World War II except for the fourteenth-century cathedral with its sixteenth-century frescos. Alternatively, a left turn on entering Kalambaka leads to less commercialised **Kastraki** village, which is on the route up to the monasteries, and a quieter place to stay. Opportunities abound for experienced rock climbing enthusiasts. Enquire locally about guides and organised climbs.

Dactylorhiza
sambucina, *a wild
orchid found on the
Katara Pass*

Tour 4 • Meteora Monastery Trail (17km/10 miles)

As the Pindos mountains meet the Plain of Thessaly, twenty-four lofty pillars of precipitous rocks create an awe-inspiring geological phenomena formed from deposits left by a sea which covered the plain, a score or more million years ago, and then sculptured by erosion into the weird pinnacles and crevices seen today. It attracted monks and hermits as early

A huge selection of ikons are for sale outside the Meteora monasteries

A spectacular view of Ag Triada monastery situated on top of a pinnacle high above Kalambaka

as the tenth century who found the seclusion they sought for a life of worship within the many caves on the rock faces. The area developed into a privileged religious retreat and in the fourteenth century the first monastery on a rock was founded by Athanasios, a monk from Mount Athos. He chose the largest rock in the area which he called Meteora 'in the air', because it seemed suspended between heaven and earth. The monastery became known as the Great Meteora which also gave its name to the area of surrounding rock. Myth and mystery shroud the original scaling of these sheer rock faces but in all probability a form of primitive scaffolding was employed. Access after the monasteries were built was either by winch, in a net suspended from a rope, or by climbing retractable ladders. Over the next 200 years other monks, drawn by the opportunity to immerse themselves in monastic life without outside interference, built many more monasteries and small monastic communities.

The monasteries, with their wooden balconies and red-tiled roofs, crown the summits of seemingly impossible needles of rock. Besides providing a fascinating insight into life in such a cramped space they also contain a rich collection of frescos and religious artefacts. Monasticism began to decline in the eighteenth century and the fact that six monasteries are still functioning today, out of a total of thirty or more, is due in no small measure to the development of tourism.

Todays' visitor need have no fear of being winched up in a net, or of climbing ladders, for they have been replaced by steps which can add up to a great deal of climbing in the course of a day. Kiosks for drinks and ice-cream can be found amongst the colourful displays of religious artefacts outside the monasteries of the Grand Meteora and Varlaam. There is no guarantee that refreshments will be available, especially outside the main tourist season, so it is as well to go fully prepared. The usual rules of dress are strictly applied. No shorts for men or women and no trousers or sleeveless dresses for women.

Start from Kalambaka by taking the road to Kastraki which leads along a good well surfaced road round the monastery circuit. En route to the first monastery of Ag Nikolaos, pass the chapel of Doupiani which was the communal church of the early monks before the monasteries were built.

Ag Nikolaos is approached by a path which divides into steps for a quick ascent or continues as an easier winding route. A more novel way is to ride up on the donkey which occasionally stands patiently waiting for custom. This intimate monastery is a fitting introduction to the larger monasteries which follow. Inside are some expressive sixteenth-century frescos by the monk known as Theophanis the Cretan. The bell tower is a good vantage point for looking down on the slender point of rock on which once stood the monastery of Ag Moni.

A few twists of the road further on is the monastery of **Rousanou** or Ag Varvara (St Barbara) which is now a nunnery. Welded to the edges of the pinnacle on which it stands, the monastery is reached across a narrow bridge above a chasm. The frescos here are well preserved and illustrate clearly the medieval conception of heaven and hell. For walkers a path leads off through the woodland, from the monastery path, to emerge on the road above where a right turn leads to the monasteries of Ag Triada and Ag Stefanos. Shortly after Rousanou take the left fork for Varlaam and the Great Meteora monasteries. The right fork leads to the last two monasteries of Ag Triada and Ag Stefanos.

Varlaam is one of the earliest monasteries and approached by climbing nearly 200 steps. The church (*katholikon*) is a gem and the frescos compelling if not at times quite gory. In the refectory, now a museum, is a collection of icons and books and the tower containing the windlass system is well preserved. To save walking back up to the road there is a connecting path to the Great Meteora monastery next door.

Standing at around 500m (1,640ft) above the surrounding countryside the **Great Meteora** is the oldest and most imposing of the monasteries. The winching house dominates the view from the entrance side of the rock where a tunnel cut through the rock leads to steps which climb to the top. Until as late as 1923 access was only by way of rope ladders or the nets hauled up by winch. As befits the status of this monastery the church is sumptuously decorated with a gilded screen, wooden throne and lecterns inlaid with ivory and mother of pearl. Maybe the fact that Theophanis had a hand in painting many of the frescos in the vicinity at this time explains a recurring theme, found yet again in this monastery, which depicts the gory martyrdom of saints. A visit to the kitchens proves interesting and to the refectory, now museum, which houses valuable relics.

Return along the road and fork left to the last two monasteries. Ignore two roads off left the second of which is the route back to Kalambaka.

Ag Triada (Holy Trinity) sits snugly atop its lofty perch with room even for a little cultivable land. Impressively situated on a pinnacle high above Kalambaka it is reached by a flight of 140 steps which wind up the sheer rock face. The climb is well worthwhile for the views alone.

The road ends at the nunnery of **Ag Stefanos** where a bridge spans the steep gorge separating the nunnery from the main mass of rock. It provides a superb view of the cultivated plain below and the Pinios river which crosses the Plain of Thessaly to flow through the Vale of Tempe into the Aegean. Complete the circuit by returning back along the road and taking the first turning right back to Kalambaka. To continue into the Zagorohoria return to Ioannina over the Katara Pass and pick up Chapter 7. Athens is reached through Trikala and Karditsa to Lamia where there is the choice of either joining the 'motorway' or taking a more leisurely route via Levadia, Thiva and Elefsina. For Halkidiki, Olympos and Pilion, Chapters 9 & 10, follow the E92 through Trikala then east to Larissa. At Larissa, either join the E75 'motorway' to go north through the Vale of 'Tembi' to Olympos and Halkidiki or stay on the E92 for Volos and Pilion.

Exploring Meteora On Foot

The area is full of paths which connect some monasteries and lead to interesting smaller churches and hermits caves for those with time to explore on foot. Some routes are fairly straightforward but some of the paths, especially descending down to Kalambaka, can be precipitous and tricky underfoot. Do not attempt if unsure! The two short forays below are easily accessible.

1. Behind Kastraki, a path leads up through the woods past the large white church, and a much smaller church with old frescos, to the monolithic rock (Roka) which dominates the skyline.

2. About 1km (½ mile) from Kastraki along the upper road to Kalambaka, take a track up left towards the gap and white cross where the rocks almost converge. The track leads to a small church. In one of the caves, beyond the church, is a small chapel. A path also winds

One of the earlier monasteries at Meteora, believed to date back to the fourteenth century

up through the bushes to a complex cave system in the right hand rock face then continues up to the white cross.

Additional Information

Places to Visit

Ioannina
Archaeological Museum
Open: daily 8.30am-3pm. Closed Monday.

Municipal Museum
Open: Every day 8am-3pm.

Ancient Dodona
Open: Mon-Fri 8am-5pm.
Sat & Sun 8.30am-3pm.

Meteora Monasteries
Ag Nikolaos
Open: every day 9am-6pm.

Rousanou
Open: every day. 9am-1pm & 3pm-6pm.

Varlaam
Open: daily 9am-1pm & 3-6pm. Closed Friday.

Great Meteora
Open: daily 9am-1pm & 3-6pm. Closed Tuesday.

Ag Triada
Open: summer 9am-6pm.
Winter 9am-1pm & 3-5pm.

Ag Stefanos
Open: 9am-1pm & 3-6pm. Closed Monday.

Metsovo
Tositsa Museum
Open: daily 8.30am-1pm & 4-6pm.
Closed Tuesday.

Nekromantion of Ephyra
Open: daily Sunday & Holidays.
8.30am-3pm.

Parga
Castle
Open: 8am-8pm.

Perama
Cave
Open: every day 8am-7.45pm. Closes at sunset in winter.

Metsovo Ski Centre (Karakoli)
☎ (0656) 41312/41211/41249

Accommodation

HOTELS
* = Open all year

IGOUMENITSA: TELELEPHONE PREFIX 0665
*Xenia Motel** (B)
2 Vass Pavlou
☎ 22282/23282

*Hotel Astoria** (C)
147 Agion Apostolon
☎ 22704/22245

*Hotel El Greco** (C)
86 Ethnikis Antistasseos
☎ 22245

*Hotel Epirus** (C)
20 Pargas
☎ 22504, 23474

*Hotel Oscar** (C)
149 Agion Apostolon
☎ 23338/22675

IOANNINA: TELELEPHONE PREFIX 0651
*Hotel Palladion** (B)
1 N. Botsari
☎ 25856/9

*Hotel Xenia** (B)
33 Dodonis
☎ 25087/9, 77301/5

*Hotel Acropole** (B)
3 Vas Georgiou ☎ 25535/26560

*Hotel Astoria** (C)
2a Paraskevopoulou
☎ 20755/25438

*Hotel Brettania** (C)
11 Central Square
☎ 26380

*Hotel Dioni** (C)
10 Tsirigoti
☎ 27032/27864

*Hotel Esperia** (C)
3 Kaplani
☎ 27682/3, 24111

*Hotel Galaxy** (C)
Pirou Square
☎ 25432/25032/25056

*Hotel King Pyrros** (C)
1 J. Gounari
☎ 27652/29830

*Hotel Olympic** (C)
2 G. Melanidi
☎ 25888/22233

*Hotel Vyzantion** (C)
Dodonis
☎ 23898/28453

KALAMBAKA: TELELEPHONE PREFIX 0432
*Motel Divani** (A)
☎ 23330/22583-4

Motel Xenia (A)
☎ 22327/22400

*Hotel Edelweiss** (B)
☎ 23884/23966

Hotel Famissi (B)
☎ 24117

*Hotel Aeolikos Astir** (C)
4 Ath. Diakou
☎ 22325/23455

*Hotel Atlantis** (C)
G. Kondyli & Pindou
☎ 22476/22924

*Hotel Galaxias** (C)
31 Hatzipetrou
☎ 23233/23029

*Hotel Helvetia** (C)
45 Kastrakiou
☎ 23041/23800

*Hotel Kefos** (C)
1 Koupi
☎ 22044

Hotel Odyssion (C)
Kastrakiou
☎ 22320

Hotel Olympia* (C)
97 Trikalon
☎ 22792/23292

Hotel Rex* (C)
11a Kastrakiou
☎ 22372/22042

KASTRAKI: TELEPHONE PREFIX 0432
Hotel France
☎ 24186

METSOVO: TELEPHONE PREFIX 0656
Hotel Victoria* (B)
☎ 41771/41761

Flokas Pension* (B)
12 Tr. Tsoumaka
☎ 41309

Hotel Apollon* (C)
☎ 41844/41833

Hotel Bitounis* (C)
☎ 41545

Hotel Egnatia* (C)
L. Tositsa
☎ 41263/41485

Hotel Galaxy* (C)
Central Square
☎ 41202/41123

Hotel Kassaros* (C)
Tr. Tsoumaka
☎ 41662/41346

Hotel Olympic* (C)
3 J. Stamou
☎ 41337/41383

PARGA: TELEPHONE PREFIX 0684
    POST CODE 480 60
Hotel Bacoli* (B)
☎ 31200/31740

Lichnos Beach Motel & Bungalows (B)
☎ 31257/31422

Hotel Valtos Beach (B)
Valtos
☎ 31610/31005

Hotel Achilleas (C)
Krioneri
☎ 31600

Hotel Acropole* (C)
Ag Apostolon Square
☎ 31239/31515

Hotel Alkyon (C)
40 Martyron
☎ 31022

Hotel Avra (C)
3 Ag Anastassiou
☎ 31205

Hotel Della's (C)
☎ 31655

Hotel Olympic* (C)
1 Skoufa
☎ 31360/31491

Elias Karayiannis (Furnished Apartments)
☎ 31225

PERAMA: TELEPHONE PREFIX 0651
Hotel Ziakas* (C)
☎ 28611/30001-2

PREVEZA: TELEPHONE PREFIX 0682
Hotel Margarona Royal* (B)
☎ 24361-8/27568

Hotel Zikas* (B)
☎ 27505-9

Hotel Dioni* (C)
4 I. Kalou
☎ 27381-2/28287

Hotel Metropolis* (C)
1 Parthenagogiou
☎ 22235/27581

Hotel Minos* (C)
11 21st Octovriou
☎ 28424/27424

CAMPING
* = Open all year

Ag Triada
Kalambaka*
☎ (0432) 22309

Igoumenitsa
Kalami Beach
Plataria
☎ (0665) 71245

Sole Mare*
Ladochori
☎ (0665) 22105/22158

Ioannina
Limnopoula Camping
Naftikos Omilos
☎ (0651) 25265/26319

Kalambaka
Filoxenia
☎ (0432) 24446

Theopetra
☎ (0432) 81405-6

Kastraki
Caves
☎ (0432) 22289

*Kastraki Vrachos**
☎ (0432) 23134/22293

*Meteora Garden**
☎ (0432) 22727/23119

Magiorka
*International**
☎ (0432) 22239

Parga
Elea ☎ (0684) 31010/31130

Enjoy
Lichnos
☎ (0684) 31171

Lichnos
Parga
☎ (0684) 31371/31171

Parga
Krioneri ☎
(0684) 31161

Valtos ☎ (0684) 31287

Preveza
Indian Village ☎ (0682) 22382/27185
Kanali ☎ (0682) 51733
Kalamitsi Beach ☎ (0682) 23268

Monolithi
Kanali
☎ (0682) 22347/51394

Nikopolis Beach
Monolithi
☎ (0682) 23104

Local Festivals

Ioannina 'Epirotika' festival every July & August. Music and theatre performances and occasional Classical drama in the ancient theatre at Dodona. Information. ☎ (0651) 20090 Kalambaka & Kastraki. Easter celebrations & local dances.

Transport

Buses leave Athens daily for Corfu via Igoumenitsa, Trikala (for Meteora) and to Ioannina. Daily buses also link Preveza with Igoumenitsa via Parga. There are daily services from Ioannina to Athens, Igoumenitsa, Preveza and over the Katara Pass to Metsovo and Kalambaka (Trikala). In Ioannina, most services leave from the main bus station on Zosimathon but a smaller bus station on Vizaniou serves Arta, Dodona and Preveza. A frequent bus sevice connects Trikala with Kalambaka.

By train from Athens or Thessaloniki, change at Farsala onto the Volos-Kalambaka line.

Daily flights Athens   Ioannina and 4 weekly Ioannina   Thessaloniki. Olympic Airways Ioannina
☎ (0651) 26518
Ferries dock at Igoumenitsa from Ancona, Bari and Brindisi in Italy as well as the regular ferry service to and from Corfu.

Tourist Information Centres

EOT Information Office:
Ioannina
2 Napoleontos Zerva
☎ (0651) 25086

Port of Igoumenitsa
☎ (0665) 22227

Preveza Municipal Information office:
Eleftheriou Venizelou
☎ (0682) 27277

Tourist Police
Preveza
☎ (0682) 22225

Igoumenitsa
☎ (0665) 22302

Ioannina
☎ (0651) 25763

Kalambaka
☎ (0432) 22813

7

ZAGOROHORIA AND THE VIKOS-AOOS NATIONAL PARK

Buried deep in the Pindos mountains, north of Ioannina, the region of Zagoria is one of great natural beauty and picturesque villages. Densely wooded for the most, the topography is exciting showing remarkable diversity for such a relatively small area. Hills and valleys punctuated by rivers or streams appear around every bend in the road, each one steeper or deeper than the next but none more so than the beautiful Vikos Gorge. Nearby Astraka, rising in sheer rock pillars to a lofty 2,456m (8,056ft), stands sentinel in overwhelming grandeur. Dotted about this region and with barely a square inch of land to cultivate are some forty-six villages of imposingly rugged, stone built houses. Stone, one of the few natural resources, features strongly in all constructions including the old trails, the snake path which winds up a near vertical cliff face and the bridges. Single, double and triple span pack-horse bridges are yet another attraction of this bewitching region of Greece. Vikos is not the only gorge. To the north of the region, by Konitsa, is the Aoos Gorge which is perhaps more accessible and probably for that very reason, a little less frequented.

If first impressions from touring around the region by car are good then, rest assured, they will be strongly reinforced if the opportunity is seized to explore at least some of the countryside on foot. It was the wealth of wild flowers, the variety in broad leaved trees and the richness of the fauna in terms of wild boar, wild bears and wild goats that persuaded government in 1973 to declare this area of the Pindos, which includes Mount Tymfos and the Vikos and Aoos Gorges, as National Park. Although this is a superb area for walking, the tours on foot are limited to the three most spectacular regions.

The inhospitality and infertility of the region proved a good defence against the Turks when they occupied the rest of Epirus in the Middle Ages. Finding outright domination in this mountainous country impossible, the Turks allowed Zagoria certain privileges. They allowed them to collect and pay taxes through elected representatives and, in exchange,

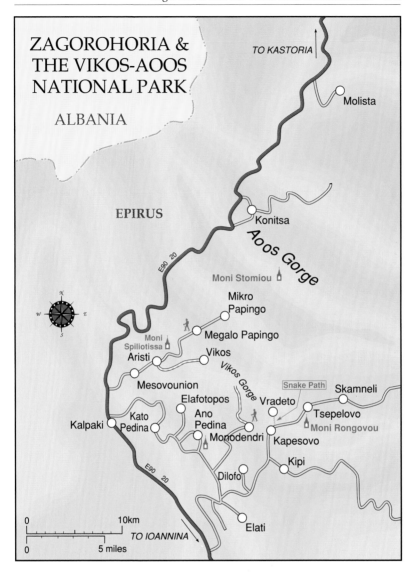

ZAGOROHORIA &
THE VIKOS-AOOS
NATIONAL PARK

ALBANIA

TO KASTORIA

Molista

EPIRUS

Konitsa

Aoos Gorge

E90 20

Moni Stomiou

Mikro
Papingo

Moni
Spiliotissa
Aristi

Megalo Papingo

Vikos

Vikos Gorge

Mesovounion

Elafotopos

Snake Path

Skamneli

Vradeto

Kalpaki

Kato
Pedina

Ano
Pedina

Tsepelovo

Moni Rongovou

Monodendri

Kapesovo

Dilofo

Kipi

0   10km

TO IOANNINA

Elati

0   5 miles

the villages were left with considerable autonomy. The region became a refuge for others escaping the Turks. With the influx of new skills and an increased work force, Zagoria grew steadily in prosperity as merchants started to build trade with central Europe. Zagoria remained in the hands of the Turks until 1913 but it had lost its privileges almost half a century earlier. With its trading power lost to an industrialised Europe, steady depopulation set in and only now is it turning to tourism in the hopes of keeping the region alive. New roads and assistance to help the residents restore property up to modern standards is slowly opening the region up but this is an area for lovers of the countryside and natural beauty so it is never going to attract mass tourism.

Turkish influences are still to be seen but only inside the houses, particularly in the sleeping quarters. Low platforms scattered with cushions and rugs line the rooms which are used for sitting and resting by day but for sleeping on at night. The people themselves are of Vlach origin. Originally migrant shepherds, the Vlachs have for centuries led a more settled existence in villages although many still keep large flocks of sheep and migrate into the hills for the summer months. Their language has a distinct Romance influence which may tell something of the Vlach origins although some believe it may have been an influence of the earlier Roman presence. Slav connections cannot be entirely discounted especially since the name Zagoria is apparently Slavic meaning the region behind the mountain.

Tour 1 • The Zagorian Villages (170km/105 miles)

Although the distance might suggest that this tour could be completed within a day, it is more likely to run into several days and could easily expand to fill whatever time is available, especially if any of the walks are to be attempted. Accommodation is not yet too freely available but there are rooms in a number of villages including Monodendri, Vikos, and Megalo and Mikro Papingo. Some of these are in traditional style and promoted by the National Tourist Office. There are also two modern hotels, Hotel Dracolimni built in traditional style with thirty-one rooms at Tsepelovo and Hotel Pindos, situated at 1,200m (3,936ft), at Skamneli.

The roads are all hard surfaced and generally good throughout. Within Zagoria, fuel (not unleaded) is available only at the village of Kipi although there is a chance to fill up just before leaving the main Kozani road to enter the region. Again on the main road, there is fuel also at Kalpaki located just before the turn off to Aristi and Papingo. Shopping is next to impossible too with only the very basics generally available in the village shops and fresh bread is not one of them.

Leave Ioannina heading north-west to enter the agricultural plains immediately beyond Perama. Sheep in great flocks are not an unusual sight here and they can create a road hazard. The shepherds are equally aware of the danger to their animals and do not hesitate to take command of the traffic to police the sheep across the road. The plain still persists after turning right to join the main Kozani road but the fringe of mountains away to the right draws steadily closer. Monodendri (19km/12 miles) is signposted off the main road and from here a long, steady climb commences through limestone mountains covered in evergreen oak into the heart of Zagoria.

Ignore the turnoffs to Elati but follow shortly afterwards to Kipi (9km/ 6 miles) and Tsepelovo (20km/12 miles). Over on the right shortly is the first of the pack-horse bridges but this one is only small. There is a second, much grander, beyond the left turn for Dilofo and encountered in a small scenic gorge. The river beneath this high single arched bridge is significant only in winter after heavy rain and with the snowmelt of spring but from April onwards is dry. Bridges remain the theme for the moment as some of the best bridges in the region are in this area. Turn right for the short diversion to **Kipi** and, if the magnificent scenery is not too distracting, keep an eye down right before the village to see a triple humped pack-horse bridge which is as aesthetically pleasing as any. A track leading down to the bridge provides the opportunity to inspect and photograph it at close quarters. Kipi, like many of the Zagorian villages, broods silently and defensively on the hillside. The odd whitewashed house stares out from the jumble of sombre stone built houses with heavy slate roofs. The filling station is mostly unattended and the owner relies on motorists to announce their own presence. The small general store in the square reached as the village is entered functions also as a café and there is another *kafeneon* nearby.

Return to the last junction to continue to Tsepelovo and Skamneli. The magnificent scenery of wrinkled, rolling wooded hills, distant ravines and snow sprinkled summits provides a backdrop that demands only one pace, slow. Churches too are built in the same sombre stone with a cloister almost the same size as the church itself like the one passed near **Kapesovo**. This tiny village lies off the road to the left and, round the corner, is a rough wide track off left signposted Vradeto. Stop here to see a beautifully engineered Snake Path on the near vertical face of the hill opposite. It can be seen from the car but a short walk will give a much better view. Allow at least an hour if the temptation to walk up the snake path is irresistible and longer if it is to be followed all the way to Vradeto. Start off along this track and turn off left to follow a lesser trail down to cross an arched bridge. From here the trail starts to wind impossibly up the face of the hill in a series of loops. The best views of it are looking down but the views from it towards Kapesovo are just as startling.

Moni Rongovou lies to the right before Tsepelovo is reached. Many of the churches of the region have elaborate carved wooden alter screens and fine wall frescos painted by local artists. Rongovou monastery is worth inspecting for its wall paintings and carving but, be warned, many of the churches are kept locked and it is not always possible to inspect without prior arrangement for which there is no system other than enquiry at the nearest village. **Tsepelovo** blends well into the hillside and there is no real view of it until it is reached. Without Hotel Dracolimni the main square would possibly pass unnoticed although there is a part time periptero and a small, very basic general store and *kafeneon*. To see Tsepelovo there is no option but to leave the car and wander through its narrow streets to find the upper square. Apart from the hotel restaurant, it is possible to find only simple meals in very basic conditions. The road continues from the main square skirting the heart of the village then on to **Skamneli**. A steady climb along a good road quickly brings a fresh sense of isolation with the mountains rising in steady peaks to the left and a barrenness of wandering uplands to the right. Almost the first building noticed as the square at Skamneli is entered is the attractive Hotel Pindos. This is another sleepy village where some footwork is required to see the best of it. It has a number of old churches including the monastery of Agia Paraskevi, all of them stoutly built in local stone.

The next stage to Monodendri requires some back tracking through Tsepelovo past Kapesovo and Dilofo to the junction signposted Monodendri. It is another chance to see again the splendid scenery which looks so different from another aspect and it is easier too to pick out Monodendri and the Vikos Gorge across to the right after passing Kapesovo. The road to Monodendri divides to serve Elafotopos but keep around to the right to reach first the village of **Vitsa** which is located just below Monodendri. Vitsa is another village of square grey stone houses built a little on the lines of a tower house often with no lower windows, or at least very small ones, again with defence in mind. On the approach to Monodendri the road divides and both approaches serve the village. The narrow road down to the right leads to the lower part of the village where there is space to park and where the route down to the gorge starts. The upper road leads to the top of the village which is more convenient for much of the accommodation. Walking between the points through the narrow streets is no problem so it little matters which option is chosen on a casual visit.

Combining some fine architecture, an interesting maze of narrow streets and a superb position on the edge of the Vikos Gorge, **Monodendri** is one of the most visited villages of the region. Many of the houses are hidden behind fortified walls leaving only a restricted view through the heavy grey stone porches. Usually with austere lines and mostly without balconies, the only relieving colour to the houses comes from the brightly painted window shutters.

The footpath out to the Vikos Gorge is signposted from the lower square and the actual route through the gorge is detailed in the walk which follows. For the casual observer there is not too much to see and no convenient viewpoint of the gorge itself from the early part of the walk. The best view is obtained by walking out to the monastery of Agia Paraskevi which is also signposted from the lower square. Although it is possible to drive there, it is a better option to leave the car in the village and enjoy a 10 minute walk out along the stabilised track. The monastery sits on a rock which hangs over the Vikos Gorge. Although unused, the heavy outside doors are unlocked at least up to 3pm, and daytime visitors can just wander in to look around the tiny rooms and enjoy the extraordinary views. Those with a head for heights, certainly not vertigo sufferers, can mount the steps behind the monastery to walk a broad ledge along the side of the gorge. Part way along, built on the ledge and seemingly blocking progress, is a small church but it seems like revealing the end of

The three arched bridge at Kipi

The Snake Path to Vradeto, a marvellous feat of engineering

the story to disclose that it is nothing more than a front wall with a doorway. Once through it broadens out into a cave area which was once the refuge used by the villagers in times of danger. The walk along the ledge continues a little further but becomes even more dangerous.

The onward journey from here leads to the villages which lie at the other end of the Vikos Gorge. Although it is no distance as the crow flies, it is a lot further by road. Back track to follow signs to Elafotopos. **Ano Pedina** is the first village along here and just on the right as the village is entered is Moni Evangelistra. It is another interesting old village spread on the hillside which offers some accommodation with an Auberge and rooms to let in a traditional house. Continue ahead and take the road to Kato Pedina. Most maps show the main route incorrectly through stony Elafotopos, there seems no point in going to this village. The road through Kato (meaning lower) Pedina follows along a fertile plain and by-passes the village itself then heads down a wooded valley, passing a World War II memorial on a hill to the right, to join the main road just beyond Kalpaki. Motorists seeking fuel should initially turn left here but otherwise turn right towards Konitsa.

The road off right to Papingo is a good wide road which climbs steadily through densely wooded rolling hills soon to pass through the small village of Mesovounion. The trees seem even taller and more verdant in this part of Zagoria. **Aristi**, the largest village in this part, looks modern with hotels and a restaurant. Just as the village is entered there is a track off to the right to the village of **Vikos**. Be warned, the track is unsurfaced for the whole 5km (3 miles) of its length but it is drivable with care and the views along it are quite spectacular. Vikos village is a good access point to Vikos Gorge and even the casual visitor might be tempted to walk the paved path a little way to catch a bird's eye view down into the mouth of the gorge at the end where the turquoise waters of the Voidomatis river flow. Much of the gorge is dry from April onwards throughout the summer but the source of the ever flowing Voidomatis is close to this end of the gorge. Those with the energy who would like to see the source need only walk to the bottom of the gorge and a little way along to find it. There is some accommodation in the village and it does have a café.

Aristi itself is beautifully situated with panoramic views around the hillsides. The road narrows through the village then descends steadily towards the valley bottom and the Voidomatis river. There is some roadside parking on the left as the river is joined which is convenient for visiting the deserted **Moni Spiliotissa**. The monastery snuggles into the densely wooded hillside overlooking the clear turquoise waters of the river. It is reached after 10 minutes on foot following the waters downstream. There is access to the courtyard from where some well preserved frescos over the doorway can be seen and higher up the hillside, perched on top of a rock, is the bell tower. Driving on, the road shortly crosses the river and on the right here is a favoured car park and picnic spot from where the cool, clear waters of the river can be enjoyed at leisure. The road ahead snakes its way through fifteen tight bends up the end of a ridge and passengers, at least, can enjoy dramatic views down into the gorge and of Moni Spiliotissa perched on the edge over the river. Once through all the bends the road still climbs, but less steeply, to Megalo Papingo.

The rock towers rising perpendicularly to the summit of Astraka provide a dramatic backdrop to the Papingo villages. First reached is **Megalo Papingo** which is clustered on the hillside and divided by the road through to Mikro Papingo although this is not immediately obvious on entry. The road to Mikro Papingo swings right at a cobbled section in front of the church and immediately left to follow up the valley. Megalo Papingo has many fine stone built houses in the traditional style of the region, some have been converted into tourist accommodation. Eating facilities are fewer but Kaliope Ranga offers a good kitchen and rooms in atmospheric surroundings. Her place is reached by heading right at the church as you enter the village and continuing along the cobbled road to the right. There is no sign outside so it is a question of looking through the open doorways on the left to find a courtyard with tables. One of the local specialities is *pitta*, not the familiar variety but one made from flour, eggs and cheese which is not only very tasty but a meal in itself. Their home made rose wine is very palatable too. If you are not driving, surprise them by asking for *tsipouro* which is a strong spirit best likened to ouzo without the aniseed flavour. It is available here and from most regions in northern Greece.

The other half of the village, where most of the accommodation is to be found, lies directly ahead up to the left of the church where there is also a small store and café. Megalo Papingo is connected by footpath to the Vikos Gorge and also to Mikro Papingo.

Mikro Papingo is quickly reached by road and there is room to leave the car outside the church. It is impossible to take it further. From there entry to the narrow streets of this small village is through the gateway. There is at least one café bar, Pension Dias, and a number of houses have rooms. Mikro Papingo is a favoured place for walkers since there is a path which leads directly to the Vikos Gorge and another which climbs up towards Astraka opening a whole number of possible walks. (see Walk 2 on pages 181-182).

There is no alternative but to return to the main road by the same route, enjoying again the ever changing mountain scenery so unique to this dramatically beautiful part of Greece. Turn right to follow the E90 north for the 23km (14 mile) journey to Konitsa. Soon after passing the viewpoint and picnic area on the left, the road drops down onto a plain to cross the Voidomatis river and reveals a view to the start of a gorge which eventually develops into the Vikos Gorge. Taking advantage of this location is the aptly named Hotel Farangi (Hotel Gorge). Judging by the birds in flight and the odd huge nest perched ludicrously on top of a telegraph pole, the storks too enjoy this richly cultivated plain where the Voidomatis and the Aoos rivers merge. Where the road crosses the Aoos

Ambling Between The Papingos

There is a fairly direct footpath between Megalo and Mikro Papingo which takes about 30 minutes one way. There is not too much parking space at either village so, once parked, its not impractical to walk to the other, although sound footwear is needed. Starting from the entrance to Megalo Papingo keep ahead to where the road ends at a traditional mansion. Take the grassy path to the left of the traditional mansion and descend to cross a stream before meeting the road. Turn left along the road and look shortly for the signposted path down right to Mikro Papingo. Cross the bridge at the bottom of the valley and follow as the path initially leads left along the stream before swinging right and up to the road. Turn right on joining the road for Mikro Papingo.

river, the old high arched bridge to the right is partly masked by a wood and girder construction alongside. Beyond the bridge the start of the Aoos Gorge can be seen which is again another good walking area. Details are given in Walk 3 on pages 182 & 183. Almost immediately over the river is the right turn which leads up to Konitsa.

After all the small Zagorian villages, **Konitsa** feels unmistakably like town. Shops surround the main square and crowd into all the narrow streets. For those short on the notes, there are two banks and for those pining for fresh bread, there are bakers. And there are shops to supply just about everything else. There are hotels too but the most modern of these is the Aoos Hotel back on the main road, just after the turn into Konitsa. One of Konitsa's claims to fame is that the mother of Ali Pasha was born there. The Turks occupied the town in 1440 and remained there until the Greeks recovered it in 1913. Much of the Turkish influence was destroyed in 1948 when the town came under fierce attacks from the communists who intended to make it their capital. Parts of the Turkish bazaar and quarters, including a minaret, still remain and can be found nearer the river.

The Aoos Gorge is another spectacularly beautiful gorge cutting deep into the Timfi mountains and carrying the fast flowing Aoos river. Part way up the gorge lies the restored Stomiou Monastery but the only way there is on foot.

Walk 1 • The Vikos Gorge

This is a truly spectacular walk which falls into the same category as the Samaria Gorge in Crete but it is much wilder and more isolated. It is a tougher walk too with a significant downhill stage at one end and an

(opposite) The Vikos Gorge, a paradise for the avid rambler

Wild Flowers Of The Vikos Gorge

With a geology of limestone and dolomites, an endless variety of habitats, a favourable climate and protection from grazing animals, this gorge teems with plant life. In parts the gorge is well forested and broad leaved trees such as the hornbeam (*Carpinus betulus*), the hop-hornbeam (*Ostyra carpinifolia*), the hazel (*Corylus avellana*) represent just a few of the species commonly present. Spring is not so early in these parts so perhaps May and June might be the best months for flowers. Some are earlier than this like the *fritillaries* or hellibores (*Helleborus cyclophyllus*), seen in the woodland on the first descent, and *Saxifraga paniculata*, found on the rocky ledges.

The narrow section of the gorge, at the south end, has some of the more interesting crevice species, as the saxifraga mentioned, and is the only section of the gorge where the rare, blue flowered, *Ramonda serbica* can be found. Orchid species are scattered throughout and include *Orchis mascula*, *Orchis tridentata*, *Orchis provincialis*, *Listera ovata* and the saprophytic bird's nest orchid, *Neottia nidus-avis* which grows only in the woodland. The rest of the flora is varied and includes perennial honesty, *Lunaria rediviva*, *Geranium macrorrhizum*, *Myosotis sylvatica*, *Salvia glutinosa*, *Digitalis lanata*, *Campanula persicifolia*, *Arum italica*, *Iberis sempervirens*, *Convolvulus cantabrica*, *Lilium candicum* and many more species besides.

In the northern section, where the gorge opens out, the ground is more exposed to the heat of the summer sun leading to a distinct change in the flora. Here, species like *Salvia* and *Pistacia lentiscus* which thrive in these drier conditions are more commonly found.

equally tough climb out. The way is stony and difficult underfoot in parts and it is not a walk to be undertaken casually. Good footwear is essential and it is equally important to carry water. Snakes are another good reason for wearing shoes which completely cover the feet. The chances are that none will be encountered but they are around, including the poisonous horned viper. Unlike the Samaria Gorge, transport at either end is not laid on, nor is there a regular local bus but it is worth bearing in mind that there is a taxi at Aristi. The distance by road between the two ends of the gorge, Monodendri and Vikos village, is 55km (34 miles). For backpackers there is no problem but for car drivers some planning is required since the walk is too long to return the same day.

Monodendri lies at the southern end of the gorge and at the other lie the villages of Vikos, Mikro and Megalo Papingo. The shortest distance, around 10km (6 miles), is between Monodendri and Vikos and this requires around 5½ hours walking but it is necessary to allow 7 to 8 hours for the Papingo villages. For those not planning an overnight stop and without support transport, the practical option is to walk to a mid point and return in one day and to repeat this from the other end on another day. The walk is described starting from Monodendri.

Follow the sign 'Pros Vikon' for the start of the walk from the lower square in Monodendri. This leads onto a narrow paved way which heads steadily downhill through woodland to the bottom of the gorge, reached after around 50 minutes. The views promised on the way down are realised in full as you reach the dry river bed at the bottom. Not one, but two gorges face you but the Vikos Gorge is the one to the left running north. The route of the walk is very poorly waymarked with red dots but just occasionally they do turn up when needed. Head over the stony river bed to find the path along the right side. It does not last long and it is back to the river bed for a short while until the path leading up the left side is located.

The route leads a little way up and stays on the left for a while. At an extensive scree section, the path traverses initially then zigzags back down to the river bed. After around 5 minutes difficult walking on the boulder strewn river bed, look for the small cairn on the left for the path which leads up the hillside again. The path now remains on the left bank for the remainder of the walk. Almost all the difficult sections lie in the narrow part of the gorge where there are sometimes some steep banks to negotiate on loose shale. At one point a large boulder blocks the way and it has to be climbed over. The sound of running water announces the Magas Lakkos Gorge which joins from the right. The river which enters here flows north-west through the Vikos Gorge towards Albania and the sea, except that it disappears underground within a few hundred metres. For half way walkers this is roughly the mid point and an easily recognised landmark.

Once down on the level, around the point where the Lakkos Gorge joins, the walking becomes much easier and the path more distinct. Eventually, as the village of Vikos draws near, a sign post indicates Vikos ahead and the Papingo villages off to the right. Either way there is some tough uphill walking to come and the Papingo route has a long traverse across a steep slope. The source of the Voidomatis river is reached immediately beyond this sign and the dry, stony river bed is suddenly full and flowing with water. Walkers heading to the Papingos will see it but others will have to divert along this path for the short distance to the river.

The climb out of the gorge up to Vikos is along a paved footpath which leads to the edge of the village. Turn right for the café bar and rooms.

Walk 2 • Mikro Papingo to Gamila Refuge (for Astraka)

This walk is relentlessly uphill, climbing from Mikro Papingo at 1,000m (3,280ft) to the refuge at 1,950m (6,396ft) and takes around 3 hours. It can be treated as a day hike or used as a stage for further walks in the mountain. The refuge is open from early June onwards, earlier by request for groups, and simple, basic meals are available. The hut has twenty-two

The Wild Flowers Of Astraka

The flora here is very different from that seen in the gorge. One or two species found in the lower woodland here, like the *helleborus cyclophyllus* and the *Muscari neglectum*, occur in both habitats but at higher levels the flora becomes truly alpine.

One of the first to flower is *Primula veris*, one of only two native primulas, which is found around the mid-May. Other early species include *Scilla bifolia, Corydalis densiflora, Crocus veluchensis, Gentiana verna, Narcissus poeticus*, found on Astraka plateau, the small, yellow flowered cushion plant, *Draba heterocoma*, a species of the familiar garden *aubrieta, A. intermedia* and the rock clinging saxifrages like *S. marginata*. The majority of the flowering species follow later than this and a fine display continues throughout June and July. Although a number of eminent botanists have visited this beautiful area, the catalogue of plants is far from complete and there remains much still to be found.

beds and can accommodate 30 people. The water supply is piped spring water and there are basement toilets but no showers. Visitors planning an overnight stay should take a sleeping bag lining. A phone number for prior enquiries or booking is given in the Additional Information which follows. From the refuge there are a number of possible walks including Dragon Lake (2,050m/6,724ft), Astraka summit (2,456m/8056ft) or Gamila (2,497m/8,190ft).

The refuge sign (Καταφυγιον) in Mikro Papingo directs to the start of the path ascending the mountain. The first part is through woodland but the trees gradually thin out and, after about 1 hour, the woods are left behind. Red dots mark the route but even these can be confusing, especially when the dry fountain is reached after 1 hour 45 minutes. Here a sign indicates right to Astraka (an alternative route to the summit) and a path also continues ahead. Stay ahead but keep a wary eye on the red dots which are not so easily followed over this stony ground. Trees, if any, are solitary at this height and away to the right the slopes rise to meet the towering rock face of the Astraka plateau. When the refuge finally comes into sight there is still plenty of uphill work left but the way to it is clear.

Walk 3 • The Aoos Gorge

This walk penetrates the gorge only as far as Moni Stomiou and is altogether a much easier walk than either of the preceding two. For those seeking the line of least resistance, there is a broad but unsurfaced track to follow all the way but others may choose the footpath which broadly parallels the track but higher up the hillside. For those interested in the wild flowers, the footpath is the better option. The return distance to the monastery on foot is around 11km (7 miles) and the walk requires a minimum of 4 to 5 hours.

From the junction of the Konitsa road with the main Ioannina road, start out by heading through the lower part of Konitsa towards the river. Cross the river by the old bridge and turn left to follow the track along the riverside. The gorge is wide to start with but it soon starts to narrow. At the weir, reached after around 30 minutes, the track ends for a time and from here it is possible to continue either by walking along the concrete wall or on part of the stony river bed by the wall shortly to reach a path. The steep sides of the gorge close dramatically around with further progress. Soon after the point where the path widens back into track, there are choices to be made. Those choosing to walk by the path must look for the route off right indicated by a red arrow whilst others simply need to continue ahead on the track.

The path up to the right here very shortly joins an old trail and the way now lies to the left. Some agility is required along here as the path, perched on the hillside is quite narrow in places. Following close to the cliffs at times, some of the most interesting flowers are found along here including the rare *Ramonda serbica* better known from the Vikos Gorge. The path eventually descends to join the track and from here the monastery, which has tantalised with its red roof and white walls for some time, is quickly reached.

The rare Ramonda serbica *can be found in the Vikos Gorge*

Additional Information

Accommodation

HOTELS

* = Open all year
The full address for the accommodation listed below should include Zagorohoria, Ioannina.

Aristi
*Hotel Zissis** (C)
☎ 0653 41088/ 41147

Kipi
Arteme Rooms
☎ 0653 51262/ 0651 23880

Konitsa
*Hotel Bourazani** (B) ☎ 0655 22783
*Hotel Aoos** (C) ☎ 0655 22079

*Hotel To Farangi** (C)
☎ 0655 22045/23171

Gamila Refuge (Astraka): The refuge itself is not connected by phone but messages for the manager of the refuge, Panos Sotiropoulos, including bookings can be made through Dias Pension at Mikro Papingo.

Megalo Papingo
*Agnandi Pension** (B)
(four rooms)
☎ 0653 41123

*Saxonis' House** (B) (ten rooms)
☎ 0653 41615

Kalliope Ranga, rooms
☎ 0653 41081

Soteres Karpouzes, rooms
☎ 0653 41176

The following are traditional settlements run by the EOT and the telephone number for reservations ☎ 0653 41088, applies to all.

Spiti Archimandriti (three rooms)
Spiti Ioannidi (five rooms)
Spiti Lagou (six rooms)
Spiti Mouza (six rooms)

Mikro Papingo
Dias Pension (A)
(five rooms)
☎ 0653 41257

Monodendri
*Monodendri Pension** (B)
(four rooms)
☎ 0653 61233

Vikos Pension (B)
(seven rooms)
☎ 0653 61232/61370

Skamneli
Hotel Pindos
☎ 0653 81280/81379

Tsepelovo
*Hotel Dracolimni**
☎ 0653 81312/18/81150

Transport

Local Transport: The Zagorian villages are poorly served by local transport. Buses from Ioannina visited the main villages on a daily basis and, whilst these are useful for getting into and out of the area, they are of little help for travelling between the villages.

Tourist Information Centre

EOT Information Office: Napol Zerva, Ioannina ☎ 0651 31456. This office supplies information on the Zagorian region.

8

WESTERN MACEDONIA

Macedonia is one of the largest regions of the country extending from the Albanian border eastwards across much of the northern region, rubbing shoulders with the former Yugoslavia and Bulgaria, to meet up with Thrace. It includes Thessaloniki, the capital, Halkidiki (Chapter 9) and, rising on its southern flanks where it joins Thessaly, Mount Olympos (Chapter 10). Macedonia (1912) and Thrace (1920) were the last to escape the Ottoman yoke to enter under Greek sovereignty. The Macedonia of antiquity was a larger region but divided under the 1913 Treaty of Bucharest with the major part passing to Greece and the remainder divided between former Yugoslavia and Bulgaria. Greek fears have been heightened with the fragmentation of former Yugoslavia and the claims for recognition by Macedonia. Fiercely opposed to their use of the name Macedonia, the Greeks insist that it should be recognised as Skopje and strengthening this insistence is the suspicion that territorial claims could eventually follow. Such is the local concern that visitors could be asked to share their views on this matter.

Western Macedonia is vibrant with mountains, verdant with forests and punctuated by lakes and pretty villages but the topography changes travelling eastwards towards Thessaloniki to a gentler landscape where cultivation increases in importance. Climatically the western region is more Balkan than Mediterranean and suffers extremely cold winters with snow and very hot summers. The rainfall too errs much on the generous side which helps to keep the countryside looking so green. Perennial rivers, in such short supply in Greece, feature here, like the Aliakmon near Kastoria and the Axios which flows into the sea south-west of Thessaloniki.

Totally without beaches, this area is less visited than many other parts of the country but, apart from great natural beauty, it competes equally for highlights. Those featured in this tour include Kastoria, delightfully situated on the neck of a peninsula which juts out into Lake Kastoria, Edessa, which boasts the best waterfalls in Greece, the ancient site of Pella, birthplace of Alexander the Great, and the capital of the region, Thessaloniki.

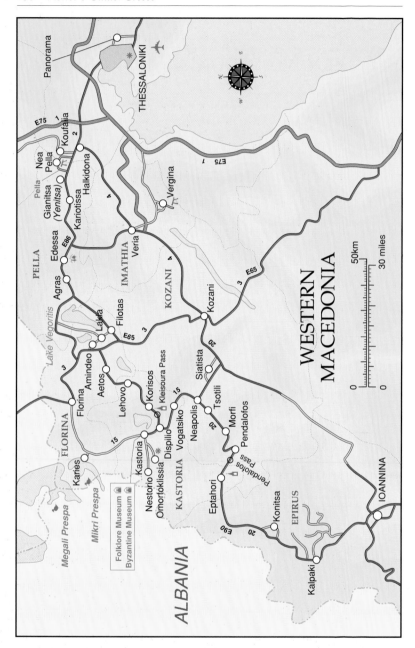

Traditional flat bottomed fishing boats on Lake Kastoria

Colourful frescos decorate the external walls of the Church of the Black Madonna on Lake Kastoria

Tour 1 • Through The Mountains To Kastoria (145km/90 miles)

For quite some time the road winds along a valley which penetrates into the heart of the mountains. Magnificent scenery from the Smolikas serpentine massif rising to the east and the mighty Mount Grammos to the west is seen afresh around every bend and twist in the road. Eventually, the route crosses over the northern tip of the Pindos range and the scenic impact reduces to more ordinary proportions. The roads are generally good although not fast and the journey requires around half a day.

Heading north from Konitsa, the presence of the mountains is soon felt as the road starts to climb. A wide gravel river bed on the left near Molista only trickles with water but, with penetration into this scenic narrow valley, there is suddenly flowing water. The road switches over the Sarandaporos River but continues to share the same green and wooded route. Small villages tucked away, cradled in the folds of the mountain slopes, are masked by trees and more trees. Everything seems suddenly within grasp as the valley narrows even more and leads unexpectedly straight into **Eptahori**, the first significant village en route. Sitting in a bowl amongst naked hills, little is seen of the village from the road except the filling station and tavernas but there is an excellent overview looking back just after climbing away from it. On leaving Eptahori a sign advises if Pendalofos Pass (1,443m/ 4,736ft) is closed. A short distance beyond lies a picnic area with fountain.

Descend on the far side to the village of **Pendalofos**. Even after leaving the peaks behind, wooded mountain scenery persists for a short while until down amongst the low rolling hills. Cultivation slowly takes over in the form of grain crops and fruit orchards. Keep straight on at a major cross roads at Tsotili (left here may be a new road under construction for Kastoria) to head shortly into agricultural **Neapolis**. The left turn for Kastoria is from the centre of the village, after a large church also on the left, but unsigned from this direction! The road is narrower but still good and particularly narrow crossing the two girder bridges which follow. Hedges and green fields add a distinctly European touch before the scattered village of Vagatsiko is reached. Beyond there a new road system is joined where Kastoria is clearly signposted. An increase in traffic density and the sight of the lake warns that Kastoria is on hand. Hotels are located by the lake on the approach or in the centre which gets very congested with traffic, particularly on Wednesday when the market is in full swing.

Attractively located across the isthmus, **Kastoria** is a town of some elegance with many old traditional houses. It is rich in churches, some fifty-four, mainly Byzantine and medieval. Walking around the streets, it is hard not to be aware that Kastoria is heavily involved in the fur trade. Large boards covered with stretched fur constructed from many tiny pieces are often placed outside the small factory workshops to dry. The ability to match and join scrap pieces of imported mink has brought prosperity to the town. This trade has flourished since the sixteenth and seventeeth centuries and still does in many small workshops found on virtually every main street. It was fur wealth which built the many fine neo-Classical houses which are now one of the attractions. The best part of town for catching a flavour of its former grandeur is in the south-east, down by the lakeside. In this quarter is the outstanding Folklore Museum, formerly a mansion of the Avatzis family. Inhabited until 22 years ago, it now provides the opportunity to peep into an old life-style, to see the furnishings, the old kitchens and clothes as well as the fur workshop. The Byzantine Museum is also worth a visit to see the well displayed collection of ikons.

A footpath constructed around the edge of the promontory provides a lakeside walk which takes just over the hour. This is the best way to find the church of the Black Madonna, Panagia Mavriotissa, and be ensnared by Papa Gabriel who delights in waylaying unsuspecting tourists to show off the two churches and a traditional house. The two churches which stand together are decorated inside and out with old frescos originating from the period of construction. St Mary's Church, the larger, is eleventh century whilst the sixteenth-century chapel is dedicated to St John. Opposite is the traditional house which also has a small shop selling ikons and handicrafts in the lower room.

An interesting side trip from Kastoria is to the Prespa lakes which will have particular appeal to bird watchers. Megali Prespa lies mostly in former Yugoslavia but Mikri Prespa falls largely within Greece. They have been designated National Park to protect the many birds, especially large breeding colonies of herons, spoonbills, egrets and the pelicans, particularly the vulnerable Dalmatian pelican.

Tour 2 • East To Thessaloniki (215km/133 miles)

There are two points of interest along the way: Edessa with its waterfalls and the ancient site of Pella which closes mid afternoon. Those wishing to break their journey with an overnight stop might consider Edessa but, be warned, it is expensive because of the pressure on accommodation. Alternatively there is the pleasant and quietly situated Motel Fillipos just beyond Pella down the road towards Veria. The road over Kleisoura Pass, reached fairly soon after leaving Kastoria, has been recently improved and now presents no difficulties.

Leave Kastoria by the same road initially but turn left at the southern end of the lake following signs to **Florina**, shortly to pass Hotel Marina on the right. Tall, slender poplar trees, sprinkle the fields of wheat and barley as the route slips through fertile valleys postponing an inevitable confrontation with the bare mountains ahead. But not for long, although the mountains, partially clad in oak and pine, are not so naked as they earlier appeared. The climb over them leads through the Kleisoura Pass into the

The old well in the grounds of the Folklore Museum in Kastoria

The huge cascades of Edessa waterfall

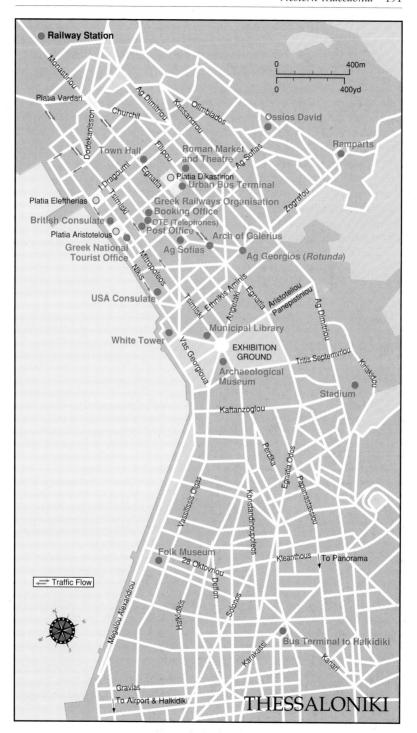

Railway Station

Monastiriou

Platia Vardari

Ag Dimitriou

Churchil

Olimbiados

Kassandrou

Ossios David

Ramparts

Dodekanisson

Town Hall

Filipou

Roman Market and Theatre

Ag Sofias

I Dragoumi

Egnatia

Platia Dikastirion

Urban Bus Terminal

Platia Eleftherias

Tsimiski

Greek Railways Organisation Booking Office

Zografou

British Consulate

OTE (Telephones)

Platia Aristotelous

Post Office

Arch of Galerius

Greek National Tourist Office

Mitropoleos

Ag Sofias

Ag Georgios (*Rotunda*)

Nikis

USA Consulate

Tsimiski

Ethnikis Aminis

Angelaki

Egnatia

Aristoteliou

Panepistiniou

Ag Dimitriou

Municipal Library

White Tower

Vas Georgioula

EXHIBITION GROUND

Tritis Septemvriou

Kiriakidou

Archaeological Museum

Stadium

Kaftanzoglou

Perdika

Egnatia Odos

Papanastassiou

Vassilissis Olgas

Konstandinoupoleos

Folk Museum

28 Oktovriou

Delfon

Kleanthous

To Panorama

Megalou Alexandrou

Halkidikis

Solonos

Bus Terminal to Halkidiki

Karakassi

Kanari

Traffic Flow

Gravias

To Airport & Halkidiki

THESSALONIKI

0   400m

0   400yd

nomos of Florina. At **Lehovo** village a barrel maker works by the roadside amidst the red-roofed houses and beyond the landscape mellows to softer, green cloaked hills themselves soon to yield to plain. Villages skip by including Aetos and, once beyond, Edessa traffic is surprisingly directed left towards Florina only to turn right within a short distance to be directed around the south end of Lake Vegoritis. The countryside remains unremarkable for a time without even a glimpse of the lake until beyond Diganos. A sea of red poppies ripples in the wake of passing cars where the road winds between limestone hills hiding pockets of cultivation. A couple of bumpy level crossings demand caution as the route heads into an ever narrowing orchard filled valley on the approach to Edessa. Strawberries, cherries; vendors ply their wares along the roadside. Signs indicate the waterfalls as Edessa is reached. They are located in the heart of the town surrounded by all the trappings of tourism but there is plenty of space for parking.

Apart from a splendid situation on a steep bluff, **Edessa** has little to commend it. Except, of course, for the waterfalls which attract tourists by the coachload. Plunging, crashing, rolling down from the mountains, the river courses through the town and falls in huge cascades over the edge of the cliff to be hungrily received by fertile plains below. Spray splashed concrete steps, walkways and platforms allow visitors to spectate from every possible angle.

The onward route from Edessa starts with a quick wind down on to the plain and, apart from storks' nests in lofty places and cucumber sellers by the roadside, the drive is unexciting. A sign to Nea Pella warns that the ancient site is close. Whilst the site lies to the left of the main road, parking is on the right.

Pella, once the capital of the kingdom of Macedonia at the time of its greatness, was the birthplace of both King Philip II and Alexander the Great. Founded when the capital of Macedonia transferred from Aigai to Pella around 400BC, it flourished for a time but declined after destruction by the Romans in the Battle of Pydna (168BC) and with the rise of Thessaloniki around 148BC. Not located until 1957, excavations have since revealed an extensive city but, apart from a few restored columns, it is mostly foundations that are on view. One of the main attractions is the mosaic floors from around 300BC. A site plan is displayed near the entrance but to find the House of the Lion Hunt, the most impressive building on the site, simply head for the standing columns. It takes its name from the subject depicted on the mosaic floor and whilst some of the mosaics have been left in situ, others have been transferred to the museum across the road. Determined visitors can also track down an extensive agora, an acropolis, many houses and shops and a circular sanctuary to Demeter and Kore. Across the main road, the small modern museum is worth a visit if only for the outstanding mosaics transferred from the site including the Lion Hunt but there are also many sculptures and a remarkable series of terra-cotta figures.

Once underway again, Thessaloniki is well signposted. For Motel Fillipos, turn right through Halkidona at the Veria road which is the first major junction after Pella. The ring-road system around Thessaloniki is incomplete and confusing at the moment so it is simpler to follow directly into the city even for those passing through to continue on to Halkidiki. Those not wishing to stay in the city centre might consider **Panorama**, 10km (6 miles) north-east of the centre. Perched on a hill, the aptly named Panorama looks down over the city to the gulf and is distinctly up-market. Its village character has long since merged into suburbia but it remains distinctive and is well served by shops, tavernas and a large supermarket. One local *zakaroplastion* (cake shop) is famed for its *trigona*, a local speciality comprising vanilla custard in a filo pastry cone. Convenient too is the bus service into Thessaloniki which is both regular and frequent.

Named after the sister of Alexander the Great, **Thessaloniki**, or *Salonika* ✳ to use an older name, sits in a bowl of hills overlooking the Thermaikos Gulf. Looking at the very modern face of the city today, it is hard to appreciate that it hides some 2,000 years of history which once saw it as the second most important city in the Byzantine Empire. A succession of fires at the end of the nineteenth century culminated with a fire which devastated the city in 1917. Immigrants from the population exchange of 1922 compounded problems which led to a replanning programme for the city centre which did not reach completion until the 1950's. Now it is laid out on a grid system with all the main streets running parallel to the sea making orientation and getting around relatively easy. It is a busy port, a university town, capital of Macedonia and an important Balkan trading centre. As the second largest city in Greece, comparisons with Athens are inevitable but one thing is certain, it does not suffer the same air quality problems as the capital. It is more modern, more bustling in an industrious way, more cosmopolitan and even the people are different in appearance, they are taller and more European to the extent of blue eyes and fair hair. Unlike Athens, the historical interest is not so concentrated in the centre but lies more in the monuments which survived, dotted around the city, and the older quarters lying to the north-west of the the modern city. Central Thessaloniki, in the area west of the White Tower to Venizelou Street, offers excellent shopping. Visitors searching for jewellery, leather, fur, copper or bronze will have lots of fun.

City Sights

Arch of Galerius: This great triumphal arch was erected around AD303 ⊓ to commemorate the victory of the Roman emperor Galerius over the Persians. On its piers are four zones of bas-reliefs set one above the other which show scenes from the battles.

The Rotunda: Built around AD306, possibly as part of the design which ⊓ incorporated the Arch of Galerius, it was converted into the christian church of Ag Georgios before the end of that century and decorated with

Via Egnatia

Egnatia road, the main route through the city follows the course of the old Roman military road, Via Egnatia. This route, started around the second century BC, was designed to connect Rome with the east. Both Edessa and Pella lie along the route which terminated at Kavala until the conquest of Thrace in AD46 after which it was extended to Byzantium, the modern Istanbul. Colonies were settled along its route, inns were built and it was generally kept in good repair until it lost importance around the fourth century AD as Milan replaced Rome as the starting point.

some fine mosaics. Much later, during the Turkish period it gained a minaret and became a mosque. Now, temporarily closed, it is preserved as a monument.

The White Tower: A conspicuous landmark near the sea front, this was built in the fifteenth century and later served as a prison. Restored in 1985, it now houses a small museum of the city's development and the energetic can climb to the top to enjoy the views from this 100ft (30m) high vantage point.

Palace of Galerius: Opposite the Rotunda and consisting only of low walls, it is easy to get an overview. Interesting here is the octagonal room which may have been a throne room later converted to a church.

The Archaeological Museum: This museum may not quite rival the National Museum in Athens for content but beats it hands down in presentation. It traces in artefacts the history of Macedonia and Thrace from the prehistoric through until around the fourth century AD all clearly labelled in both Greek and English. Particularly outstanding is the Vergina exhibition which displays finds from the Royal Tombs of King Philip II of Macedonia excavated only in 1978. Apart from the skeleton of the king, there are massive amounts of gold. The wreath of oak leaves and acorns so delicately crafted in pure gold, now over 2,000 years old, would challenge any modern day artisan given the same tools. The same extraordinary craftsmanship and artistic feeling was evident too in the other objects which included golden jewellery and works in bronze.

The Folk Museum: A well presented and colourful exhibition. Tableaux and models depicting period scenes of everyday life in housing, weaving, traditional costumes and arts and crafts. Possibly the finest museum of its type in Greece.

The Ramparts and the Acropolis: There are extensive Byzantine ramparts located at the highest part of the city which started existence in the fourth century. They have been patched and rebuilt over various periods, the latest being around the fourteenth century. Originally 8km (5 miles) long with towers along its length at irregular intervals, only about half the ramparts now remain, some of the towers but none of the gates. A well preserved section starts at the circular keep known as the Chain Tower, a contemporary of the White Tower, and runs northwards enclosing the Acropolis crowned on its summit by Eptapirgion, a fortress with seven towers which now houses the State prison. Below Eptapirgion is the old Turkish quarter, or what remains of it as modern developments are destroying the character. The small and very old church of Ossios David is worth visiting for the exceptional twelfth-century frescos.

Thessaloniki has many early churches, two have already been mentioned, but most were used as mosques for a time before reconsecration and many also suffered from the fire of 1917 and the earthquake of 1978. Many of the original features have been lost but there is a constant programme of restoration. It is worth touring those which are handily placed in the central region which includes most of the important ones.

Ag Sophia: An eighth century domed church which probably took its inspiration from its illustrious namesake in Istanbul. It is a transitional design with a basilica and isles which typifies early Christian style but with elements from a cross layout with dome which was gradually evolving. Here, a mosaic in the dome depicts the ascension.

Ag Dimitrios: Built over a crypt and extensive Roman baths, this church takes the name of the patron saint of Thessaloniki who was martyred here at the command of Galerius by incarceration in the crypt. It has the distinction of being the largest church in Greece and was built in the fifth century as a double-aisled basilica. Largely destroyed in the fire of 1917, it was restored over a period of years in its original style except for the wooden roof.

Panagia Akhiropiitos: One of the earliest Christian churches still in use, it was built as a basilica with nave and two aisles and completed around AD470. Remnants of old mosaics can be seen under the arcades of the galleries while the frescos outside the nave are thirteenth century.

The well-preserved mosaic on the floor of the House of the Lion Hunt at Pella

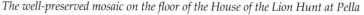

Additional Information

Places to Visit

Kastoria
Byzantine Museum
Open: daily 8.30am-2pm, closed on Mondays.

Folk Museum
Open: daily 8.30am-6pm.

Pella
Site and Museum
Open: daily 8.30am-3pm, closed on Mondays.

Thessaloniki
Archaeological Museum
Open: daily 8am-7pm, Saturday, Sunday and holidays 8.30am-3pm and Monday 12.30-7pm.

Folk Museum
Open: daily 9.30am-2pm closed on Thursdays.

Accommodation

All those listed below are open all year.

EDESSA/PELLA: TELEPHONE PREFIX **0381**
Hotel Katarraktes (B)
4 Karanou
☎ 22300/2

Hotel Xenia (B)
41 Pilipou Parasissos
☎ 22995/6

Hotel Alfa (C)
36 Egnatia
☎ 22221/2

Hotel Fillipos (B)
Halkidona (near Pella)
☎ 0391 22125

KASTORIA: TELEPHONE PREFIX **0467**
Hotel Xenia du Lac (A)
Dexmenis square
☎ 22565

Motel Maria (B)
☎ 74696/7

Hotel Tsamis (B)
Dispilo (3km outside town)
☎ 43334

Hotel Acropolis (C)
16 Gramou
☎ 22537

Hotel Anesis (C)
10 Gramou
☎ 29410

Hotel Europa (C)
8 Ag Athanasiou
☎ 23826/7

Hotel Kastoria (C)
122 Nikis
☎ 29453

Hotel Keletron (C)
52 11th November
☎ 22676

Hotel Lazos (C)
☎ 24895

Hotel Orestion (C)
Platia Dassaki
☎ 22257/8

THESSALONIKI: TELEPHONE PREFIX **031**
A free Thessaloniki/Halkidiki booklet lists hotels in town and in Halkidiki and contains a street map which is useful for locating the places mentioned throughout this chapter. All those listed below are open all year.
This is a selection from a list of more than thirty hotels available from the Tourist Office.

Makedonia Palace (de Luxe)
Megalou Alexandrou
☎ 837520

Hotel Capitol (A)
8 Monastiriou
☎ 516221

Hotel Electra Palace (A)
5a Aristotelous Square
☎ 232221/30

Hotel Panorama (A)
26 Analipseos
☎ 941123/29

Hotel Astoria (B)
20 Tsimiski/Dodecanissou
☎ 527121/5

Hotel Capsis (B)
28 Monastiriou
☎ 521421/10

Hotel City (B)
11 Komninon
☎ 26942

Hotel Metropolitan (B)
65 Vas Olgas/Flemming
☎ 824221

Hotel Olympia (B)
65 Olympou
☎ 235421

Hotel Amalia (C)
33 Ermou
☎ 268321

Hotel Continental (C)
5 Komninon
☎ 277553

Hotel Park (C)
81 Ionos Dragoumi
☎ 524121

Hotel Pella (C)
65 Ionos Dragoumi
☎ 524221/4

Hotel Vergina (C)
19 Monastiriou
☎ 516021

PANORAMA: TELEPHONE PREFIX 031
Hotel Nefeli (A) ☎ 42002
Hotel Panorama (A) ☎ 41123
Hotel Pefka (C) ☎ 41153/41790

Transport

Kastoria
It is connected by regular bus services
to Athens, Thessaloniki, Florina, Kozani
and Ioannina. There is also a local
airport with flights to Athens.

Thessaloniki
Air
Thessaloniki has an international
airport which receives both schedule
and charter flights from most parts of
Europe. Internal flights connect with
Athens, Ioannina and a limited number
of islands including Rhodes, Crete and
Mytilene. Tourist Police (airport)
☎ 425011 ext 215221

Road
An extensive timetable of buses con-
nects Thessaloniki to all major towns.
There is no central bus station, Athens'
buses (6 daily) depart from 100, 26
October Street but consult the Tourist
Office for other departure points and a
full timetable.

Rail
Thessaloniki is the link for most of the
international services. The line out to
former Yugoslavia serves Edessa but
most of the internal destinations lie to
the south. Katerina (for Mount
Olympos) and Larissa lie on the route
south to Athens and also served are
Volos (for Pilion) and Trikala (for
Meteora).

Festivals

Thessaloniki
Dimitria Festival October/November.
A festival of drama, music, and ballet.
Fire Walkers, 21 May. The villagers of
Langada and Ag Eleni (about 20km/12
miles north from Thessaloniki) perform
a ritual barefooted dance on burning
charcoal embers to celebrate the feast
day of St Constantine and St Helen.

Tourist Information Centres

Kastoria
Municipal Information Office
The Town Hall
☎ 24484

Thessaloniki
Greek National Tourist Office
8 Aristotelous Square
☎ 271888

9
HALKIDIKI

Halkidiki (Chalkidiki) is the largest resort area on mainland Greece outside Attica. Looking at the map, the shape of this three-fingered peninsula biting deep into the Aegean sea alone is enough to excite interest. It boasts the longest coastline of any prefecture in Greece and much of it is sandy. Only in 1960 did the Greek National Tourist Organisation move to promote the region and it was not until 1968 that significant investment started. Progress has been steady rather than spectacular and now it features in the brochures of most major tour operators. Of the three peninsulas, Kassandria, the most westerly and the one nearest to Thessaloniki, has received the most attention. Perhaps because there is so much coastline and so many opportunities it has no major developments but a host of small resorts. It is a playground for the people of Thessaloniki who flood out to it at weekends and help fill the resorts in the main season. The same comments, but to a lesser degree, apply also to the Germans. It is the nearest resort area of Greece which can be conveniently reached by an overland drive.

Sithonia, the central peninsula, is more rugged, more mountainous and more than a few steps behind in tourist development. It might seem contradictory now to relate that, at Porto Carras, is has the largest resort in Halkidiki but a drive around the scenic coastal road of the peninsula reveals many untouched villages.

Even more rugged and mountainous is the most easterly peninsula, Mount Athos. It is a self-administered part of Greece totally dedicated to the worship of god. The population is exclusively male and ecclesiastic. Women are expressly excluded. The region is closed to visitors except those holding a permit.

Driving around the Halkidiki peninsula there is not the same feel of history as in other parts of Greece. It does have a history, and a long history judging by the finds in the cave at Petralona which date back 700,000 years, but the threads have been broken too often for it to persist into the present. Many prehistoric settlements have been discovered along the

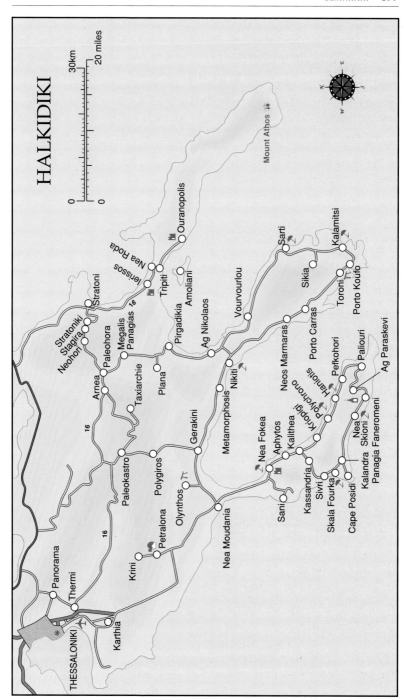

HALKIDIKI

30km
20 miles

THESSALONIKI
Panorama
Thermi
Karthia
Krini
Petralona
Olynthos
Polygiros
Paleokastro
Gerakini
Nea Moudania
Sani
Nea Fokea
Aphytos
Kalithea
Kassandria
Sivri
Skala Fourka
Kalandra
Cape Posidi
Panagia Faneromeni
Nea Skioni
Paliouri
Ag Paraskevi
Pefkohori
Hanlotis
Polychrono
Kriopigi
Porto Carras
Neos Marmaras
Metamorphosis
Nikiti
Vourvourlou
Ag Nikolaos
Pirgadikia
Plana
Taxiarchie
Megalis Panagias
Paleohora
Arnea
Neohori
Stagira
Stratoniki
Stratoni
Ierissos
Nea Roda
Tripiti
Amoliani
Ouranopolis
Mount Athos
Sikia
Sarti
Kalamitsi
Toroni
Porto Koufo
16
16
16

coastline indicating that the region was well populated by 4,000BC. There is evidence of further colonisation by southern Greeks about the eighth century BC but a century later the Macedonians invaded to drive them out and install the Bottiaeans, people from just south-west of the present day Thessaloniki, and it became known as Bottice. Around the mid-fifth century BC, following the Persian Wars, it joined the Athenian League and later, in the Peloponnesian Wars, it became a battle ground for a fight between the Athenians and the Lacedaemonians. Many of its cities were wiped out and to survive it united to form its own Halkidikian League under the leadership of Olynthos, the most important city. The Spartans used force to bring it to an end in 397BC but their domination quickly faded and the League sprang back into prominence and regained considerable power. Both Athens and King Philip of Macedonia asked to join but the League became suspicious of King Philip and terminated their alliance. Halkidiki asked Athens for help when King Philip marched against them but it came too late to save the sacking of most of the cities of the league and of Olynthos. Halkidiki was absorbed into Macedonia. From then on the history is punctuated with attempts to rebuild followed by devastation. King Kassander built a new city for the survivors of Olynthia and Potidaea and named it Kassandria. In the following year he also built Thessaloniki for other displaced settlements. In 168BC the Romans conquered the region and brought new colonists from their own country. They too suffered a siege by the Goths in AD269 which lead to enormous devastation. The region was again devastated by the Huns in the sixth century and this time the destruction is believed to have been almost total.

Its more recent history is equally turbulent. In 1821 Halkidiki played an important role in the Greek revolution. Unfortunately, their uprising against the Turks was premature and they were defeated. The Turks extracted a terrible revenge; they set fire to the villages and took the sword to the people. Many fled, some never to return. Slowly, some refugees did return and by 1830 the reconstruction of Halkidiki started again but it was not until 1912 that they actually gained freedom from the Turks. In the population exchange of 1922 it received a mass influx of refugees from Asia Minor who formed new towns. Almost all the villages in the region with the prefix Nea to their name, like Nea Moudania, date from this time.

Settled now to a much more peaceful existence, the people of Halkidiki are principally farmers who produce olives, nuts, grapes, vegetables and honey, a major product. Fishing, forestry, mining and tourism too all contribute to the local economy.

Starting from Thessaloniki, the exploration of the region is presented in three tours which link together to make a continuous tour if desired. The early part of the access road from Thessaloniki is being widened but generally the roads are good throughout the region.

Tour 1 • The Kassandra Peninsula (190km/118 miles)

As far as the driving is concerned, one day is adequate to cover the distance but with the caves at Petralona and a host of small resorts around the Kassandria Peninsula to visit more time may be required. Accommodation is available in most of the resorts but difficulty can be anticipated in high season when the tour operators take up a large slice of the available beds.

The precise route for escaping Thessaloniki to the east is determined by the road contractors at the moment but diversions are well signed and, once clear of the city, there is a good dual carriageway all the way to Karthia. Follow signs initially to Nea Moudania through an undulating countryside splashed with fields of grain and clumps of trees. Long before Nea Moudania is the left turn to the caves at Petralona.

The caves lie around 800m beyond the village of **Petralona** in the foothills of Mount Katsika. They were first explored and mapped out in 1959 by Ioannis Petrocheilos and a year later, amongst the remains of bears, panthers and hyenas, was found a human skull of the Neandertal type. Lighting and walkways have been installed and part of the cave is open to the public under the control of a guide. A museum section inside the entrance displays old tools and other findings as well as tableaux depicting the life of the cave dwellers. The highlight is the large hall with its dramatic array of stalactites and stalagmites.

Back on the main route, Nea Moudania is quickly reached and a traffic light junction, rare outside large towns. Straight on leads to Kassandria and, shortly afterwards, the sight of sea on both sides of the road marks the entry onto the peninsula. The first village reached is **Nea Fokea**, divided by the main road. The fishing village character still prevails and tourism is low key. It has its share of beaches, the best at the north end, tavernas and accommodation. Just to the south of the village, by the sea shore, is the Tower of St Paul built around the start of the fifteenth century for defence purposes. Aphytos, the next village, is one of the older communities which managed to persist through all the turbulent periods of history. A short diversion takes you down the narrow streets into the old village perched on a cliff. The beach below, a fair downhill tramp, is only a narrow sandy strip without much in the way of facilities.

Founded only after 1922, **Kalithea**, with its grid layout, is unmistakably modern. The road through the village is colourfully decked with all the trappings of tourism, souvenir shops, tavernas and fast food places. To escape this atmosphere simply head for the long stretch of sandy beach which is far enough away from the road to make it peaceful and private although it is adequately served by tavernas. The Hotel Ammon Zeus on the front takes its name from the fourth-century BC sanctuary to Ammon Zeus found in this area. Much of the accommodation, which is mainly rooms, lies on the inward side of the main road but there are underpasses for the benefit of pedestrians. Kalithea is also the junction where the road

The deserted beach at Vourvourlou

Haniotis beach, decked out with sun beds and umbrellas

divides to cross the peninsula but this tour continues first down the eastern side.

A succession of villages follows, each separated by only a few kilometres of open road. **Kriopigi** is the first of these, small, inland and with tourist accommodation but it is hard to describe as a resort. Just off the main road to the left is **Polychrono**. This modern purpose built resort has a good long ribbon of sandy beach unimaginatively backed by a road but with plenty of facilities in the way of shops, bars, tavernas and accommodation. The next resort to the south, and again off the main road to the left, is the modern development of **Haniotis**. Up to 1935, the village occupied a site some 2km (1 mile) inland from its present position. With the lavish use of flower beds and pedestrianised ways, it has managed to create a character which sets it apart from the other resorts on the peninsula. The long sandy beach is just as neatly decked out with sun beds and umbrellas. Last of the line of these east coast resorts is **Pefkohori**. This fairly large village straddling the main road had a life before but has now mushroomed in response to tourism. The sandy, fine shingle beach is long and narrow with jetties at intervals and a road directly behind. The quieter part of the village lies inland of the main road.

Following the coast road still, the grandly named Hotel Marina on the right faces a natural, picturesque lagoon over to the left which is totally bereft of moorings or buildings. After the level run down the peninsula to this point, climbing into the low pine covered hills to cross over to the west coast provides an interesting contrast. The two inland villages encountered, **Paliouri** and **Ag Paraskevi**, are both small, sleepy and offer little in the way of tourist facilities but there is some older style architecture to see. Views from this elevated position while descending towards the west coast are of a wandering coastline and blue sea against a foreground of rolling dark green hills splashed yellow by the Spanish broom. Squeezed by the hills, the road along the west runs close to the sea and even the narrow strip of land between is put to good use in growing olives. Just before reaching Nea Skioni, the small white church, Panagia Faneromeni, on the sea edge with a seating area behind is an invitingly peaceful and tempting picnic spot. Inside the church, if it is unlocked, are some partly preserved seventeenth-century wall frescos showing the crucifixion and the burial of Christ.

Turn left shortly for the small fishing village of **Nea Skioni**. With its fish tavernas and boat building activity it manages to look more typically Greek than many of the villages on the peninsula yet Nea Skioni developed only after 1930 when the inland village of Tsaprani was deserted. There is plenty of sandy beach running to the north and tourist accommodation. The road north follows a narrow ribbon of sandy beach passing through Mola Kalina, a scattering of rooms and developments. From here the route drifts inland to cut across Cape Posidi so a left turn is required to head for Kalandra and visit the cape. **Kalandra** is one of the older villages of the region where older style balconied houses mingle with the new. The isolated and beautiful Cape Posidi, a short drive further on, is dedicated to the campers. Beaches are not in short supply although they are mixed sand and shingle.

Skala Fourka, the next resort along the main route, is blessed with a wide run of sand enclosed by pine covered hills. A relaxing atmosphere is created by tavernas serving directly on to the beach and the accommodation not crowding too close to the sea front. Expect nothing more than a small resort. Even smaller with more of the same is **Sivri**, the next call, which is barely worth the diversion to see it. The route back to Kalithea, to complete the circuit, passes through **Kassandria**, the largest town on the peninsula. It is not especially notable but it does offer a wider range of shops and banks.

Tour 2 • Sithonia Peninsula (200km/124 miles)

With its sharper hills, and greater abundance of trees and wild flowers, Sithonia is scenically more attractive than Kassandria and far less developed. Virtually the only road, and a good road too, follows the coastline connecting all the towns and villages. The interior remains virtually uninhabited. Travelling down the east coast first has the advantage of good views over to Mount Athos, haze permitting. With far less reason to stop than on the Kassandria Peninsula, one day will be sufficient time for most.

From Kalithea some backtracking is required to Nea Moudania before turning right to head for Sithonia. For the real history buffs there is a diversion off left shortly for the ancient city of **Olynthos**; there is little to see but the outline of the street plan, open cisterns and a few mosaics which are hard to find. Olive groves and cereal fields punctuate this rich agricultural area until the quarries of Gerakini come into view. It is immediately back to pastoral scenes and the silver grey of the olive trees all the way to Metamorphosis. It is a quiet place, at least out of high season, with a narrow strand of sandy beach lapped by the Aegean. There are the usual tavernas aiming to please mainly the Greek tourist but otherwise there is little in the way of facilities. Further along the coast, at another traffic light junction, lies **Nikiti**. Turn right, down towards the beach, for the tourist part of town and for the tavernas grouped at the sea edge. The road does continue to the left, as a track, along the beach edge for quite some distance to provide access to the various rooms and apartments along the front. It is a quiet place to stay and a good base for exploring the eastern part of Halkidiki otherwise it has little else to commend it.

Continue on along the main road to cross the head of the Sithonia Peninsula through a boulder strewn landscape and keep ahead following signs to Sarti. Pine covered mountains rise inland with progress down the east coast of the peninsula. Turn left to follow signs to Vourvourlou and be prepared for a maze of uncharted roads laid out some time ago probably in connection with the Professor's Community. Sometime in the 1960's, professors from the University of Thessaloniki laid out a model community on the headland here in such a way that the houses blend unobtrusively into the landscape. It appears to have essentially a seasonal population although there is a taverna and supermarket. Turn left on reaching a T-junction, 4km (2 miles) from leaving the main road, and left again at the next T-junction to reach a car park area and the beach. The whole area is picturesque with a cluster of nine small offshore islands, sand spits and endless secluded sandy bays and coves which makes it a great place for nude bathing.

Back on the main road travelling south again, there is the occasional flirtation with the sea and view of Mount Athos. Eye catching amongst the wild flowers along the route is *Campanula lingulata* which displays narrow blue bellflowers grouped at the top of its tall stems but the compact form which grows on the rock face is hardly recognisable as the same plant. The drive here is through the wild scrub and pine covered hills, without either habitation or cultivation but there are occasional glimpses of a rocky sea shore and more distant views over to Mount Athos. Olive groves reappear to warn of habitation but, apart from two houses, there is still nothing. A sign indicates Plakanitsi beach and camping off left and shortly after is the turn into the village of Sarti. Developed by the returning refugees after 1922, **Sarti** might be small with a permanent population of less than 1,000 but it is fairly self-contained with a bakers, a bank, seafront tavernas and plenty of accommodation. The sandy beach is especially pleasing for its view over to Mount Athos. The country outside is goat country and, apart from sometimes stopping the traffic, large goat pens dot the hillsides. Turn right for a diversion to **Sikia**. It is hard to immediately appreciate that Sikia, caught in the bowl of a hill, is actually larger than Sarti. Named after the fig tree, Sikia is one of the oldest villages on the peninsula which, in Byzantine times, belonged to several Mount Athos monasteries but chiefly Megisti Lavra. During the Turkish occupation, with their traditional love of the sea and their secure refuge, the Sikians were inclined to piracy. They were at the forefront of all the struggles throughout the fight for independence and even today that free spirit still exists but the people here also have a reputation for hospitality. It is worth a stop to see some of the houses in the older quarter.

The road shown on most maps which leads on from Sikia across the tip of the peninsula is nothing more than a rough track which makes returning east to rejoin the main road the best option. The journey around the southern tip passes two inviting beaches, Sikia beach seen soon after rejoining the road and, shortly afterwards, Kalamitsi which requires a slight diversion left. Cistus and other dwarf shrubs cloak the hillsides here but a reafforestation programme is in hand judging by the extensive new pine plantations. **Porto Koufo** sprawling around a small lagoon is the most southerly village on the peninsula and just a little further north is **Toroni** which requires a short detour off to the left down a stabilised track.

It is only a very small community administered by Sikia but it does have archaeological remains to explore. The site was occupied from around the eighth century BC through until the sixteenth century and systematic excavations were started in 1974. Today the visible remains are of extensive fortifications, some possibly as early as the Classical period but with much later additions, and early Christian basilicas. Perhaps the most eye catching remains are those of the medieval Castle of Lecythus on the rocky headland to which there is no access for the general public but, for those with the energy, the acropolis is there to be roamed.

A ribbon of sandy beach stretches northwards attracting numerous small developments which can be seen from the road as, shortly, can Kelfos island. After all the pine and scrub on the hillsides, the appearance of vineyards is quite startling but they merely announce **Porto Carras**. Built by the ship owner John Carras, Porto Carras is a unique holiday complex which includes a model farm for growing citrus fruit, olives, almonds and grapes on an extensive scale. The excellent Porto Carras wine is produced here on site. The complex has hotels, a marina and a full range of sporting and cultural facilities for 3,000 guests as well as providing homes for an army of permanent staff. The sporting opportunities include water skiing, yachting, tennis, golf and horse riding. Just north of here is Neos Marmaras, the largest town on the peninsula which owes a considerable part of its own success to the neighbouring Porto Carras. Like the other towns incorporating Nea in the name, it developed after the population exchange in 1922 and swelled in 1970 when the nearby mountain community of Parthenon decided to abandon their own village to settle there. A track leads up into the mountains to Parthenon and beyond to the summit of Mount Itamos (811m/2,660ft) but it is too rough for a car and best done on foot. **Neos Marmaras** is well equipped with shops, accommodation, tavernas and restaurants and fairly buzzes with activity. The harbour too is busy with a regular service down to Porto Carras and excursions for Skiathos, Skopelos and Alonissos.

The first landmark on the way north again is an old monastic complex, now in a state of collapse, and afterwards a road down to Lagomandra beach but expect nothing more than a taverna and a few rooms. Small developments like this occur along the route but nothing too organised. Further north still, the landscape is dominated by the barren rock formations which characterise the head of this peninsula. The tour now returns to Nikiti ready for the start of Tour 3.

Tour 3 • Halkidiki Interior (235km/146 miles)

Here is the opportunity to visit Ouranopolis to press your nose against Mount Athos and this is about as close as ordinary mortals are allowed, unless you take to the sea. A cruise around the peninsula gives a different perspective and a sighting of some of the monasteries. The return route

visits Arnea, undoubtedly the prettiest village in Halkidiki, before crossing high over Mount Holomon towards Polygyros. This is a diversion
point for those wishing to return to Thessaloniki otherwise the tour
completes the circuit back to Nikiti.

Head east from Nikiti, this time cutting across the head of Sithonia
towards and into Ag Nikolaos. Turn right following signs to Pirgadikia
for a twisting climb through olive and pines before winding back down
towards the sea. Ahead, on a rocky headland reaching into the sea,
Pirgadikia dominates the horizon but there is some weaving around
inlets and sandy bays before it is reached. Clustered up and around the
bay sheltered by the headland, Pirgadikia is a peaceful village depending
on fishing and farming for its existence. The present community was
started by returning refugees after 1922, possibly on the site of an earlier
settlement, but it shows signs of recent expansion. Not too much stirs but
there are tavernas and rooms in the village. Without the benefit of a coastal
road for the final link to Mount Athos, the route turns inland for a fairly
lengthy detour via Megalis Panagia and Paleohora. It is a steady climb
away from the coast through a landscape dominated by cultivation and
a variety of wayside shrines. There is a sharp and unsigned right hand
turn just before the village of Plana. From thereon it should be a peaceful
drive unless it is early August. **Megalis Panagias** is a place of pilgrimage.
According to legend, a devout woman of Revenikia, moved by a dream,
searched at a spot outside the village to find the miraculous ikon of the
Virgin Mother. A church was built there in 1863 and rebuilt after an

A pastoral landscape in Halkidiki

Mount Athos, The Holy Mount

The wild and mountainous peninsula is a self administered part of the Greek state dedicated to the holy community. The population is exclusively male and only male visitors are allowed. Greeks may visit on production of their identity cards but aliens are required to have a pass. The issue of permits to aliens to visit Mount Athos is limited to ten each day. Only males can apply. To acquire a permit it is first necessary to obtain a letter of commendation from the government which is best done through the consulate in Athens or Thessaloniki. The applicant is expected to have some special interest in religion, art or architecture or claim to have. Preferably in the same city, take the letter to the Ministry of Foreign Affairs who will issue a permit for a 4 day visit valid for a month and which may specify the day of entry. In summer when the pressure for permits is at its height, it may not be possible to get desired dates. There is a regular ferry service from Ouranopolis to Dafni, the main port on Mount Athos and, on boarding, visitors will be asked to relinguish both their permit and passport which can be reclaimed later from the police at Karies.

There are twenty monasteries of which seventeen are Greek, one Bulgarian, one Russian and one Serbian. They are scattered around the peninsula, mostly near coastal areas but there are no roads and travel is by foot, on donkey or by boat. Footpaths criss-cross the island to the confusion of many visitors. Divorced from the modern world, even time has a different meaning and they still use the Julian Calendar which puts them some thirteen days behind the rest of Europe. Its early history is somewhat clouded but in one legend it owes its origins ironically enough to a woman, the Virgin Mary, but it officially celebrated its first 1,000 years in 1963 dismissing all very early claims to its foundation. History becomes a little clearer from about the seventh century. Peter the Athonite is known as one of the very early monks but he, like others of his period, lived in a cave or simple hermitage. The first monastery, the Great Lavra, was built around AD963 and others quickly followed until around the fifteenth century when there were as many as forty with a total population of around 20,000. After the fall of Constantinople, the religious community managed to keep on good terms with the Sultan but it ran into real trouble during the War of Independence. The monks fought alongside the Greeks who were badly beaten and Mount Athos went into decline, especially when southern Greece won its independence.

Some of the monasteries practice a common style of living (*cenobia*), in which all the monks dress alike, pool their resources and share the same fare whilst the others have an idiorhythmatic life-style of living apart, providing their own clothes and finding their own food.

earthquake in 1932. Ever since the ikon was found it has been a place of pilgrimage, festivities start on 1 August and end on the 15. To find the church, head a little up the Gomati road just before the village but do not expect to see the miraculous ikon, it was stolen in 1979.

A cultivated landscape slowly gives way to forests of deciduous oak before Paleohora is reached and the sign indicating Ierissos to the right. Neohori follows quickly in a countryside verdant with forest of pine and broad leaved trees and, just before Stagira, look for the park on the right with the statue of Aristotle amidst the ruins of a Byzantine fortress. **Stagira** claims to be the birthplace of Aristotle but in reality he was born at nearby ancient Stratoniki. His modern statue stands in a fine country setting next to the ruined tower of Madem Aga. There are some simple facilities too including bench seats and drinking water. This area was historically important for mining silver which some suggest was used in the ancient coinage of the region. Mining in the surrounding hills came to an end around the seventeenth century. The village itself has many modern white houses built in the traditional style with overhanging balconies. It almost merges into the next village, Stratoniki.

After reaching the coast, a fast road leads southwards through masses of pink oleander dashed with yellow broom and dotted with blue campanulas. It stays close to the sea shore but not offering too many glimpses until much nearer to Ierissos. One or two hotels, boat builders along the shore and a small harbour give no hint of the former importance of the ancient town where **Ierissos** now stands and all that remains is the ruins of a castle and a Byzantine church. The land, marked here in a patchwork quilt of wheat and barley, shrinks giving a view of the sea on both sides even before Nea Roda is reached. Just beyond this village is the location of the canal cut under the direction of Xerxes in the Persian Wars. The plan was to provide an easy route for the Persians after a previous attempt by Mardonius' fleet in 490BC to round the Mount Athos Peninsula had resulted in a disasterous loss of ships and men. From here the road switches to the south coast passing through sandy Tripiti and hugs the shore line revealing bay after bay of golden sand with strategically placed hotels along the way. Enter **Ouranopolis** and turn left at the tower to head for a large car park with money collecting attendant, rare for Greece at the moment.

After the drive through isolated and deserted countryside, the joyful hubbub in this thriving little resort and the sight of people milling around the souvenir shops and diners filling the long line of shaded tavernas comes as a shock to the senses. It is an appealing resort in its own right but the big attraction which brings visitors by the coachload is the boat excursion to view Mount Athos. Another popular excursion from here, also by boat, is across to the island of Amoliana.

Ouranopolis was built on land owned by the Mount Athos monastery of Vatopediou only in 1922 by the returning refugees from Turkey. The tower of Proshorion which dominates the village is much older and was built by Vatopediou for defence somewhere around 1344. It was rebuilt to some extent following earthquake damage in the nineteenth century. Hand knotted rugs and carpets made from goats hair and incorporating designs based on motifs from the Mount Athos frescos are the chief local handicraft. Curiously enough this skill, and the art of dyeing with vegetable dyes, was taught to them by Mrs J. N. Lock, an Australian, in 1928.

To reach **Arnea** return by the same route as far as Paleohora andd from there follow the Thessaloniki sign. Look for parking in the platia then enjoy a wander through the narrow streets crowded by tall traditional tower houses, some gleaming white and others of stone but all with projecting wooden balconies. It has a longer history than many villages in the region but it was burnt by the Turks in 1821 and deserted for a while. Many of the houses have been restored but modern ones are still built in this style. Follow signs to Taxiarchis from Arnea. This narrow road winds and twists up the forested mountain, tunnelling through the broad leaved trees and their dappled shadows. Not until the road starts to descend do the trees release their grip to allow views to the top of Mount Holomon. There is a taverna on this section and a Sunday lunch here could see you dancing and singing with the Greeks. After a fairly steep descent with a few hairpins, the Paleokastro junction is quickly reached. It is straight on for Thessaloniki which is well signed or a left turn for those returning to Nikiti or other parts of Halkidiki. The way south is clear but a new road is under construction which parallels the existing road down to Polygiros. From there a fast road runs down to the coast at Gerakini and familiar territory.

(opposite) The modern statue of Aristotle stands in a fine country setting in the park at Stagira

Wayside shrines, like this one in Halkidiki, are a common feature by the roadside

Additional Information

Place to Visit

Petralona
Caves
Open: daily 9am-6pm.

Accommodation

HOTELS
* = Open all year

KASSANDRIA: TELEPHONE PREFIX **0374**
Ag Paraskevi
Hotel Aphrodite (B) ☎ 71228

Afytos
Hotel Afitis (B) ☎ 91237

Haniotis
Hotel Pella (B) ☎ 51679
Hotel Ermis (C) ☎ 51245
*Hotel Hanioti** (C) ☎ 51323
Hotel Plaza (C) ☎ 51246
Hotel Strand (C) ☎ 51261

Soussouras (B)
Bungalows
☎ 51251

Dionyssos Inn (B)
☎ 51632

Dionyssos (C)
Furnished apartments
☎ 51402

Kalandra
Hotel Mendi (A)
☎ 41323/6

Kalithea
Athos Palace (A)
(Hotel and Bungalows)
☎ 22100/10

Pallini Beach (A)
(Hotel and Bungalows)
☎ 22480

Hotel Ammon Zeus (B)
☎ 22356/7

Hotel Belvedere (C)
☎ 22352/22910

*Hotel Delfini** (C)
☎ 22355/22567

Paliouri
Hotel Xenia (B)
☎ 92277/92291

*Hotel Nostos** (C)
☎ 92240

Giannokos (B)
Bungalows
☎ 92214

Thermavos (B)
Bungalows
☎ 92146/92204

Pefkohori
Pension Flegra (B) ☎ 61454
Pension Fox (B) ☎ 61244

Alexander Furnished Apartments (C)
☎ 61225

Dioamontopoulos Furnished Apartments (C)
☎ 61568

Dimtra Furnished Apartments (C)
☎ 61396

Ioli Furnished Apartments (C)
☎ 61043

Polychrono
Hotel Akroyal (C) ☎ 51500
Hotel Geogios (C) ☎ 51693

OURANOPOLIS: TELEPHONE PREFIX **0377**
Eagles Palace (A)
Hotel and Bungalows
☎ 22747/8

Aristoteles (B)
Bungalows
☎ 71296

Pension Iliovassilema (B)
☎ 71372

Xenia
Motel and Bungalows
☎ 71202/71265

Skites (C)
Bungalows
☎ 71140

Sithonia: Telephone prefix 0375
Neos Marmaras
The following three are all in the Porto Carras complex ☎ 71338:
Meliton Grecotel (de Luxe), Hotel Sithonia (A) and Village Inn* (B)

Hotel Skouna (B) ☎ 71183
Pension Glaros (B) ☎ 71205

*Hellenico Spiti** (C)
Furnished Apartments
☎ 71052

Miramare (C)
Furnished Apartments
☎ 71444

Nikiti
Pension Sithonia (B)
☎ 22788/22374

Elia (C)
Furnished Apartments
☎ 22786

Nikos (C)
Furnished Apartments
☎ 22465/22377

Pigadikia
Pension Panorama (B) ☎ 93230

Sarti
Sarti Beach (B)
Furnished Apartments
☎ 41450

Manolis House (C)
Furnished Apartments
☎ 41571

Vourvourou
Pension Diaporos (B)
☎ 91313/91384

Camping

All the following sites open only in the summer season.

Kassandria region: Telephone prefix 0374
Ag Paraskevi
Porto Loutra
☎ 71123

Kalandra
Kalandras Camping
☎ 41345

Kryopigi
Kryopigi Camping
☎ 51037

Nea Sykion
Anemi Beach
☎ 71276

Paliouri
Paliouri
☎ 92206

Sithonia region: Telephone prefix 0375
Ag Nikolaos
Lacara
☎ 91444/56

Akti Armen
Armenistis
☎ 91487/97

Neos Marmaras
Areti ☎ 715723
Castello ☎ 71095
Europa Beach ☎ 71078

Kalamitsi
Porto ☎ 41346

Porto Koufo ☎ 41346

Nikiti
Mylos ☎ 22041/2
Sylva ☎ 22496

Tourist Information Centre

The nearest is in Thessaloniki, see Chapter 8.

Local Transport

With such a low indigenous population, the local transport is not well developed and cannot be relied upon to travel around the peninsulas. Most villages are connected to Thessaloniki and services can be hourly from the bigger centres.

10
MOUNT OLYMPOS AND PILION

Two areas of outstanding natural beauty, Mount Olympos and Pilion, lie at opposing ends of a range of mountains which has a dominating influence on the entire region. Its climatic effect on the plain of Thessaly is extraordinary. Already enclosed to the west by the Pindos and to the south by Parnassos, the plain is sealed off from maritime air completely by the Olympos, Ossa and Pilion ring to the east. As a consequence the Thessaly plain enjoys a continental climate with cold winters, too cold for olives to be grown and very hot summers. It is the most important region in Greece for the production of cereal crops.

Some very early settlements like Sesklo, Dimini and Iolkos near Volos stretch back to millenniums BC and the importance of the region, especially in Mycenaean times, can be assessed by the number of myths centred on Thessaly. The Argonauts set out in their quest for the Golden Fleece from Iolkos. Chiron, the centaur, was there for the send off as Thessaly was the home of the centaurs. It was Chiron who taught Asklepios the art of healing. The best known legend centres on Mount Olympos as the mythical home of the Gods. As in many countries, place names are used and re-used in many different localities and there are more than a few mountains bearing the name of Olympos. There is one in Evia, Laconia, Arcadia, Lesbos and another in Cyprus but the one here, the one straddling the borders of Macedonia and Thessaly, is the undoubted home of the Olympians.

Early Greek religions were dedicated to the Earth Mother but at some stage an awareness of the sky gods grew. The transition between the two is uncharted but the great pantheon of gods, the twelve Olympians, was firmly established by the time of Homer. Each god represented a different aspect of the human soul and each had different responsibilities. High on Mount Olympos, on the peak of Ag Antonios (2,817m/9,240ft), a shrine to Zeus was discovered and excavations have yielded pottery, inscriptions and coins. There are remains of another shrine too, this time to Apollo, at the more comfortable altitude of 700m (2,296ft).

Apart from its association with the gods Mount Olympos is a beautiful

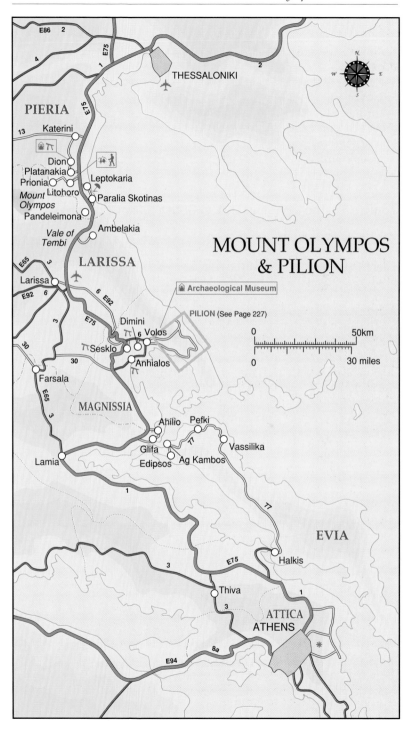

MOUNT OLYMPOS
& PILION

PILION (See Page 227)

area, a mecca for walkers and botanists alike. The flora is especially rich containing species which can be found nowhere else and is protected by National Park status. Litohoro, a sparkling little village, is the most convenient base to explore this region. Nearby, on the Macedonian side, is ancient Dion. Excavations in recent years have revealed temples, baths and some fine mosaics which make it a worthwhile detour.

Further south lies Pilion, another area of natural beauty with a wholly different character. It is not the mountain which is the main attraction, and Mount Pilion is significant at 1,618m (5,307ft), but the lushness of the wooded countryside and the delightful villages full of traditional houses.

Tour 1 • To The Mountain Of The Gods (100km/62 miles)

West bound traffic heading through Thessaloniki is usually channelled at some point onto Ignatia street from where Athens signs can be picked up. There is no option but to use the Athens 'motorway' for traffic ultimately heading south. It is a toll road but at least on the stretch to Litohoro there is only one pay booth located fairly soon after the start, just south of the Axios river. The road begins as dual carriageway but soon reverts and, contrary to what might be expected, roadside filling stations and canteens occur along the route. If the scenery is unremarkable to start with, all that changes when the Olympos massive comes into view. Once past Katerini, keep an eye open for the **Dion** sign on the right and follow. The ancient site is close to the modern village of the same name. At the cross roads reached on entering the village, where Hotel Dion stands on the left, turn right to reach the site very shortly.

From around 500BC Dion grew as a sanctuary to Zeus and to Demeter with a stadium for games and a theatre. It was important to the religious life of Macedonia but never achieved the status of a city. Philip II brought his troops to celebrate triumphs or to sacrifice ahead of campaigns and one notable occasion was prior to the invasion of Persia. It was sacked by the Aitolians in 220BC but was quickly regained and rebuilt. Eventually, it became a Roman town complete with a bishop and survived until the third century AD but it was laid waste by Alaric never to recover.

A modern road divides the site with the greater part of the ancient city on the west side. The ruins are largely at foundation level but strategically placed elevated viewing platforms offer a better perspective of the important areas. The remains of Roman baths indicate a very substantial building. It included various areas for cold baths, hot baths and for relaxation. The sculptures of the Asklepios family displayed in the museum were found in a place of worship in this baths complex. Nearby is a small theatre or odeon which was once covered. A network of footpaths leads to all parts of this extensive site which was once enclosed by fortified walls, still intact in parts. Near the eastern perimeter lies a building complex which included workshops, baths, two atriums, a chapel and a hall. Outstanding here is the magnificent mosaic depicting Dionysos' triumphal epiphany. Near here too is the river Helopotamos, earlier known as Vaphyras, which was navigable in ancient times. A footpath leads to the jetty area where there are remains of storerooms which may have been a port in ancient times.

Outside the main site and across the road lies the partially submerged sanctuary to Isis. Copies of sculptures now stand in the places where the originals were found. Nearby is the sanctuary of Demeter from around 500BC, the oldest known sanctuary in Macedonia. The offerings found there are displayed in the museum. Further south is a small theatre built in the reign of Philip V. It is unusual for a Greek theatre in that, apart from being built on an artificial hill, the seats were constructed of large bricks.

The modern museum lies back in the village amongst a cluster of souvenir shops and restaurants. Spacious and well laid out, many of the finds from Dion are displayed here as well as some early Iron Age finds from an extensive cemetery nearby.

The onward route to Litohoro means a return to the motorway but only as far as the next exit. The village is reached after a gentle climb over 4½ km (3 miles). **Litohoro** is a small modern town standing at the foot of the mountain. Although at no great altitude, only 300 to 400m (984 to 1,312ft), it has the feel of an alpine village. It may be an association of ideas with the snow capped mountain on hand but it could be equally inspired by the neat trimness of the village and the remarkable cleanliness. Unusually, this philosophy extended into the hotels too and Hotel Myrto reflected this fully. The platia remains the hub and is the terminus for the buses. Most of the restaurants are in this region, although a number lie opposite the park which is passed on entering the village. Also in the park region is the Tourist Information Office and nearby a small office of the Greek Alpine Club, tucked down a side street but well signposted. The latter is manned by part-time staff and open only in the summer months, from mid-June onwards.

Litohoro is an excellent base for exploring and walking Mount Olympos. Whilst scaling the very heights might appeal only to the very fit or vastly experienced walkers or climbers, there is much walking to be enjoyed on the mountain without tackling the peaks. There are three stages in the ascent. The first is from Litohoro to the spring at Prionia (1,100m/3,608ft), the second from Prionia to Refuge A (2,100m/6,888ft) and the final stage from the refuge to the summits (2,817m/9,240ft). For most walkers treading the well worn paths a guide is hardly necessary but Kostas Zolotas, who also runs Refuge A, is the official guide and knows the mountain better than anyone. He also speaks both English and German.

From Litohoro To Prionia (1,100m/3,608ft)

There are two ways to achieve this stage, either on foot or by car or taxi. A good road climbs from Litohoro over 18km (11 miles) to terminate at

The dramatic peaks of Mount Olympos

Walking through the spectacular Enippeas Gorge

The Enippeas river flowing down from Mount Olympos

The atmospheric ruins of Ag Dionysios monastery

Prionia. At the moment the first 7km (4 miles) are asphalted and the rest remains as stabilised track which is very dusty but kept in good order. There are plans to extend the surfaced section a little each year with the ultimate aim of providing a minibus service for walkers while restricting private cars. Much of the climbing in this 40-minute journey is achieved in the first part and, while the road is not difficult to drive, it must be taken slowly. Almost immediately after the current end of the hard surface is a viewpoint and stopping place on the left. Higher still, after 10km (6 miles), is the Stavros refuge which belongs to the Greek Mountain Club of Thessaloniki. It is open for most of the year offering both food and accommodation. After around 16km (10 miles), there is a track running back to the left which is signposted to the Monastery of Ag Dionysios.

The track down to the monastery is rough and the best option is to leave the car at the top and walk. It takes around 20 minutes to reach the atmospheric ruins which are now undergoing restoration after destruction by the Germans during World War II. There is a solitary priest in residence. A footpath leads a little way below the monastery to the Enippeas river.

The forest road terminates at Prionia which has parking space for a number of cars. A wooden and very basic taverna entered through saloon style swing doors adds rustic character as do the mules which are stationed there throughout the summer. The taverna sells drinks and simple meals in season. There is a spring too, opposite the taverna.

Walking this stage, from Litohoro to Prionia, is tough. The route follows along the scenic Enippeas Gorge but is constantly rising above and dipping down to cross it. The river is crossed four times in total. In summer the waters are low enough for this to be no problem but it is very different in spring when the snows are melting so it is wise to seek local information before June. The route, which is the E4 and waymarked with red dots, starts from the top of the village keeping the river on the right. This section requires around 5 hours walking time which makes it a tough day if the intention is to continue to Refuge A. For scenic excitement, this is the finest section of the walk and, for those interested in walking it for this reason, the alternative is to taxi to Prionia and walk the return to Litohoro. The flowers along this section are good only until early summer and they quickly fade as the flora moves higher up the mountain.

From Prionia To Refuge A (2,100m/6,888ft)

For anyone not too keen on walking, there is always the option of being taken up on horse back. This can be arranged at the Stavros refuge, or at Prionia, as mentioned above. The route for walkers is fairly straightforward. There is no drinking water available until the refuge is reached. The path is clear, easy to follow and without any sense of danger. Although the signs suggest about 2½ hours and the young and fit achieve this, 3 hours or longer is perhaps a more average time. For anyone interested in flowers, it could be a lot longer. The first part benefits from the woodland shade but eventually the trees thin out as the rocky limestone starts to dominate the scenery. Benches are positioned at strategic points in the lower part but they too run out.

Refuge A, or Spilios Agapitos, is situated on a rocky balcony and not easily seen until reasonably close. The start of the season depends on the snow situation but the hut opens sometime around the end of May or early June. It is a well ordered and well run refuge with sleeping accommodation for 90 people. Anyone planning to spend the night is advised to make a reservation by telephone and should take a sleeping bag liner; blankets are provided (Mount Olympus Refuge A [Spilios Agapitos] managed by Kostas Zolotas. Telephone for reservations on 0352 81800 in season and 0352 81329 at other times). Electricity is by generator which is switched off at 10pm sharp and there is no admittance after that time. The hut has running water, toilets and very cold showers. Food and drinks are available at a reasonable cost considering its location.

From Refuge A To The Peaks (2,817m/9,240ft)

Crowning this mountain is a dramatic group of peaks, Mytikas, Skala, Skolio and Stefani, of which Mytikas, standing at 2,817m (9,240ft), is the highest. The route, marked in red dots, starts from the back of the refuge and passes beneath Skala. Although it is possible to walk much of the way without too many problems, the final assault on this peak is both difficult and dangerous requiring nerve and a head for heights. It is possible to reach some of the other peaks too, like Skala and Stefani, but these are still very difficult if a little less so than Mytikas. Snow lies very late around some peaks and proper equipment is required if they are to be tackled.

All high mountains carry a health warning and this is certainly true of Olympos. Bad weather can arrive at any time. The peaks invariably cloud up around midday and on some days the clouds descend well below the refuge. Walking above the refuge is not for the inexperienced.

A Short Stroll Through The Enippeas Gorge 9km (6 miles)

There is the opportunity for a short circular walk which explores part of the spectacular Enippeas Gorge just below Prionia. Park the car at the head of the track leading down to the Monastery of Dionysios (see above). Keep to the left of the monastery to find the path down to the river, reached in around 25 minutes. Follow the E4 sign to Prionia which leads away to the right on the same side of the river. The sign suggests 1 hour to Prionia but for most mortals 1½ hours is probably more realistic. Shaded at times and easy to follow, the footpath climbs gently uphill crossing the river twice before Prionia is reached. From here it takes around 20 minutes walking along the track to reach the car.

Flowers of Mount Olympos

A very high mountain close to the sea, limestone geology, and a long period of geographical isolation are the influences which have helped to shape the very rich flora of this region.

Exactly which species are seen depends critically on the timing of the visit. Spring comes to the lowlands around the village sometime in March or April but it arrives much more slowly at higher levels. May sees more flowers blossom but it is not until June that things start to move above Prionia with virtually nothing in flower above the refuge at that time, depending on the lateness of the snow. July and August are the best months for flowers at the higher altitudes.

It is not practical to list here the vast catalogue of species but the few mentioned were recorded in the first week of June and were found between the monastery of Dionysios and Refuge A. Several species will be found higher in the mountains throughout June. In the woods near the monastery were a number of orchids including twayblade *(Listera ovata)* and the bird's nest orchid *(Neottia nidus-avis)*, both of which are common throughout Europe. *Pinguicula hirtella*, a lover of wet flushes, was found down by the river. Nearby was the charming blue and white flowered *Aquilegia amaliae* which also loves damp places and grows to an altitude of 2,200m (7,216ft). The route up towards Prionia uncovered more orchids including

Fritillaria messanensis

Saxifraga sempervirens

Viola graeca

Orchis simia (*Monkey Orchid*)

Orchis tridentata (Toothed Orchid), *O. quadripunctata* (Four Spotted Orchid) and the Monkey Orchid, *Orchis simia*. Another woodland species found growing in these parts was *Pyrola rotundifolia*. The star was the endemic *Jankaea heldreichii* found growing in a rocky crevice. It has a rosette of silvery leaves and blue flowers not unlike an African violet, both are of the *Gesneriaceae* family. More colonies were noticed higher up the mountain but none were in flower.

Above Prionia many of the species already mentioned persisted for some time. At higher levels, a mass of lily of the valley (*Convallaria majalis*), almost masked a number of *Fritillaria messanensis*. The ubiquitous blue flowered *Viola graeca* was inescapable. There is also a yellow form which is only occasional here but predominates on the south and west slopes of the mountain. Also common along the footpath was the pink flowered *Polygala nicaeensis* with occasional clumps of glistening white *Iberis sempervirens*. Rock crevices are home to some of the more interesting species and to two saxifrages in particular; *Saxifraga sempervirens* with its arched purple flowering stems and the white or sometimes delicate pink-flowered *S. scardica*. On the approach to Refuge A was a high altitude orchid, the beautiful, yellow *Orchis pallens* which flourishes up to around 2,300m (7,544ft). Finally, two species found in the region of the refuge which always warn that melting snow is not too far away, *Corydalis densiflora* and the yellow draba, *D. athoa*.

Tour 2 • Into Magnetic Magnesia and the Pilion (165km/102 miles)

Heading south it is again difficult to avoid using the toll road but it has the advantage of speed. There are two pay stations on the section down to Volos, the first guards the entrance to the Vale of Tembi (Tempe) and the second is located just beyond Larissa. It is possible to avoid the second by leaving the motorway at Larissa and taking the E92 which is signposted to Volos from that point. The roads are good the whole way and the journey requires only a few hours which leaves plenty of time for sight-seeing on the way down. The choice of Vizitsa as a base from which to tour the Pilion rested on its location and character, especially its beautiful platia. A number of other bases would serve equally well for exploring the region, Kala Nera perhaps if a seaside resort is preferred or Makrinitsa for another village of character.

A short distance down the motorway, **Leptokaria** is signposted off to the left. This is the first of a series of seaside towns, including Paralia Skotinas and Paralia Pandeleimona. At one time targeted for tourist development, this region attracted investment for a time but, with only narrow beaches and perhaps sharing too much of the cloud from the mountains, it soon lost popularity in favour of Halkidiki. There is plenty of accommodation in these resorts and, for those who prefer to stay by the sea, it offers an alternative to staying in Litohoro. Seen from the motor-

way, and near to Pandeleimona, are the substantial remains of a medieval fortress built by the Crusaders strategically placed to guard both the entrance to the Vale of Tembi and the Thermaic Gulf. Near here too is an information centre. The road sweeps almost suddenly into the Vale of Tembi. Like a huge slice taken from the mountain, the vale divides the two naked limestone massives, Olympos and Ossa. Through the vale flows the abundantly watered river Peneios, green under the plane and willow and the lushness that moisture brings. After killing the serpent Python at Delphi, Apollo came here to purify himself in the waters of the river. He fell in love with the nymph Daphne, daughter of the River Peneios, but she resisted his advances and fled begging her father to save her. He did so by turning her into a laurel tree. There is a divergence in the myths here but in the most romantic Apollo took a sprig of Laurel back to Delphi to plant by the Kastalian fountain.

The oasis of the Vale of Tembi lasts the whole of its 10km (6 miles) length. There are a number of lay-bys and parking places mainly on the right. Half way through the vale, on a hillock to the left, stands the Kastro

tis Orias (Castle of the Beautiful Maiden), a Frankish guard post. Once through the vale the vegetation changes to normal arid Mediterranean broken by olive groves. Larissa marks the parting of the ways for those preferring the toll free E92 route to Volos. Beyond Larissa, the plains with their acres of golden wheat dominate the view. The road to Volos leaves the motorway to the right only to sweep round and cross beneath it. It remains a fast road all the way into the busy port. Just before Volos are two

minor ancient sites both of which will require a short detour off to the
right. The first is **Sesklo** which claims to have the oldest acropolis in
Greece from 6,000BC as well as foundations of a palace. A little further on,
almost on entering Volos, is the turn for **Dimini**. Here are two beehive
tombs, another ancient acropolis and walls surviving from 1200BC and
before.

Parking in **Volos**, as usual in larger towns, is a problem but the roads are
laid out on a grid system and there is plenty of street parking to the north
of the main through routes.

Volos is the capital and economic centre of the prefecture of Magnesia.
It nestles beneath the green slopes of the Pilion mountains which rise to
the north-east. They peak at 1,610m (5,281ft) which is high enough to
attract winter snow and make a ski resort worthwhile. Founded only in
the nineteenth century, Volos now boasts a population of around 71,000.
The port handles much of the produce of Thessaly as well as passenger
traffic for the Sporades. There is not too much to persuade the casual
visitor to stay over long, except perhaps for the Archaeological Museum
which houses finds from the Bronze Age, very early pottery and sculptures from the sixth and fifth centuries BC. The work of modern Greek
artists is exhibited in the Municipal Gallery housed in the Town Hall.
Shoppers are best served in the area behind the quay and pedestrianised
streets just across the main Dimitriados street. The lively Friday market is
one of the highlights of the week. It fills the back streets with colour and
noise in the eastern quarter and is well worth a visit. At some time in the
past, there was a train which ran from Volos on a scenic route up to Milies,
near Vizitsa. Some effort has already been made to restore a section of the
route and the plan is to run the train as a tourist attraction. It seems miles
away from completion but the track, in the meantime, is popular with
walkers.

Signs to Argalasti and Agria lead in the right direction for Vizitsa. Once
through the town, the road follows first along the coast, shortly passing
through the unremarkable village of Agria. It is back to the coast at the
village of Malakion, the first of three small resorts of which Kala Nera is
the brightest. The road by-passes this resort but a brief diversion leads
along a tree-lined road looking onto a sandy, shingly beach. It is well
served by tavernas, café bars and with plenty of accommodation on hand,
at least fifteen hotels. Back on the main route, the left turn to Milies and
Vizitsa is quickly reached. A good road winds and twists its way into the
hills and, on reaching the bakers shop on the right advertising cheese
bread (see Feature Box) turn right into Milies. The road squeezes through
the village centre and continues on to terminate at the lower platia in
Vizitsa.

Vizitsa, like many of the Pilion villages, is draped over a wooded
hillside. A number of the tower houses have been restored by the EOT
(Greek National Tourist Office) to a high standard for use as tourist
accommodation. A cobbled trail leads from the lower square to an upper

platia sitting on an elevated balcony. Leafy green under the shade of huge plane trees, this large, secluded square is entirely devoted to serving the social needs of the village, leisurely eating, drinking and conversation. Territorially, the space is divided between three surrounding tavernas, one perched even higher on its own balcony. For the rest of the village, and there is not much more, it is a question of wandering around the narrow cobbled streets. The one and only village shop, located on the entrance road, serves just the most basic of needs.

Tour 3 • The Pilion (206km/128 miles)

The Pilion takes its name from the range of mountains which forms the peninsula enclosing the Pagasitic Gulf. Much of the central area is remarkable for its lush vegetation of broad-leaved trees and abundant streams in total contrast to the nearby mainland. If that seems enigmatic then so does the climate. It is said to be cooler and more agreeable in summer and mild in winter and, to cap that, there is sufficient snow on top of Agriolefkes, which reaches an altitude of a mere 1,350m (4,428ft), to run a successful winter ski resort. Beech, oak, chestnut and apple all grow with vigour and scattered randomly amongst all this greenery is a collection of charming villages, each one the same but each one different. It is a chance to roll back the years for the villages have remained unchanged over a long period. Some of the mansions have been restored but there is little in the way of modern development. Throughout the period of Turkish rule, Pilion managed to retain some independence and continued to trade with Europe. Many of the traders flourished and used their wealth to build fine mansions in a tower house style with a stone lower section supporting a half-timbered projecting second floor. Many of these houses are in a state of disrepair but restoration of many, supported by the EOT, is in hand. Two villages have been sufficiently restored to put them firmly on the tourist trail, Makrinitsa foremost and Vizitsa to a lesser extent. The churches too are distinctive, built in a low wide style and often with a separate bell-tower.

The area is good for walking too, it is riddled with old cobbled trails and footpaths between the villages. Unfortunately, there are no published maps for walkers although the Tourist Office in Volos has some information and may be able to help. There is one walk which is easy to find and follow; it is along the old railway line already mentioned. The most scenic start is from the old station, Paleostathmos, at Milies. It is a convenient place to start, and finish, since the old station has been converted into a taverna which is locally well known for the quality of its food.

Touring the villages can take time and even this modest tour which captures the heart of the Pilion can spill over to a second day or more without too much stopping. Even though the roads wind and twist, sometimes unnecessarily so, they are generally well surfaced and good to

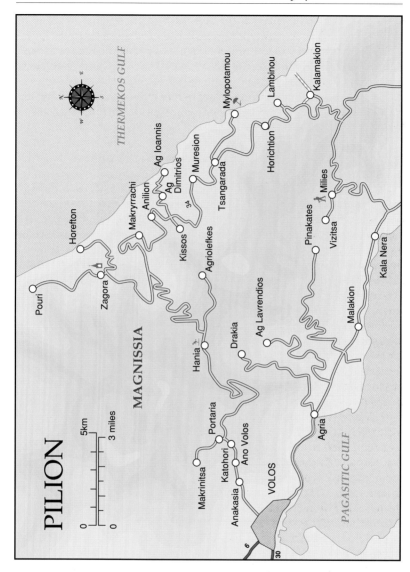

drive with the provision that an ever watchful eye is kept open for the occasional pot-hole. One local explanation for the winding nature of the roads, offered in all seriousness, was that the road builders were paid by the kilometre. Fuel is not a great problem and is available in a number of the villages.

On leaving Vizitsa it is worth sparing a glance at the vertical rock cutting on the left just outside the village. This uninspiring habitat is home to the magnificent *Campanula incurva* which clings to the rock face and covers itself with huge pale blue urn-shaped bells, surely the largest bells of any *campanula.* The narrow roads through **Milies** discourage thoughts of stopping but there is room for parking near the church and platia. The village tumbles and sprawls around the hillside but it does have a small centre with shops. A number of houses here have also been restored as guest houses.

Turn left on reaching the junction. Chestnut trees shade the way on the climb towards the crest and there is a junction to watch for signposted Tsangarada. Pilion is another good area for wild flowers and the June roadsides are littered with purple vetch, yellow broom and pink cistus. Lambinou is no more than a sleepy hamlet but the excursion needed from the road is very short.

High up, the road clings to the mountain side faithfully following contours around endless convolutions, like a cornice on a verdant cliff which slides incessantly into the blue waters of the Aegean. The coastline changes with every bend along the drive which is one of the most scenic in Greece. The scattered hamlet of Horichiton slides past with barely a notice and beyond the route cuts inland a little to negotiate one of the deeper valleys. The sign for Tsangarada is passed but, before the village centre is reached, there is a turn off down to **Mylopotamou**, one of the finest beaches on the peninsula. It is a fairly lengthy wind down to the parking area near the bottom. From here steps lead down to the beach. Two small sandy bays linked together by an archway through the rock are lapped by the clean waters of the Aegean. Their natural beauty is in no way impaired by the café bar or taverna which are tucked away above the beach area. This is a locally popular beauty spot so expect it to be crowded in high season, especially weekends.

Tsangarada is strung out along the mountainside at different levels and is another of the villages which is difficult to appreciate without exploring it on foot. Hidden amongst all the vegetation are at least a dozen hotels or pensions but the pride of the village is the 1,000-year-old plane tree in the main square. The road continues its tortuous route following the folds of the mountain which become more exaggerated now as the valleys cut still deeper into Mount Pilion. The hamlet of **Muresion**, set in apple growing country, slips by and the road off left to Kissos is reached next. Shortly after this, turn right to pass through the village of Ag Dimitrios and continue down to the sea front at Ag Ioannis. Here the road looks onto a long sweep of course sand and shingle beach on one side and a line of tavernas, hotels and supermarkets on the other.

Back on the main road, another deep ravine forces a long detour en route to **Makryrrachi**. One of the larger villages, Makryrrachi has suffered an attack of modern concrete structures which dilute the influence of the traditional Pilion homes. Another detour around the mountainside, passing the road off left to Hania which is eventually the return route, leads on to **Zagora**. This is the largest village in the Pilion. Its prosperity in earlier times was due in no small part to the nearby port of Horefton from which it was able to export textiles, silk, ribbons and fruit. The two Byzantine

Regional Specialities

Both the cheese bread (*tiropsomo*), and the olive bread (*liopsomo*), are irresistible once tried and the best known bakery for these lies at the junction of the Milies road. They are made in large, flat rounds which you can buy also as halves or quarters. There are two specialities to look out for on the taverna menus too; *spetzofai*, a spicy sausage and pepper stew, and *kouneli stifado* which is rabbit stew. The local *tsipouro*, a strong alcoholic drink best likened to ouzo without the aniseed flavour, is especially good in this region and inexpensive.

churches of Ag Giorgios and Ag Kiriaki are both worth a visit for their finely carved ikon screens. **Horefton** itself is no longer a port but a pleasant fishing village with a sweep of coarse sand and shingle beach backed by woodland. It has a surprising number of hotels, furnished apartments and pensions scattered around as well as tavernas and campsites.

There is some backtracking up the winding road to Zagora to continue on to **Pouri**, the end of the line. The road terminates in an area for parking and turning around. Only a small village which almost tumbles into the sea, it has an invitingly shaded three-tiered platia ranging up the steep hillside worth trying for the views out to the Aegean.

Returning from here covers the same ground until well past Zagora but, viewed from a different perspective, it could almost be totally new. Turn right at the junction to head over the mountain towards the Pagasitic Gulf. A long winding climb with a few tight bends thrown in leads over the mountain pass to the village of **Hania,** not so much a village as a collection of tourist facilities now that the ski resort has developed nearby. Expect hotels, tavernas, gift shops and honey but blink and it might be missed. The short diversion up to the snow centre to see the ski facilities ends in a car parking area. From there a cobbled footpath leads the rest of the way to the facilities which includes a café.

A downhill section follows from Hania with excellent views to the Pagasitic Gulf and over Volos, particularly at lower levels. The turn to **Makrinitsa** arrives with the village of Portaria. Not without justification, Makrinitsa is built up as the showpiece traditional village. Ranging down the mountainside, its central platia, at 625m (2,050ft), provides an elevated view down onto the gulf. It was founded in 1204 by refugees from the sacking of Constantinople but its proximity to Volos accounts for its past prosperity. There are some fine restored tower houses but equally it has some fine churches, six in all plus a monastery. Beware, to see all the churches means walking to the bottom one at 300m (984ft) and up to the

The clear blue waters of the Aegean at Mylopotamou beach

A peaceful platia in Vizitsa

Many fine traditional houses make Makrinitsa the showpiece village of the Pilion

Fresh fish is a popular buy at Volos market

To Pinakates On Foot

This short easy 45-minute walk starts from Vizitsa. Most maps show a road between the two but in reality although there is a track there is no access for motor vehicles from Vizitsa. Set off straight ahead from the right hand side of the lower square car park, ignoring the trail off right to the upper platia. At the first fork take the path to the right which leads down to join the track; go right here. The track winds around the hillside but divides before the village, keep right for Pinakates. To say it is a sleepy village might be an overstatement, certainly not much seems to move, but the village shop in the small platia does serve drinks.

top one at 800m (2,624ft). Fortunately one of the finest churches, Ag Ioannis, is conveniently sited right by the main platia and the Monastery of Theotokos is by the clock tower.

The route back to Vizitsa leads first down to Volos, cutting across the eastern corner of the town, before heading out on the now familiar coastal route via Kala N.

Tour 4 • And Back To Athens

Volos lies 326km (202 miles) from Athens and the quickest way, if time is important, is back via the fast National road. There is a much pleasanter route which involves a short ferry crossing from Glifa to the island of Evia then crossing the island to emerge at the bridge joining the mainland. From here the National road can be joined for the final leg to Athens. The distance is a little longer, about 370km (229 miles) in total, but it is a much slower route. If an overnight stop is planned, the best option is to choose one of the northern resorts on Evia, like Pefki or Vassilika. After Vassilika accommodation seems to dry up completely until down at Halkis.

Additional Information

Places to Visit

Dion
Site and Museum
Open: Monday 12.30-7pm, Tuesday to
Friday 8am-7pm and Saturday and
Sunday 8.30am-3pm.

Volos
Archaeological Museum
Open: daily 8.30am-3pm. Closed on
Monday.

Accommodation

There is an excellent booklet printed in
English which lists some 180 hotels,
pensions and traditional settlements in
Volos and Pilion. Each entry is accompanied by a photograph and relevant
details. This is available from the Union
of Hotel Keepers of Magnesia Area, 47
Korai, Volos ☎ 0421 20273. A selection is
listed below:

HOTELS
AGHIOS IOANNIS: TELEPHONE PREFIX 0426
Hotel Aloe (B) ☎ 31241 & 0421 27949
Hotel Galini (C) ☎ 31234
Hotel Kelly (C) ☎ 31231
Hotel Sofoklis (C) ☎ 31230/31531
Pension Sevilli (B) ☎ 31238

Manos (C)
Furnished Apartments
☎ 31110-1

HANIA: TELEPHONE PREFIX 0421
Hotel Hania (B) ☎ 96421
Hotel Manthos (C) ☎ 96402

HOREFTO: TELEPHONE PREFIX 0426
Hotel Katerina (C) ☎ 22772
Hotel Maraboy (C) ☎ 22534/22200
Hotel Votsala (C) ☎ 22001/22830
Pension Erato ☎ 22445

Dimitios (C)
Furnished Apartments ☎ 22803-4

Hermes (C)
Furnished Apartments ☎ 23071/22771

KALA NERA: TELEPHONE PREFIX 0423
Hotel Izela (C) ☎ 22379

Hotel Argo (D) ☎ 22371
Hotel Helena (D) ☎ 22296
Hotel Victoria (D) ☎ 22219
Pension Alcyon (B) ☎ 22364/22169
Pension Rodia (B) ☎ 22100/22070

LITOHORO: TELEPHONE PREFIX 0352
Aphrodite ☎ 81415

Dion (nr Litohoro)
Hotel Dion ☎ 0351 53682

Enipeas ☎ 81325
Leto (C) ☎ 22122
Markesia ☎ 81831
Myrto ☎ 81398/81498
Park ☎ 81252/81263

MAKRINITSA: TELEPHONE PREFIX 0421
Archontiko Repana (A)
Traditional Pension ☎ 99584/99067

Archonitiko Karamarli (B)
Traditional Pension ☎ 99570

Pension Theoflos (A) ☎ 99435
Pension Tzimerou (A) ☎ 99348

MILIES: TELEPHONE PREFIX 0423
Two more Traditional Pensions:
Evagelinaki (A) ☎ 86714
Paluios Stathmos (A) ☎ 86425

PORTARIA: TELEPHONE PREFIX 0421
Hotel Portaria (B) ☎ 99014
Hotel Pelias (C) ☎ 99290-1
Pension Tis Marios (A) ☎ 99535

TSANGARADA: TELEPHONE PREFIX 0423
Hotel San Stefano (C) ☎ 49218

Alkioni (A)
Traditional Pension ☎ 49334

Fakistra (A)
Traditional Pension ☎ 47866/49470

Pension Kentayros (B) ☎ 49233
Pension Konaki (B) ☎ 49481

VIZITSA: TELEPHONE PREFIX 0423
All the following are traditional
pensions:

Contoy (A) ☎ 86793
Kyriakopoulou (A) ☎ 86373

Karagianopoulou (A) ☎ 86373
Vergou (B) ☎ 86293/86480

VOLOS: TELEPHONE PREFIX 0421
Hotel Park (B)
2 Diligiorgi ☎ 36511-5

Hotel Alexandros (B)
3 Topali ☎ 31221-4

Hotel Nefeli (B)
10 Koumounourou ☎ 30211-3

Hotel Adamitos (C)
3 Athen. Diakou ☎ 21117-9

Hotel Iolkos (C)
25 Dimitriados ☎ 23416

Hotel Kypseli (C)
1 Ag. Nikolaou ☎ 24420/26020

Hotel Argo (D)
165 Dimitriafos ☎ 25372

Hotel Iasson (D)
1 Pavlou Mela ☎ 26075/24347

CAMPING
* = Open all year

Litohoro
Plaka
Apollon ☎ 0352 22109
Delfini ☎ 0351 23476 & 0352 22419
Helena ☎ 0352 22148/81280
Minerva ☎ 0352 22177-8
Olympus Zeus ☎ 0352 22115/7

Platamonas
Afroditi ☎ 0352 91300
Castle ☎ 03532 41252

Volos - Pilion
Kato Gazea
Hellas*
☎ 0423 22267

Platanias
Louisa Camping
☎ 0423 65660 & 0421 42456

Kato Gazea
Marina
☎ 0423 22277/22167

Sykia
Kato Gazea
☎ 0423 22279

YOUTH HOSTEL
Litohoro
Cosma Doumbioti 2
☎ 0352 81311/82176

Transport

Frequent services to Thessaloniki and to Katerina; 3 buses daily to Athens. The nearest railway station lies 9km/6 miles away, to the north-west.

Buses
There are two bus companies providing a service to Athens, KTEL and OSE (10 buses daily). Buses also run to Larissa (9 daily), Litohoro, Katerini, Thessaloniki (4 daily), Trikala and Kalambaka (3 daily).

There is an excellent local bus service which radiates out from Volos to the Pilion villages. Unfortunately, these services are only really convenient for visitors based in Volos and not helpful for touring around between the various villages.

From Volos buses run daily to: Milies/Vizitsa (6), Portaria/ Makrinitsa (8), Promira/Platania (3), Makryrrachi/ Zagora (via Hania, 1), Horefto (1), Ag Ioannis/ Kissos (2), Afissos (5), Kala Nera (8) and Zagora/ Pouri (3).

Trains
There are daily trains to Athens (9),Thessaloniki via Larissa (8), Larissa (12) and Kalambaka (4).

Ferry Boat Services
There are two boats daily which ply the route Skiathos, Skopelos (calling at Glossa), Alonissos and return. In addition there are direct boats to Skopelos calling at Skopelos Port.

Tourist Information Centres

Litohoro
Municipal Information Office
The Park
Open: only in high season.

Volos
Riga Fereou Square ☎ 0421 36233

Tourist Police ☎ 0421 2709

GREECE FACT FILE

Accommodation

Hotels

These are classified by the National Tourist Office of Greece (NTOG—EOT when in Greece) into De Luxe, AA and A class which are subject to a minimum price structure only. Bars, restaurants and swimming pools are the facilities that you expect to find but, on a cautionary note, the class in itself is not a guarantee of the standard of service. Mostly, higher grade hotels are found in the bigger cities and in regions where there is a demand.

In addition there are B, C and D classes for which the room rates are fixed by the NTOG. These hotels are obliged to display their category and price behind the door of each room. There is no C in the Greek alphabet so this class is represented by the gamma sign 'Γ.' Extra charges described as taxes or service may be added to the final rate and you need to check each time. Note that the charge is a room charge, not a charge per person and may or may not include breakfast. Room charges are seasonal with low, mid and high season rates. It is possible to bargain, especially for a stay of three days or more, but you are most likely to succeed when business is slack out of high season. Generally the C class hotels have rooms with bathrooms as do many of the D class but here it is not obligatory. Away from big cities, these hotels are often family run and offer a good level of cleanliness and comfort. The lower grade hotels may not have bar or restaurant facilities, except for breakfast.

The Tourist Office itself runs a chain of Xenia Hotels (A, B & C class) scattered throughout the country which are often delightfully situated. These are detailed, where appropriate, at the end of each chapter. There are a small number of motels too offering bed and breakfast accommodation and these are mostly located on main road sites.

Pensions

Accommodation of this kind in small hotels or private houses can also be very good. Again, the standards are controlled and graded by the NTOG but you really need to take each one on its own merit and do not hesitate to inspect before you commit yourself. At best they are very good with private bathroom facilities and a kindly Greek family to fuss over and take care of you.

Villas and Apartments

There are many scattered around popular tourist locations. Many are in the hands of letting agencies who place them with tour operators. One technique for searching them out is to read through the holiday brochures of companies who specialise in this type of accommodation. Many of these villas are often not in use until late May or early June so, if you are around before then, it is possible to make private arrangements on the spot, sometimes at very attractive rates.

Rooms
In the main tourist areas, there are generally plenty of private houses offering rooms. And, if you are looking for budget accommodation, some of these will be hard to beat. If you arrive in Greece by ferry, the chances are that you will be met at the dockside by a dancing cluster of assorted 'Room to Let' notices, otherwise enquire at the local NTOG office or with the Tourist Police who also help in these matters.

Traditional Settlements
This is a recent development organised by the NTOG in which old houses have been restored in their original architecture but now with modern facilities. At present there are three locations in the Peloponnese, five locations in northern Greece and three on islands. Precise locations are given in the appropriate chapters. Reservations for these can be made at the NTOG head office in Athens and further details can be obtained from NTOG offices in home countries.

Camping
Camping in areas other than on official camping grounds is not permitted in any part of the country. It is something which the Greek authorities tend to get uptight about, especially in popular tourist regions. However, there are now an increasing number of camp sites appearing for both caravans and tents. These are often set in attractive locations. Standards vary as always, some are well equipped with modern facilities and are open all year round. Other sites are run by the NTOG and again the rates for all the services are fixed. Further details from: Association of Greek Camping, 102 Solonos Street, 10680 Athens ☎ 362 1560

Banks

When you think of changing money, try to think of it as a morning job. This advice will become much clearer when you study the bank opening hours which are: Monday to Thursday 8am-2pm. Friday 8am-1.30pm.

In large cites and in popular tourist locations, certain banks may open for a short period in the late afternoon. The best place for changing money in Athens outside the accepted banking hours or at weekend is at: National Bank of Greece, 2 Karageorgi Serias Street. Open: Monday to Thursday 8am-2pm & 3.30-6.30pm. Friday 8am-1.30pm & 3-6.30pm. Saturday 9am-3pm. Sunday 9am-1pm.

Some banks now have 'hole-in-the-wall' cash dispensers which will accept Eurocheque cards. Oddly enough, foreign services are not always available through these tills on Bank Holidays when most needed!

The only round the clock banking service, seven days a week, is provided by the Agricultural Bank of Greece at East Air Terminal (International). At West Air Terminal, the National Bank of Greece is open from 7am-11pm, seven days a week.

Climate

The weather is very often the main consideration. Some people enjoy hot weather, others do not so, if you have the freedom, you can choose for yourself.

The flowers tell you that spring is in the air as early as March but the temperatures do not start to rise significantly until April and May. In coastal regions both these months are delightful, fresh, warm, certainly warm enough for shorts on sunny days, but still with a risk of the odd rainy day. Generally the region has a Mediterranean climate which means mild, wet winters and hot, dry summers. That gives a picture of the rainfall, plenty of rainy days in the winter months but generally becoming dry through April and May with summer rain largely confined to short thunder storms. It is a very different picture in the mountain regions which are much colder in winter, often with snow on the high peaks, and slightly cooler in summer with a higher risk of rainy days.

June sees the temperatures warming steadily towards summer heat with the evenings and nights becoming warmer too. Throughout July, August into September, the heat is really on. Hot by day and hot by night. It seems much easier to sleep in the heat of the day than in the night-time heat. The days are made more bearable by the wind, the Meltemi, which blows incessantly throughout, rising and fading with the sun. However, the Meltemi only affects the eastern half of the mainland and does not reach over to Epirus or to the western side of the Peloponnese. It feels much more humid in those areas without it.

High summer is not the best time for touring unless you are prepared to stay in the mountain areas where the temperatures are still high but the air feels fresher and where, blissfully, it cools off in the evening.

Sometime, usually late in September, a short unsettled spell brings an end to the summer heat. Temperatures fall significantly and the air feels fresh again. Good weather continues through October into November but with an ever increasing risk of rainy days. The risk of rain is significantly higher in the mountain regions.

The above picture describes an average pattern which is not the same as a forecast. The summer is reliably hot but there can be a fair variation from the norm in spring and autumn.

Average Daily Temperatures

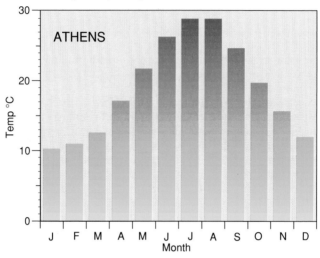

Average Monthly Rainfall

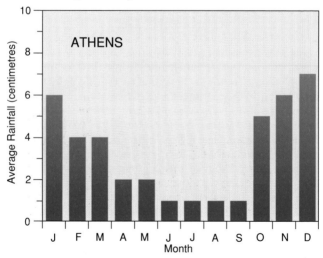

Average Daily Temperatures

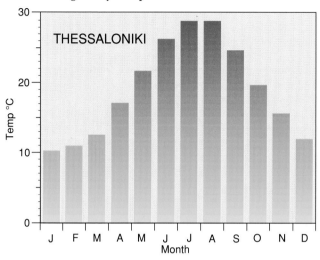

Average Monthly Rainfall

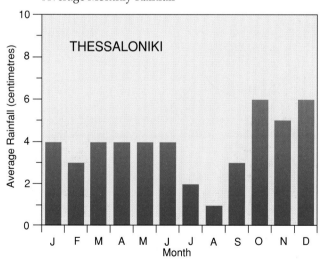

Crime and Theft

The incidence of crime and theft is rising in Athens and other large cities but it still remains at a relatively low level. There is no need to feel threatened in any way, even throughout the evening but it is sensible to be cautious late at night, especially women on their own.

Many hotels have safety deposit boxes available for guests at a small charge. Otherwise, keep valuables out of sight. This is particularly true if you have a car. Cameras, personal stereos and the like are best carried with you but if you need to leave them in the car make sure they are locked in the boot.

If you are unfortunate enough to suffer a loss through theft or carelessness then report it to the tourist police by dialling 171.

If your loss includes a passport then you will need to contact your Embassy. See page 241.

Currency & Credit Cards

Foreign currency in excess of $1,000 US must be declared on entry. Failure to comply may result in fines or confiscation. There is no limit on gold or gold coins. Importation of the Greek *drachma* too is limited to 100,000.

There are controls on the exportation of currency. Tourists can take out up to 20,000 *drachma* plus foreign currencies up to $1,000 US. Higher amounts are allowed if there has been an import declaration.

Money Matters

The local currency is the *drachma* which is indicated by drx or simply Dx (ΔP) before the number. *Drachma* notes commonly in circulation include 10,000, 5,000, 1,000, 500, 100 and 50 with coins of 50, 20, 10 ,5, 2 and 1 *drachma* value. (Avoid bringing home coins and low value notes since most banks refuse them).

Travellers cheques, Eurocheques and hard currencies are freely accepted at banks, Post Offices and Exchange Bureaus. Major credit cards and charge cards are also widely accepted in hotels, shops and restaurants in the large cities. In provincial regions, their use is mostly restricted to hotels and sometimes to only the larger ones. When driving in the countryside, do not count on credit cards to pay for fuel.

Although it is possible to get a cash advance on a credit card, there still seems to be some suspicion of this transaction. Only certain banks will co-operate and the best ones to try are the National Bank of Greece and the Commercial Bank. There is a minimum size of transaction, around 15,000 *drachma*.

Always take your passport when changing money. Even though the production of a passport may not be a necessary requirement, the Greeks rely on them as a means of identification. You may even be asked for it when purchasing an internal flight ticket. In terms of commission, the cheapest place to change money is at a bank and the worst place is usually the hotel reception.

Disabled Facilities

While there is an awareness of this problem, few practical steps have been taken to improve matters. As yet only the international hotels provide anything like adequate facilities. Street ramps are starting to appear in the main cities but in other places the pavements are non existent or barely fit for even the most able.

Embassies and Consulates

Foreign Embassies and Consulates in Greece are:

Australia
37 D Soutsou Street & An Tsocha
115 21 Athens
☎ 6447303

Canada
4 I. Genadiou Street
115 21 Athens
☎ 7239511-9

New Zealand
15-17 Tsocha Street
115 21 Athens
☎ 6410311- 5

USA
Embassy-Consulate
91 Vass. Sophias Avenue
115 21 Athens
☎ 721951-9 & 7218 400

UK
Embassy-Consulate
1 Ploutarchou Street
106 75 Athens
☎ 7236211-19

Vice Consulate
45 Thessaloniki Street
Kavala
☎ (051) 223704

Vice Consulate
2 Votsi Street
Patra
☎ (061) 277329

Consulate
8 Venizelou Street
Eleftherias Square
Thessaloniki
☎ (031) 278006/269984

Electricity

Mains electricity in Greece is supplied at 220 volts AC with just a few rural districts still on 110 DC. Electrical equipment should be fitted with a continental two pin plug or an appropriate adapter used.

Greek Time

Greek normal time is 2 hours ahead of GMT. The clocks advance one hour for summertime starting the last Sunday in March and ending the last Sunday in September.

America and Canada: Greek normal time is ahead of time in America, 7 hours ahead of Eastern Standard, 8 hours ahead of Central,

9 hours ahead of Mountain and 10 hours ahead of Pacific Time.

Australia and New Zealand: Greek normal time is 7½ hours behind South Australia, 8 hours behind New South Wales, Tasmania and Victoria and 10 hours behind time in New Zealand. These differences relate to GMT but, to take into account clock changes for Daylight Saving hours, the following corrections should be made: add 1 hour to these differences from late September to the end of March and subtract 1 hour from late March to the end of September.

Health Care

For minor ailments like headaches or tummy upsets, head for the chemist shop (*farmakion*). If you need a further supply of prescription drugs make sure to take a copy of your prescription and the chances are that you will be able to get them, and cheaply too. Most of the chemists, certainly in the large towns seem to speak English.

If it is a doctor or dentist you require, the chemist shop again should be able to assist. If that does not work then contact the Tourist Police. There are English speaking doctors and dentists in most large towns.

Problems really start if hospital treatment is required. European countries have reciprocal arrangements with the Greeks for free medical treatment, subject to certain restrictions. For this reason British visitors should take an E111 form obtained from the Post Offices. The story does not end there. To operate the scheme you need to find the local Greek Social Insurance office (IKA) who, after inspecting your E111, will direct you to a registered doctor or dentist. If you are in a region remote from an IKA office then you must pay privately for your treatment and present your bills to an IKA official before you leave Greece. Up to half your costs may be refunded. The best answer is to ensure that you have adequate holiday insurance cover.

Emergency treatment, sunburn, broken bones etc, is free in state hospitals. The situation is less happy if you require treatment as an in patient. In many of these hospitals, nursing care is restricted only to medical treatment and it is left to the family to supply general nursing care, drinks, food and even blankets. It is generally preferable to activate private medical insurance.

Health Hazards

Some of the more obvious ones can be avoided with a little care. Sunburn and sunstroke fall into this category. The sun is very burning even on a hazy day and great care is needed in protecting yourself, particularly at the start of your holiday. Sun creams help considerably but, at least for the first few days, take some very light clothing to cover up and control the exposure of your skin to the sun. A slowly acquired tan lasts longer.

Mosquitoes can be a nuisance in the evening and throughout the night. If you sit or dine outside in the evening, particularly near trees, either cover up your arms and legs or use insect repellent. An electric machine which slowly vaporises a pellet is very efficient, especially in a closed room. Anthisan cream is an effective treatment for bites, particularly if applied immediately.

Care is needed on the beach to avoid stings from jelly fish and, in rocky regions, from sea urchins. If you are unlucky enough to have a brush with the latter then it is important to ensure that all the spines are properly removed. Wearing beach shoes will give your feet some protection from stings of this nature.

Stomach upsets are perhaps the most common ailment. The excess olive oil used in cooking and over salads can be a cause of this so take care with oily foods, at least to start with. The digestive system adjusts to this within a few days and you can soon eat giant beans swimming in oil without fear. Squeeze plenty of fresh lemon over your food to counter the oil and, if still troubled, an acidic drink, like Coca-Cola, helps to settle things. Drinking wine to excess can cause similar symptoms too. More serious are the upsets caused by bad water and bad food. Generally the water in Greece is good to drink but in high summer it pays to be more careful and use bottled water which is freely available. Avoiding food poisoning is not always possible but there are elementary precautions that can help. Most tavernas prepare cooked dishes for the lunch time trade and these are left keeping warm until finally sold. If they are still there in the evening, and they often are, avoid them. Ask for something which will require grilling or roasting.

Holiday Insurance

Whichever holiday insurance you choose, make sure that the cover for medical expenses is more than adequate. It helps too if there is an emergency 24 hour contact to take care of arrangements, including repatriation if necessary. Injuries caused whilst taking part in certain hazardous pursuits are normally excluded from medical cover. Look carefully at the specified hazardous pursuits; in recent times, injuries caused by riding a moped or motor-bike have been added to the list by some insurers.

Language

Many Greeks speak good English, especially in the large towns and in tourist areas. Children learn it in state schools and most of them attend private schools as well. After all, English is the official second language in Greece and all official notices are presented in Greek and English, at least the more recent notices. Therein lies the danger. It is all too easy to expect and rely on every Greek to speak English which is clearly not the case when you move into country areas.

Some knowledge of the Greek language is not only useful to help you get by, but can enhance enormously the pleasure of your holiday. The Greeks really warm to you if you make the slightest effort with their language. Do not worry about perfection in pronunciation in the beginning, just give it a go. The Greeks are very outgoing and, if they have any English, they will try it out no matter how fractured it is. Take a leaf from their book. As long as you make an effort, the Greeks will love you for it and once you can string a few words together you might find their hospitality overwhelming.

Perhaps the biggest hurdle to getting started is the Greek alphabet itself. If you take a little time to study it, you will find it is not really so different. Isolate the letters which are unique to the Greek alphabet and the remainder generally follow the sequence of the English alphabet. The language is phonetic so time taken over learning the sounds of the letters will be well rewarded in subsequent progress. Two pieces of advice to get you started on the right foot. (1) Treat all vowels equally and do not attempt to lengthen them. (2) Avoid breaking a word down into syllables as in English, instead, follow the stress pattern indicated by the accent in the word.

The Alphabet

Capitals	Small		Name of the letter
A	α	'Αλπα	Alfa
B	β	Βητα	Vita
Γ	γ	Γαμμα	Ghama
Δ	δ	Δελτα	Dhelta
E	ε	'Εψιλον	Epsilon
Z	ζ	Ζητα	Zita
H	η	'Ητα	Ita
Θ	θ	Θητα	Thita
I	ι*	Γιοτα	Iota
K	κ	Καπα	Kapa
Λ	λ	Λαμδα	Lamdha
M	μ	Μι	Mi
N	ν	Νι	Ni
Ξ	ξ	Ξι	Ksi
O	ο	'Ομιξρο	Omikron
Π	π	Πι	Pi
P	ρ	Ρο	Ro
Σ	σ(ς) **	Σημα	Sighma
T	τ	Ταυ	Taf
Y	υ	'Υψιλον	Ipsilon
Φ	Φ	φΦι	Fi
X	χ	Χι	Khi
Ψ	ψ	Ψι	Psi
Ω	ω	Ωμεγα	Omegha

*The ι is not dotted as in English. When it is, means a stress accent.
** (ς) is used only at the end of the word.

244

Dipthongs

αι   **e** in met
αυ   **av** as in avoid or af in after
ευ   **ev** as in ever or ef as in left
οι   **e** as in feet
ου   **oo** as in mood

Double Consonants

mp   **b** at the beginning of words; mb in the middle
vt   **d** at the beginning of words; nd in the middle
tz   **dz** as in adze
gg = ng   in the middle of a word
gk = g   **g** at the beginning; ng in the middle

Numbers

The numbers 1, 3 and 4 (and all numbers ending in them) have three forms, masculine, feminine and neteur. In this list the phonetic words are given in place of the Greek.

1 — *ena (n), enas (m) or mia (f)*
2 — *theo*
3 — *tria (n), tris (m & f)*
4 — *tessera (n), tessaris (m & f)*
5 — *pende*
6 — *eksi*
7 — *efta*
8 — *octo*
9 — *enya*
10 — *theka*
11 — *entheka*
12 — *thotheka*
13 — *thekatria*
14 — *thekatessera*
etc up to twenty
20 — *eekosee*
21 — *eekosee ena (n & m), mia (f)*
30 — *treeanda*
40 — *seranda*
50 — *peninda*
60 — *eksinda*
70 — *evthominda*
80 — *ogthonda*
90 — *eneninda*
100 — *ekato*
130 — *ekato treeanda*
200 — *theakosea*
300 — *triakosea*
1000 — *hilia*

Days Of The Week:
Monday — *Theftera*
Tuesday — *Treetee*
Wednesday — *Tetartee*
Thursday — *Pemptee*
Friday — *Paraskevee*
Saturday — *Savato*
Sunday — *Kiriakee*

Months Of The Year:
January — *Eeanuareos*
February — *Fevruareos*
March — *Marteos*
April — *Apreeleos*
May — *Maeos*
June — *Eeuneos*
July — *Eeuleos*
August — *Avyustos*
September — *Septemvreos*
October — *Octovreos*
November — *Noemvreos*
December — *Thekemvreos*

Useful Phrases:
Yes — *neh*
No — *ockee*
Please — *parakalo*
Thank you — *efharreesto*
Hello and goodbye — *yasas*
Good morning — *kaleemera*
Good evening — *kaleespera*
Goodnight — *kaleeneekta*
How are you? — *tee kanete?*
Do you speak English? — *meelatee angleeka*
When? — *poteh?*
I want — *thelo*
Where is/are? — *poo eene?*
... the post office? — *poo eene to takeethromeeo?*
... the tourist office — *poo eene to grafeeo toureesmoo?*
... the museum? — *poo eene to mooseeo?*
... the bus station — *poo eene o stathmos ton leoforeeon?*
... the toilet — *poo eene ee tooaletes?*
Hotel — *ksenothoheeo*
Perhaps you have — *meepos ekehteh*
... a single room — *ena mono thomateeo*
... a double room — *ena theeplo thomateeo*
... with bath — *meh banyeeo*
... with shower — *meh dush*
Shop — *to magazee*

Market — *agora*
How much? — *posso?*
How many? — *possa?*
How much does it cost? — *posso kanee?*
How much do they cost? — *posso kanoonee?*
Open/closed — *anikto/kleesto*
Stamp(s) — *gramatossimo/gramatossima*
Envelope(s) — *fakelo(a)*
One kilo — *ena kilo*
Half a kilo — *meeso kilo*
Two kilo — *theo kila*
Apple(s) — *meelo(a)*
Orange(s) — *portokalee(eea)*
Tomatoes — *domates*
Cucumber — *angouree*
Lettuce — *maroolee*
Doctor — *yatros*
Pharmacy— *farmakeeo*
Hospital — *nosokomeeo*
Police — *asteenomeea*

Place Names

With no official transliteration, the latinisation of the Greek alphabet is open to various interpretations which leads to much confusion. The conversion of the double consonants, for example, is one cause of difficulty. The Greek mp is pronounced as b at the start of a word but mb in the middle. A Greek word starting with mp is almost invariably Latinised to begin with b but in the middle of the word both mp and mb can be observed. The Vale of Tempe is also seen as the Vale of Tembi. Vowel sounds, especially e and i, do not always strictly correspond so there is a tendency to substitute the more phonetically correct, as in Tembi, the last example. Some single consonants have no strict equivalent either, such as X, pronounced as the ch in loch, and this is Latinised to ch, which is a mile away phonetically, or h which is a little better. The village of Xora appears as Chora or Hora. All these difficulties are reflected in the spelling of place names. Pick up three different maps and it is more than likely that many of the same villages will have three different spellings. The philosophy adopted for this book is firstly to follow the spelling observed on the sign outside the village or, since many villages are without name boards, use the spelling which leads to a more accurate pronunciation.

Luggage

Since Greece is a full member of the EEC, it is very likely that, should you forget your favourite brand of toothpaste, you will be able to buy it in the shops there. All leading brands of food and products are freely available, give or take some national peculiarities. Brands of tea and breakfast cereal fall into this category. The Greeks do not normally start the day with breakfast instead they nibble the morning away with their own versions of fast food, cheese pies (*tiropitta*) and *souvlaki* in pitta bread are well favoured. However, a limited range of breakfast cereals can be bought in some popular tourist regions. With tea it is a little easier, if you have a favourite brand of tea or tea bags then it is easy to find room for some in your luggage. If you are self catering it is wise to take teacloths and rubbish bags with you.

There are a few other items which are worth considering if only to save time shopping when you are there:

A universal sink plug — this is useful when travelling.

An electric mosquito repeller and tablets — these are readily available in Greece but small 'travel' types are freely available which are a convenient size for packing and will last for years. Make sure you buy one with a continental 2 pin plug.

Insect repellent — if you prefer a particular brand, buy it at home.

Two other useful items are a compact folding umbrella, particularly if you are visiting Greece outside the main season. Rain showers tend to be short and, with the rain falling straight down, an umbrella gives good protection, better than a waterproof which can quickly make you hot and sweaty. A small rucksack is useful too, not just for if you go walking, but for general use when heading for the beach or off on a shopping trip. Walkers might consider taking a plastic water bottle. It is important to carry water when walking in a hot climate and it is difficult to buy a plastic bottle in Greece which does not leak into your rucksack. The same advice is offered to motorists too. Unless you live in a hot climate, it is sometimes hard to appreciate the constant need to drink and how that need is best supplied by nothing other than water. Simply having water on hand when needed can add a lot to your comfort level and enjoyment of the excursion.

It is rarely necessary to take a heavy jumper but it is always useful to take some thinner layers of clothing which you can wear together. Sometimes it is cool in the evening or you may feel cool after the heat of the sun. If you intend to do any serious walking, walking on country tracks as opposed to city streets, make sure you have suitable footwear.

Most basic medical requirements, plasters, bandages, headache pills can be bought in chemist shops in Greece. More than that, many drugs normally available in Britain only on prescription can be bought over the counter on demand and at reasonable prices.

Note that codeine and drugs containing codeine are strictly banned in Greece so be sure to exclude these from your luggage.

Maps

Even with a good sense of humour, you are unlikely to get too many laughs from a road map of Greece. In the main they look good but accuracy is something they are careful to avoid, or so the cynics say.

The main trunk roads are reliably marked but the position of joining roads does not necessarily relate to reality. A well placed signpost in advance of the anticipated junction would make driving too comfortable so the sign, if there is one at all, is placed immediately on the junction. This situation is improving and major routes are better in this respect. Road numbers have recently been changed so do not always correspond to roadside numbers on earlier maps. To add to the confusion there are still too many roads which, for reasons not even to be guessed at, have not yet made it to the road maps. The map of Greece supplied by the Greek National Tourist office is as accurate as any.

Newspapers & Magazines

The *Financial Times*, most British newspapers, a selection from European countries and the *Herald Tribune* are usually available in large towns and centres of tourism. Mostly they are one day late and sometimes more. Expect a fair mark up in price. The place to look for newspapers is at the kiosks (*periptera*) where you will see them displayed on racks or along the counter or in book shops which are generally few and far between.

Also available throughout Greece on the day of issue is *Athens News*, published in the English language. It contains a mix of local and international stories, an entertainment section announcing local events and concerts, a sports page, TV listings and a fairly easy crossword. The English language is constantly being pushed into areas where no man has dared before but, notwithstanding, it gives an interesting insight into local attitudes. *Greek Weekly News*, more competently produced, full of interest and with a good listing of events and concerts, is published on Saturday evening.

A selection of English and European magazines is also available, again at the *periptera*. The best locally produced English language magazine is *The Athenian* which appears monthly. Not only is it a good read but it is useful also for the comprehensive listings of cultural events.

Passports & Visas

EEC nationals should not require a passport but still do.

Nationals from USA, Australia, Canada, New Zealand, Norway, Sweden, Finland and certain other nations require only a valid passport for a stay of up to 3 months in Greece. For a stay exceeding 3 months, it is necessary to register at the Aliens Department which, in Athens, is located at: 173 Alexandras Avenue, 115 22 Athens ☎ 646 8103/770 5711 ext 379.

Local police forces too have an Aliens Department so if you are outside Athens you can report locally to obtain an extension. The whole process is long and drawn out, often requiring 2 to 3 weeks or more, and you will be asked to provide up to 6 passport size photographs. These are worth taking with you if you plan a long stay. In addition you will be asked to show visible means of support, i.e. a good number of money exchange slips. If convenient, one option is to leave the country briefly, preferably overnight, and return making sure that you get a passport stamp on re-entry. You may wish to plead ignorance of the requirements and opt to pay the fine when you leave the country which is quite small, roughly equalling the duties you would have paid for an extended visa.

Pets

Cats and dogs require health and rabies inoculation certificates issued by a veterinary authority in the country of origin not more than 12 months (cats 6 months) and not less than 6 days prior to arrival.

Photography

Signs which show a picture of a camera crossed out indicate a prohibited area for photography. Notices of this kind are posted near every military establishment, no matter how small or insignificant. Disregard this at your peril. The Greeks are still paranoiac about security and anyone found using a camera in a prohibited zone faces unpleasant consequences. The photographer is normally held in custody whilst the film is developed and inspected. It could mean overnight detention.

Photography on archaeological sites is free but if you wish to use a tripod without the insertion of a live subject then a fee is demanded.

Photography with a camera mounted on a tripod is prohibited in museums and moving pictures are subject to a fee according to the category.

Outdoors, the light for photography is brilliant. Summer haze can cause difficulties with distant shots but the use of a UV or Skylight filter is helpful here. Some of the clearest days occur in spring when a cool north wind blows. Mid-day light is harsh and contrasty, mornings and evening provide the best lighting conditions for serious photography.

Places to Visit

Ancient Sites and Monasteries
Most of the ancient sites are fenced off and there is an entrance fee to look around. Opening and closing times vary from site to site but these can be found for all the major sites either in the text or at the end of the appropriate chapter. Do not count on being able to buy site guides at all sites, sometimes only glossy books are sold. If your interest runs deeper than the information given in the chapters of this book, the best advice is to go equipped with your own guide.

Students can claim reduced fees on production of a student's card. Archaeological sites are closed on certain public holidays which include 1 January, 25 March, Good Friday and Easter Monday, 1 May and 25 & 26 December.

Museums

Here again there is a charge for admission. Opening and closing times vary but most, not all, close on a Monday. Refer to the end of the appropriate chapter for further details.

The museums too are closed, or open only for a short while, on the public holidays listed under ancient sites. In addition they have half-days on Shrove Monday, Whitsunday, 15 August, 28 October and Epiphany, 6 January.

Postal Services

Post Offices are open only on weekdays from 7.30am-2pm. They are closed on Saturday and Sunday. The exceptions are the Athens Post Offices in Syntagma Square, Omonia Square and Acropolis which also open Sundays from 9am-1.30pm and the mobile Post Office in Monastiraki Square which is open weekdays 8am-6pm and on Sundays from 8am-6pm.

Stamps (*grammatosima*) can be purchased at the Post Office, sometimes at a special counter, or at some kiosks (*periptera*).

Letters from Greece to overseas destinations are delivered fairly speedily, 4 to 6 days for Europe, 6 to 8 for USA and longer for Australia and New Zealand. For a speedier delivery, ask for express post on which there is a fairly modest surcharge but it cuts 2 to 3 days off the delivery time.

Post cards take forever, or so it seems, especially at peak holiday times. Even to nearby Europe they regularly take 2 weeks which often means you have reached home before the cards you sent. Cards go at the same postal rate as letters so you could always slip a card inside an airmail envelope and have it treated as a letter. It leaves more space on the card for writing too. Envelopes (*fakellos*) can be bought very cheaply at stationers.

Anyone staying long enough to receive mail can use Poste Restante. This system works fairly well in most large towns. The letter should be clearly addressed and marked Poste Restante; be sure that your name is clearly printed. Some identification will be required, usually passport, when you collect your letter. Letters are held for one month. A telegram, telex or fax can be sent from the Telecommunications office (OTE).

Public Holidays and Festivals

The Greek calendar overflows with red letter days; public holidays, Saints days and festivals. On public holidays, banks shops and offices

251

are closed although restaurants and tavernas normally stay open. Public transport is often interrupted too, reverting either to a Sunday service or none at all. Filling stations also close for many of the holidays. The days to watch out for are:

1 January — New Year's Day
6 January — Epiphany
25 March — Independence Day
Monday before Lent — Clean Monday
April — Good Friday & Easter Monday
1 May — May Day
15 August — Assumption of the Blessed Virgin Mary
28 October — Ochi Day
25 December — Christmas Day
26 December — Boxing Day

Easter is variable and does not always coincide with Easter throughout the rest of Europe. Accommodation can be a problem at this time so either book in advance or head for a major resort which caters for tourists.

Name-days are one reason why the calendar is so full of celebrations. It has been a long tradition for Greeks to ignore birthdays to celebrate instead the special day of their saint, and there are a lot of saints. If you see people wandering around with cake boxes neatly tied with fancy ribbon, or bunches of flowers or unusual activity around one of the many churches, then the chances are that it is a name day. The custom is for the person celebrating to offer hospitality to friends, to neighbours and to almost anyone who will partake of a little ouzo and refreshments.

Some of the big name days to watch out for are:

23 April — St George's day
All Georges everywhere celebrate their special day but in addition to that it is also the national day of Greece
21 May — Saints Konstantinos and Eleni
15 August — Assumption of the Blessed Virgin Mary
This is the day when millions of Marias celebrate and an important day in the religious calendar often marked by local pilgrimages or festivals
8 November for all Michaels and Gabriels
6 December — Feast of St Nicholas

Easter is the biggest and the most important celebration of the year. The arrival of Carnival time commences the long build up. This festival takes place throughout the 3 weeks before Lent and may commence as early as late January. Celebrations differ throughout the regions but Patra excels with a chariot parade and costume parties. Fancy dress is an important part of the tradition throughout the whole of Greece. It arises from the period of Turkish occupation when the Greeks were banned from conducting these celebrations. Driven under-cover, festivities continued with people disguised to prevent recognition. Now it is firmly rooted into the custom and fancy dress and costumes are worn at all events. The children wander the streets in fancy dress and traditionally show defiance by wearing their disguises on the last school day of Carnival.

All this comes to an abrupt end with a complete change of mood on 'Clean Monday' (Kathari Deutera), the Monday before Lent. This is a public holiday when families traditionally exodus to the country to fly kites and to picnic, which mostly means heading to a taverna. Special meat-free menus are the order of the day.

It is back to the quiet life throughout Lent which is still strictly observed by many, especially in country regions. Serious preparations for Easter start on Maundy Thursday. How hens are persuaded to lay so actively for the occasion remains a mystery but the shoppers are out buying eggs, not by the tens but by the hundreds. The rest of the day is spent in boiling the eggs and dying them red in the process. The colour red is supposed to have protective powers and the first egg dyed belongs to the Virgin.

Good Friday is a day of complete fast and widely observed. In large towns there are usually some tavernas open but in country areas it can be difficult or impossible to find food. Yellow or brown 'impure' candles are on sale everywhere ready for the evening church service. The sombre mood of the day is heightened by the continual tolling of church bells. It is a day for remembering their own dead; graves are visited and wreaths are laid. In the evening, the burial of Christ is the most moving and widely attended service in the whole of the Greek Orthodox calendar. The Epitaphios, the funeral bier of Christ, is centre stage in the services which start around 9pm. Garlanded with fresh flowers and with a gilded canopy, the Epitaphios bearing the coffin of Christ is ceremoniously taken from church in dignified candle-lit procession followed by silent mourners. The processions from all the local churches meet in the town square for a further short service. This is the most poignant moment of the evening, cafés close, tavernas close and there is not one Greek who would willingly miss it. The processions return slowly to their churches, stopping at each street corner for a short prayer.

Saturday brings an air of expectancy. Gone are the yellow candles; white candles are being eagerly bought ready for the evening service. Funereal drapes are removed in the churches and decorations of laurel and myrtle take their place. In dimly lit churches everywhere, services begin. Slowly the light intensity increases reaching full brightness at midnight when priests triumphantly chant 'Christ is risen' (Christos anesti). The sanctuary doors open to show that the Epitaphios is empty. Light from the priest's candle is passed to the congregation and that flame is rapidly passed from candle to candle until it reaches the waiting crowds outside. Fire crackers drown the clamour of the church bells as the crowd erupts in joyous celebration and greetings of 'Christos anesti' ring out loudest of all. The crowds disperse shortly carefully protecting their burning candle; it is a good omen to enter the home with the flame still burning.

Sunday is a day of out and out rejoicing. The big occasion of the day is the spit roast lamb or, in some areas, goat. Charcoal fires are lit early in the morning and the spit roasting is done with loving care over some 5 hours with copious quantities of ouzo or retsina to help things along. All those red eggs now appear and are used in friendly competition. Each contestant taps their egg hard enough to break an opponent's but not their own.

Easter Monday has no special ceremonies or rituals and passes as any normal public holiday.

Cultural Events
In addition to the major festivals listed with each chapter, local festivals are commonplace in the summer months. A word of warning too. Each town and village has its own saint's day and sometimes, depending on the local whim and the phase of the moon, a holiday is called. This decision is often not taken until the day before so there is no way you can plan for such eventualities.

Public Toilets

The most usual sign is WC with figures to indicate ladies (*gynaikon*) and gents (*andron*). Toilets with permanent attendants who demand a fee, usually found in the larger towns and cities, are normally quite clean but others can be appalling. There are also toilets in museums and at archaeological sites. Toilet paper is sometimes supplied where there is an attendant and very occasionally elsewhere. Take your own supply.

Public Transport

Buses
Buses throughout Greece are mainly operated by a syndicate of privately owned companies operating under the name of KTEL. They operate a vast network and their faded green and cream buses can be seen cruising along main roads or struggling through clouds of dust to some mountain village. Mainline buses, often air conditioned, are efficiently run and mostly leave promptly from their starting point. Tickets for these buses are often bought from an office at the terminal immediately before the journey. Tickets bought this way often have a seat number which is the number on the reverse of the seat on which you sit and not the number you sit facing. Although this is a perfectly logical system once it is understood, it takes only a few inexperienced travellers to reduce a bus to chaos within minutes. When a ticket service is not operating, or if you join at an intermediate point, it is

usual to pay the driver on entry. Local services or those on short runs mostly operate with a conductor to collect fares.

In moderate size towns, there may be two or more bus stations; local buses using one and long distance buses the others, according to destinations.

The State Railway Organisation, OSE, also operates an express bus service between major cities. They depart from railway stations and their charges are similar to KTEL.

Details of the bus services in Athens are given at the end of Chapter 1.

Trains

The railway network is not so extensive and the trains are generally slow compared to the buses. The only saving is in cost; the trains are cheaper. Trains usually have some first class compartments, although the standards are not significantly better than second class. It is possible to reserve a seat in either class, and at no extra charge, but only if you join the train at the starting point.

For a spectacular journey, try the rack and pinion line in the Peloponnese between Diakopto and Kalavrita. See Chapter 4 for more details.

Taxis

Taxis are relatively cheap and well used in Greece. In the cities it is fairly straightforward. All licensed taxis are designated by a roof sign and fitted with a meter which displays the fare in drachmas. The rate of charges and surcharges are all fixed. Within the city boundaries taxi fares are charged at the single rate and you may see 1 displayed in a solitary box on the meter. Once you travel outside the city boundary, the double rate applies so it is likely you will see the driver alter the meter so that 2 shows in the box. Legitimate small surcharges are allowed for a sizeable piece of luggage, for attending an airport, port or station for the benefit of passengers, and for late night or very early morning travel. Surcharges are permitted too at holiday times, especially Christmas and Easter. Picking up a second fare is allowed too so you may find yourself sharing a taxi.

Most of the licensed taxi drivers are good and honest but there are always a few around who regard tourists as a good source of revenue. Some of the tricks encountered include; the meter does not work, the meter set on the double rate when it should be single and, worst of all, multiplying the charge by ten which is easily done by wrongly reading the display on the modern digital meter.

Avoid unlicensed cabs where at all possible. These are not fitted with a meter and their charges can be extortionate. At the ports and airports, drivers of these cabs tend to stalk their prey on foot offering their taxi service. Obligingly, help will be offered with your luggage and you will be hustled into the cab. There will be hardly time to notice that it is an unofficial cab.

If you intend to travel a distance outside the city centre, it is common practice to negotiate your fare with the driver before you start the journey. Do not hesitate to ask two or three drivers for a quote on the fare, it is the only yardstick available.

One last word of warning, for a period of around 3 hours, between 2pm and 5pm (siesta time), it can be almost impossible to get a taxi, particularly in Athens.

Recorded Information

Time ☎ 141
Weather ☎ 148
News ☎ 115
Buses (Greece) ☎ 142
Ships (Piraeus, Rafina, Lavrio) ☎ 143
Trains (Greece) ☎ 145
Trains (Europe) ☎ 147
Road assistance (ELPA) ☎ 104

Shopping

Regulations on opening hours have changed recently to adjust to market needs. Different regions have their own views on this so there is now greater confusion than ever over opening times. Big city supermarkets and department stores open: Monday-Friday 8am-8pm. Saturday 8am-3pm.

Pharmacies: Monday & Wednesday 8am-2.30pm. Tuesday,Thursday and Friday 8am-2pm & 5-8pm.

There is also a duty rota for pharmacies so that at least one in the vicinity is open on Saturday and Sunday. Usually a note on the door of the pharmacy details the duty chemist.

The opening hours for pharmacies are fairly typical of the opening hours in small towns and villages. They argue, with some justification, everybody wants to sleep in the afternoon and nobody wants to shop.

In tourist areas, shopping hours are much more relaxed. Tourist shops in particular are open all day long.but supermarkets, butchers, bakers and the like tend to observe more restricted hours.

The *periptero*, the corner-stone of Greek society, is open all day long and from there you can buy anything from chocolate to ice creams, soap to postage stamps and road maps to matches.

Sports & Pastimes

Water Sports

Recent years have seen a big increase in the popularity of wind surfing. Many of the small bays and coves are ideally suited to this sport and boards can be hired in most holiday resorts. Lessons for beginners are generally available too at rates which are still very reasonable.

Water-skiing is available at many of the larger resorts. Further information can be obtained from: Water Skiing Association, 32 Stournara Street, Athens ☎ 523 1875

Scuba diving is subject to certain regulations in Greece. More information on this and on the best coastal regions for scuba diving can be obtained from the Greek National Tourist Office.

Tennis
There are public tennis courts in Thessaloniki, Halkidiki and Patra. Better class hotels in tourist regions often have facilities for tennis.

Golf
This is not a sport with a big following in Greece. The country boasts a total of four golf courses but only two of these are located on the mainland. One is at Glyfada just 12km (7 miles) from Athens and the other is within the Porto Carras complex at Halkidiki.

Walking and Mountain Climbing
In a mountainous country like Greece riddled with old donkey trails there are abundant opportunities for walking. Unfortunately, there are no guide books available for those interested in short rambles or day hikes, although there are a number of such walks described in these pages. Long distance walkers have the opportunity to try the E4 European Rambler Trail which winds down through Greece from north of Florina to Githion in the southern Peloponnese. Further information outlining the route is available from the EOT and from the Hellenic Alpine Club, 7 Karageorgi Servias St, Athens ☎ 3234555. The HAC also supplies information, magazines, maps and guide books relating to mountain climbing and trekking in Greece.

Skiing
Facilities for skiing are on the increase in Greece. The season starts around mid-December and continues until the end of April.

All the skiing resorts are equipped with ski lifts and have accommodation facilities. The more recent centres, at Mount Parnassos and Mount Pilion, have the advantage of even better facilities with ski schools and first aid centres. Below is a complete list of the centres:

Dirfis Ski Centre, Halkidiki ☎ 0221 25230
Falakro Ski Centre, Drama, Macedonia ☎ 0521 23054/23049
Helmos Ski Centre, Peloponnese ☎ 0692 22174/22661
Kissavos Ski Centre, Larissa, Thessaly ☎ 041 220097
Menalo Ski Centre, Peloponnese ☎ 071232243
Metsovo Ski Centre, Epirus ☎ 0656 41249
Olympos Ski Centre, Thessaly
Pangeo Ski Centre, Macedonia ☎ 051 835952
Parnassus Ski Centre, Central Greece ☎ 0234 22689/22695
Pertouli Ski Centre, Thessaly ☎ 0431 82459

Pilion Ski Centre, Thessaly ☎ 0421 25696/99136
Pissoderi Ski Centre, Florina, Macedonia ☎ 0385 22082
Tria kai Pende Pigadia Ski Centre, Naoussa, Macedonia
☎ 0332 28567

Telephone Services

Certain public telephone boxes, those marked with an orange strip at the top and usually with the word 'international,' can be used for long distance and international calls. They take only low value coins which means that conversation is constantly interrupted by a bleeping tone, a reminder to feed more money; not very convenient. Many *periptera*, the small kiosks which sell just about everything, have metered phones for public use. Some, but not all, will allow their use for international calls. These are useful in quiet locations but in a busy thoroughfare you have to compete with all the noise and bustle. The rate per call unit is not advertised so you will need to ask and the meter is often not displayed so you must rely on the vendors word for the number of units used.

Hotels have telephones for use by residents, mostly in the rooms but sometimes at reception. They charge a much higher rate per unit so it pays to ascertain the hotel rate and compare with the rate at the Telecomunications office (OTE).

The cheapest and most convenient place to make telephone calls is from the Telecommunications office, the OTE. This is normally part of or adjoining a main Post Office. If you are not sure where, look for a building with a large telecommunications dish and aerials on top, and head for that. Inside the OTE there are a number of telephone booths, mostly all international, but some still have a few dedicated to local calls. Choose a booth and note the number on the door as you enter. The call meter is set on the wall above the telephone and this should be set to zero. If not, hang out of the booth and attract the attention of the counter clerk who will reset it. Only when it is on zero can you actually make a call. The ringing tone for an international call will be unfamiliar and depends on the destination country. An engaged tone is mostly a series of rapid bleeps. Throughout the call you can see the meter which usually displays the charge directly in *drachmas*. When the call is finished head to the counter and declare your booth number and pay.

International dialling codes from Greece are as follows: UK & Northern Ireland 0044: USA & Canada 001: Australia 0061: New Zealand: 0064. The internal code for Athens is 01.

Tipping

There are no hard or fast rules on tipping and certainly no fixed percentages. Restaurants and tavernas automatically include a service charge so there is no need to tip but most Greeks pick the notes from their change leaving the small coins. If you intend to use a taverna regularly throughout your stay, a small tip will help to ensure continued good service. Taxi drivers do not normally get a tip from locals but they seem to expect it from tourists. A tip would certainly be expected if they had been helpful in finding a restaurant or hotel for you. During the Christmas and New Year period and the whole of the Easter fortnight they are legally allowed to add a fixed tip to the bill. Hotel charges also include service and it is not usual to tip here but the porter and chamber maid are normally rewarded. Otherwise it is entirely discretionary.

Travelling to Greece

The majority of visitors arrive by air but travelling by road or rail is a distinct possibility for those starting out from European destinations.

By Air
Olympic Airways operates scheduled flights to many cities in western Europe and to destinations beyond including New York in the USA, Toronto and Montreal in Canada and Melbourne and Sydney in Australia. Foreign national carriers also operate services into Greece by reciprocal arrangements. Athens is the main point of entry although Thessaloniki too receives flights from a number of European cities.

There are many charter flights operating to Greece from Europe, especially throughout the summer months, and these generally offer much cheaper fares than scheduled flights. Athens is a popular destination but charter flights also operate to the mainland towns of Thessaloniki in Macedonia, Kavala in Thrace, Preveza in Epirus and Kalamata in the Peloponnese and to a whole host of Greek islands.

Visitors from the USA, Canada and New Zealand might consider the option of flying to London to take advantage of a cheap charter flight on to Greece. The whole package can often work out cheaper. With a large population of Greeks resident in Australia, Olympic Airways offer special fares from time to time which are very competitive with alternative routes. For New Zealanders, without the convenience of direct flights, routing via Australia provides an additional option to travelling via London.

Although charter flights offer very cheap travel, it is important for the independent traveller to be aware of their limitations. The Greeks are constantly requesting that the charter flight regulations are upheld. Under these regulations, charter companies can only sell flight seats with accommodation. If you buy a 'seat only' you will probably be issued with an accommodation voucher which you will not be expected to take up. The duration of stay on a charter flight is restricted to between 3 days and 6 weeks and a further restriction, which can be the most irksome, is that you cannot leave Greece for another country during the term of your stay, except if you return the same day.

Breaking this latter restriction seems to cause most offence to the authorities, particularly if it involves a trip to Turkey, and, at worst, offenders may face cancellation of their return ticket leaving no option but to pay out for a scheduled flight home. None of these restrictions apply to scheduled flights and, if you plan a long stay in Greece, this is the best option.

Athens airport has two terminals. The West Terminal which handles Olympic Airways flights exclusively, both internal and international, and the East Terminal which handles international flights by all other carriers. Although these two terminals lie in different parts of the same complex, it is a lengthy journey around the perimeter to change from one to the other. The connecting bus service is of limited frequency out of the main season and taxis cope with the bulk of passenger transfers. Check the current taxi fare into Athens or between air terminals at the information desk on arrival. If faced with an ongoing internal flight, using Olympic Airways avoids the inconvenience of changing terminals. Both terminals have a frequent express bus service to Athens centre and regular airline buses connect with the Olympic and British Airways offices in Syntagma Square.

Internal flights are relatively inexpensive and there is a frequent service on almost all domestic routes. From Athens there are regular services to the mainland towns of: Alexandroupolis (Thrace), Kavala (Thrace), Thessaloniki (Macedonia), Kastoria (Macedonia), Ioannina (Epirus), Preveza (Epirus), Kalamata (Peloponnese) and to many island destinations.

Detailed flight information and bookings for any internal flight can be made in the country of departure by contacting Olympic Airways or national airlines with reciprocal arrangements or from leading travel agents. Domestic lines, especially on tourist routes, are well used throughout the holiday season so it pays to book in advance. The main ticket offices for Olympic Airways in Athens are located at:

Olympic Airways
6 Othonos Street
Syntagma Square
☎ 929 2555 (International) 929 24444 (Domestic) and
96 Syngrou Avenue
117 41 Athens
☎ 929 2251/4

By Rail
Rail fares to Greece mostly work out to be more expensive than charter flights, except if you are under 26 and can benefit from youth fares. Generally, you need to be young to withstand the rigours of the journey although it can be a lot more fun if you adopt the adage — it is better to travel than to arrive — and break the journey in various countries en route.

British Rail's InterRail pass, available to anyone living in Europe, allows one months free travel on all railways in Europe. There is a proviso that you pay half the price of travel in the country of issue. The holder is entitled to reduced ferry fares on Channel crossings and on certain ferries between Italy and Greece.

Also of benefit to those under 26 are the Euro train or Transalpino tickets which, although costing more than the InterRail pass, allow for a stay of up to 2 months and include all ferry crossings. One-way tickets are also available at just over half the cost. Further information can be obtained from:

British Rail European Travel Centre
Victoria Station
London SW1
☎ 0171 834 9656

USIT/Eurotrain
London Student Travel
52 Grosvenor Gardens
London SW1
☎ 0171 730 3402

Transalpino
71-75 Buckingham Palace Road
London SW1
☎ 0171 834 9656

By Road

The usual route from western Europe involves driving down through former Yugoslavia via Ljubljana, Zagreb, Belgrade and Skopje. Even with hard driving and only brief overnight stops, this requires a minimum of 4 days from England. It is not a journey to be undertaken lightly, especially the long haul through former Yugoslavia. Poor road surfaces, thundering heavy goods wagons delivering produce to and from Greece, contribute to a high accident rate along the whole of this section of the journey. At the moment, the unrest in former Yugoslavia provides the most compelling reason to seek an alternative way. Even when peace returns, it would be wise to await good reports before attempting this route.

Fortunately, there is a very attractive alternative which can also save a lot of driving. Head for Italy and use one of a number of ferry services to take you and your car to Greece. Regular services operate all year round from a number of Adriatic ports. Listing from north to south, these include:-

Venice: does not figure prominently in timetables but the ferry boat Marco Polo provides a weekly service to Patra.

Ancona: from 2 to 6 sailings daily to Greece. Most call in at Corfu (about 26 hours) and Igoumenitsa (28 hours) on the way to Patra (36 hours) but there are also express services to Patra.

Bari: not a heavy timetable but there are daily sailings via Corfu (11 hours), Igoumenitsa (13 hours) to Patra (21 hours)

Brindisi: as many as eight sailings daily, mostly via Corfu (9 hours), Igoumenitsa (11 hours) to Patra (19 hours) and at least one express daily direct to Patra.

All the above listings run between Italy and Patra in the Peloponnese but, if you are looking for the experience of sailing through the Corinth canal to Piraeus (for Athens), there are not too many opportunities. The most famous name on this route is the Orient Express which sails from Venice to Istanbul although this is a cruise ship rather than a ferry boat. There is one genuine car ferry, the Ariadne which plies the route between Ancona in Italy and Kusadasi in Turkey via Piraeus. A number of the ferry companies operating these lines have agents in the UK. Their addresses are as follows:

Karageorgis Lines
36 King Street
London WC2E 8 JS
☎ 071 836 821

Mediterranean Passenger
  Services
9 Hanover Street
London W1R 8HF
☎ 071 499 0076

P&O European Ferries
Channel House
Channel View Road
Dover
Kent CT17 9TJ
☎ 0304 203388

Viamare Travel Ltd
33 Mapesbury Road
London NW2 4HT
☎ 081 452 8231

Travelling in Greece

Driving in Greece

Driving in Greece is on the right hand side of the road and overtaking on the left. Unless there are signs indicating otherwise, the speed limits are as follows: built-up areas 50kph (31mph), outside built-up areas 80kph (50mph) and motorways 100kph (62mph).

Traffic moving along main roads outside towns has priority at intersections; in towns give way to traffic from the right. On approaching and on roundabouts, vehicles must give way to traffic coming from the right.

Unleaded fuel (*amolivthi venzini*) is increasingly available except in some remote country areas. The two grades of fuel (*venzini*) normally on offer are Apli at 91/92 octane and Super at 96/98 octane. Diesel is also widely available. Fuel is sold by the litre.

Driving in Athens city centre is subject to special restrictions. During the week, a ban on traffic is enforced according to car registration number plates where even numbers alternate on a daily basis with odd numbers. Restrictions apply between 7am and 8pm Monday to Thursday and 7am-3pm on Friday. Doctors and journalists are exempt from these restrictions at all times and foreign and hire cars, displaying a special sign, for the first 40 days.

Parking in cities is something of a problem and the best solution is not to try. Leave your car in the suburbs and walk or bus into the centre. In Athens, parking in the Green Zone is restricted to parking meters only. Other regulations ban parking within 5m of an intersection, within 15m of a level crossing or bus stop and within 3m of a fire hydrant.

Illegal parking can result in a ticket which indicates the amount of the fine and where and when to pay it. The police are not empowered to collect on-the-spot fines. In Athens, illegal parking is dealt with differently. The car's number plates are removed and there is a heavy charge made to have them released.

With one of the worst accident rates in Europe, driving in Greece demands a cautious attitude from the onset. The discipline shown by the majority of drivers in western European countries, which brings order to traffic flow, is often missing from Greek drivers. Drive with your own safety in mind. Another major hazard is the state of the roads. Pot holes are a serious danger and can be encountered unexpectedly even on well surfaced roads. Some of the holes are large enough to cause damage to tyres and wheels. A line of rocks on the road guiding you towards the centre is the usual warning of edge subsidence and there will often be no other warning signs. Minor roads, which are well surfaced, may suddenly become unmetalled.

There are two 'motorways', one links Athens to Thessaloniki in the north and the other joins Athens to Patra in the Peloponnese. Both are toll roads. These are not of expected motorway standard as it is possible to encounter frequent and sudden changes in the number of lanes, for example, and there are roadside services.

Passenger cars, trailers, motor-cycles and side-cars can be cleared through Customs for use for four months (extendable) if the owner is the holder of a corresponding 'Carnet de Passage en Douane' issued by the automobile and touring clubs of his country of origin. In the absence of such a document, motor vehicles are admitted temporarily without payment of import duty or tax by making an entry on the owner's passport whereupon a free use card is issued by the Customs.

Tourists from North America, Australia and South Africa have the right to use their automobiles for two years upon approval by the appropriate Customs Authority. Road taxes are paid for the second year.

Motorists from Britain, Germany, Belgium or Austria need only a valid driving licence from their home country, others require an International Driving Licence. These can be obtained from ELPA (address below) on production of a national driving licence and a passport or identification card. Again, passport size photographs will be required. A Green Card International Motor Insurance Certificate is enough for drivers from Britain and most European countries. Visitors from USA, Canada, New Zealand and Australia will be required to buy local short term insurance on entry. The minimum age for driving a car in Greece is 18.

Greek law states that a car must carry: a fire extinguisher, first aid kit and a warning triangle but these are rarely found in hired vehicles.

The carrying of fuel in cans is forbidden as is the use of main beam headlights in towns and cities. Safety belts must be worn at all times and do not be dissuaded from this by the fact that many Greek motorists do not use them. There are days when the police crack down hard on offenders. These occasions are usually well advertised but the news may escape you, especially if you are on the move. The same warning applies to motor-cyclists. It is mandatory for driver and passenger to wear a crash helmet.

Information on all aspects of motoring can be obtained from the Automobile Association & Touring Club of Greece, ELPA, Athens Tower, 2-4, Messogion Street, 15 27 Athens ☎ 7791 615 to 629 & 7797 402 to 405

Car Hire

Greece is one of the more expensive countries for car hire and a better deal can be arranged by booking and paying in advance of departure. The minimum age for car hire is 21 but 25 for jeeps and minibuses. Clear with the hire company usage on ferries and trips out of Greece.

International car hire companies, such as Avis and Hertz are well represented in Greece. Also present are Europe Car, Budget and Eurodollar but with fewer hire stations. In Britain, companies like Transhire ☎ 0171 978 1922, fax 0171 978 1797 offer very competitive rates. If you choose to use this option enquire which car hire company in Greece is involved. The quality of the back up service rather than the price may be the deciding factor ultimately, especially if you plan to tour widely. Wherever you are, it is comforting to feel that there is a branch of your car hire company not too far away in case of breakdown or similar problems. It is very likely that the car hire company will have membership of ELPA to cope with this situation, nevertheless, you can end up with a long drive or wait if there is a need to change the car. There are also local companies, InterRent and Just, for example, but choose carefully.

Third party insurance is compulsory under Greek law and this cost will be added to the hire charge. An additional optional insurance is collision damage waiver (CDW) and it is imperative to take it. This cannot be stressed too strongly. Should you be unfortunate enough to be involved in an accident without CDW insurance and the costs cannot be recovered from a third party then the consequences can be frightening. At best you may be faced with a huge repair bill, at worst you could end up in jail until it is fully paid.

Tyres and damage to the underside of the car are mostly excluded from the insurance cover. Take time when you are accepting the car to inspect the tyres and, if not fully satisfied, don't accept the vehicle. It is worth a moment to check that lights and indicators are fully operational. Before driving away, make sure you have the agents telephone number and a complete list of offices throughout the country.

Motor Cycles

Above comments on insurance apply also to hiring a motor-cycle or moped. There is a problem over crash helmets too. The law says very clearly that these must be worn but the chances that you will be able to hire them along with the bike are slim to nil. It is an unhappy situation which only compounds the personal dangers to motor-cyclists in a country which has a very high accident rate. If you intend to hire a motor-cycle, it is worth checking the fine print in the medical section of the holiday insurance taken out in your home country. Such is the concern over motor-cycle accidents that some companies are specifically excluding injuries arising this way.

Road Signs

Fortunately, international road signs are used throughout the country but there may be occasions when you encounter temporary signs written in Greek. Here are a few examples:

ΑΛΤ	Stop
ΕΛΑΤΤΩΣΑΤΕΤΑΧΥΤΗΤΑΝ	Reduce Speed
ΕΡΓΑ ΕΠΙ ΤΗΣ ΟΔΟΥ	Road Works In Progress
ΑΝΩΜΑΛΙΑ ΟΔΟΣΤΡΩΜΑΤΟΣ	Bad Road Surface
ΑΠΑΓΟΡΕΥΕΤΑΙ ΤΟ ΠΡΟΣΠΕΡΑΣΜΑ	No Overtaking
ΤΕΛΟΣ ΑΠΗΓΟΡΕΥΜΕΝΗΣ ΖΩΝΗΣ	End Of No-Overtaking
ΠΑΡΑΚΑΜΠΤΗΡΙΟΣ	Diversion
ΜΟΝΟΔΡΟΜΟΣ	One-Way Traffic
ΠΟΡΕΙΑ ΥΠΟΧΡΕΩΤΙΚΗ ΔΕΞΙΑ	Keep Right
ΑΠΑΓΟΡΕΥΕΤΑΙ Η ΣΤΑΘΜΕΥΣΙΣ	No Parking
ΑΔΙΕΞΟΔΟΣ	No Through Road

Accidents and Legal Advice

In the event of an accident involving personal injury or damage to property, both the law and your insurance require that it is reported to the police. To do this, dial 100 in most big cities or contact the tourist police by dialling 171 and ask their advice.

ELPA offer free legal advice concerning Greek legislation on car accidents and insurance.

Breakdowns

It is a legal requirement to place a warning triangle 100m behind the car. Next step is to dial 104 to obtain the road assistance service of ELPA (address on p264). This is available in and around all large towns in Greece.

ELPA has reciprocal arrangements with European motoring organisations, like the British AA and RAC, for road assistance, either a light repair on the spot or a tow to the nearest garage. Car hire firms are mostly members of ELPA but some have alternative arrangements for repair and assistance.

By Rail

The rail network in Greece is operated by the state-owned Hellenic Railways Organisation (OSE). Diesel trains run on narrow gauge lines in the Peloponnese and on standard gauge lines in the rest of Greece. This means that Athens has two stations which are located almost side by side. Larissis station provides services to Northern Greece and the international connections while Peloponnisos station serves the Peloponnese lines.

Most travellers book seats in advance and it pays to do so unless you prefer to travel standing in the corridor. Two classes are available and for long distance journeys, it is well worth considering first class if only for the extra space and additional comfort. First class costs around 50 per cent more than second class. There are no sleeper services but most long distance trains do have restaurant cars. Do not expect a fast journey on any line. Generally Buses are quicker, even when lunch stops are included in the reckoning.

GREECE
RAILWAY NETWORK

Tourist Information Centres

The head office is in central Athens: Greek National Tourist Office, 2 Amerikis Street, Athens ☎ 322 31 11 but this only deals with administration matters. Information for the public is supplied from two locations in nearby Syntagma Square. There are information desks at East (International) Airport and many frontier posts including Evzoni and Niki (which may be used entering from the former Yugoslavia), and the sea ports of Piraeus, Igoumenitsa and Patra.

The National Tourism Organisation of Greece, known as EOT within Greece, distributes attractively produced leaflets on all locations in Greece which include maps of the main towns and ancient sites. New stocks of up-to-date leaflets arrive in about March/April which is the best time to apply; by mid season demand often exceeds supply. NTOG addresses around the world include:

UK and Ireland
4 Conduit Street
London W1R ODJ
☎ 0171 734 599

Australia and New Zealand
51-57 Pitt Street
Sydney, NSW 2000
☎ 241 16 63

USA
645 Fifth Avenue
Olympic Tower (5th Floor)
New York NY10022
☎ 421 57777

168 North Michigan Avenue
Chicago
Illinois 60601
☎ 728 1084

611 West 6th Street
Suite 2198 Los Angeles
California 90017
☎ 626 696

Travel Information

Foreign airline ☎ 96991
East airport ☎ 969 9466
Rail ☎ 524 0601
Road ☎ 512 4910
Sea ☎ 417 2657

Useful And Emergency Telephone Numbers

Doctors on call ☎ 105
Ambulance ☎ 166
Hospitals on duty ☎ 106
Pharmacies open ☎ 107
Aliens Police ☎ 770 5711
Coast Guard Emergency Patrol ☎ 108
Police ☎ 100

Port Authorities ☎ 103
Automobile Association ☎ 104
Automobile Association & Tourist Information ☎ 174
Information/International calls ☎ 169
Telephone information ☎ 134
Telephone Numbers in Greece ☎ 132
Telephone Numbers in Athens ☎ 131
Internal telephone information ☎ 162
International telegrams ☎ 165
Domestic telegrams ☎ 155

MPC

A Note to the Reader

Thank you for buying this book, we hope it has helped
you to plan and enjoy your visit. We have worked hard
to produce a guidebook which is as accurate as possible.
With this in mind, any comments, suggestions or useful
information you may have would be appreciated.

Please send your letters to:

The Editor
Moorland Publishing Co Ltd
Moor Farm Road West
Ashbourne
Derbyshire
DE6 1HD

The Travel Specialists

INDEX

Page numbers in **bold** type indicate maps